THE WORLD NEWSPAPER INDUSTRY

PETER J.S. DUNNETT

CROOM HELM
London • New York • Sydney

© 1988 Peter J.S. Dunnett
Croom Helm Ltd, Provident House,
Burrell Row, Beckenham, Kent BR3 1AT
Croom Helm Australia, 44–50 Waterloo Road,
North Ryde, 2113, New South Wales

Published in the USA by
Croom Helm
in association with Methuen, Inc.
29 West 35th Street,
New York, NY 10001

British Library Cataloguing in Publication Data

Dunnett, Peter J.S.
    The world newspaper industry.
    1. Newspaper publishing — Economic aspects
    I. Title
    338.4'7070572   PN4734

    ISBN 0-7099-0834-2

Library of Congress Cataloging-in-Publication Data

Dunnett, Peter J.S.
    The world newspaper industry.

    Bibliography: p.
    Includes index.
    1. Newspaper publishing — Economic aspects.
    2. Newspapers — History — 20th century. 3. Freedom of
    the press. I. Title.
    PN4734.D86   1987   338.8'36107   87-20126
    ISBN 0-7099-0834-2

Filmset by Mayhew Typesetting, Bristol, England
Printed and bound in Great Britain
by Billing & Sons Limited, Worcester.

THE WORLD NEWSPAPER INDUSTRY

Contents

Figures

Tables

To J.M.D.

Preface

This book examines the changing economics of the world newspaper industry in the 1980s. It attempts to cast light on the complex relationships between readers, advertisers, owners, government policies and the other media during a period of rapid change. I hope the comparisons and contrasts between different countries will prove useful to those interested in maintaining and sustaining a free press. I hope the analysis of the economic foundations of the press will provide a useful insight for policy makers, journalists, readers and advertisers alike.

In writing this book I have been indebted to the Canadian Department of National Defence and the Social Science and Humanities Research Council for financial support. I received useful advice and encouragement from Colin Jones, Doug Kelk, James Boutilier, David Heft, Richard Pomfret and Mary Jane Spray amongst others. For word processing I owe thanks to Lori Heimbecker, Eileen Langstaff and Maureen Nelson.

1

Introduction

Newspapers are under threat all over the world from electronic competition, and in many countries there is a decline of readership. The greatest asset newspapers have is the habit factor.

Rupert Murdoch, 1985[1]

AN OVERVIEW OF THE INDUSTRY

The newspaper industry worldwide is an industry in transition. Virtually every aspect of the industry has recently undergone or is currently undergoing change. Newspapers in the developed world, the Third World and the Communist world have all been affected.

These changes have affected newspaper industry demand and supply, structure, conduct and performance. The aim of this book is to examine and analyse the economics of the changing newspaper industry in a worldwide context. The book compares and contrasts the different responses of readers, advertisers, governments and newspaper firms to the changing economic conditions, and attempts to identify current trends and future prospects.[2]

Technology has been the main engine of change. Computers have had an impact at every stage of production. Satellites, computers, fiber optics, lasers, new inks and new papers have all been important. In 1986 it was possible for a reporter to file a story, with photographs, from virtually anywhere in the world and have the story printed at different regional presses within a country all in under two hours. It was possible for the print media to individualise an advertisement to include the individual subscriber's name.

Technology has also affected the competing media both to the benefit and detriment of newspapers. Newspapers are a subsection of the broader entertainment and information industry. New technology has made all branches of that industry more efficient. A more efficient newspaper industry must compete with more, and more efficient, competitors in the 1980s; satellite broadcast, cable

1

Figure 1.1: The old and new technology

The Old

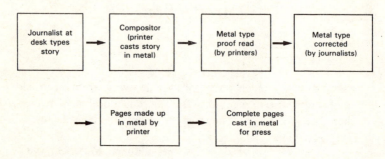

The New

television, video cassette recorders, videotext, teletext and personal computers with access to databases have all become commonplace during the current decade. These, and traditional media, impinge on the market of the established and mature newspaper industry.[3]

In the developed world the newspaper industry has a long and well documented history. Growth prospects, however, are limited for paid-for circulation daily newspapers. British circulation peaked in 1957, Australia's in 1956, the United States' in 1971, Japan's in 1981. France has seen significant decline since 1950. In southern Europe and Latin America daily newspapers have not achieved the circulation levels of northern Europe and North America, despite increased economic prosperity.[4] In the Communist world, newspapers in 1986 were still the main media instrument to propagate official policy. In China, for example, the past decade has seen a tripling in newsprint consumption, despite the rapid expansion of radio and television. In the Third World, there have been newspapers for the ruling minorities since colonial days. Daily newspapers for the growing middle-classes however have had limited success, and the economic obstacles to further growth are formidable.

Figure 1.2: The newspaper as a broker model

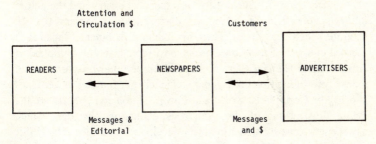

Daily newspapers and Sunday newspapers dominate the world newspaper industry. In 1985 in the United States over 80 per cent of all newsprint was used by dailies. In turn, the United States and Western newspapers dominated the world newspaper industry, accounting for over three-quarters of non-Communist newsprint consumption. Whilst a significant portion of this book is devoted to the daily papers of the Western world, in terms of their relative economic importance Third World newspapers, freesheets and minority newspapers are given a more than proportionate share of coverage.

The newspaper industry is an extraordinary industry with many unique and unusual characteristics. It sells a joint product in that it sells news and entertainment to readers and then sells those readers to advertisers. It is a broker between readers and advertisers. In the twentieth century advertising has become the essential base for newspapers and much of the media outside the Communist world. At the same time, newspapers have an unusual quasi-public service status in many countries and are expected to be socially responsible and act accordingly. Reflecting this expectation all countries have special newspaper legislation.

Marshall McLuhan observed that those media such as newspapers that mix programming and advertisements are a form of 'paid learning'.[5] If they could, advertisers would pay potential customers to listen to their sales pitch. They cannot, so instead they pay for a 'free' show on television and a highly subsidised one in the daily newspapers. Advertisements are part of the show. Critics of the press, McLuhan noted, deplore the frivolity of what the press selects as newsworthy, but in reality newspaper owners only attempt to give the public what it wants. The power and influence of a press baron lies not in the specific messages carried in his paper but rather in his ownership of the medium.

The book is organised into two sections. The first three chapters are of a general nature and examine the basic conditions of supply and demand, the structure of the newspaper industry and the nature of newspaper firms' conduct and performance. Chapters 4 to 10 examine specific countries. The United States, Britain and Japan each merit a chapter of their own because of their size and complexity. Australia and Canada share a chapter. Three other chapters extend the analysis of the first three general chapters to examples of the Third World, the Communist world and Europe. India and Nigeria are the prime illustrations of the numerous economic obstacles which newspapers must surmount in newly developing countries. The USSR and China exemplify newspapers in the planned economies of the Communist countries. For Europe, West Germany is used as a case study of the high circulation mature market typical of northern Europe, whilst Italy, Spain and Greece typify the stunted and frustrated development of the newspaper market of southern Europe, and also of Latin America. The examples cited demonstrate the extent to which economic forces impact on the newspaper industry in the Third World, developed world and Communist world in the 1980s.[6] They demonstrate how economic forces continue to determine the nature of the newspaper industry and the very nature of the newspaper product manufactured, including, as Marshall Macluhan pointed out a quarter of a century ago, editorial content.

A BRIEF ECONOMIC HISTORY OF NEWSPAPERS

With the invention of movable type by Johan Gutenberg in the mid-fifteenth century the technical ability to mass produce the written word came into being. The social and psychological consequences of Gutenberg were widespread, radically changing the very way in which man saw himself. Marshall McLuhan claims print enabled man to develop a private point of view, to become detached and disinterested. Print enabled man to create new perspectives of time and space. In time, it contributed to the rise of nationalism, industrialisation, mass markets and universal literacy. It rendered memory and the scholastic oral tradition obsolete. The ability to repeat the message in written form meant social, political and economic power.

The origins of modern newspapers can be traced to England.[7] The *Oxford Gazette*, which soon moved to London to become the *London Gazette*, first appeared with government approval in 1665. The first daily was the *Daily Courant* which appeared just after the turn of the century. In the British colonies of North America the

Franklin brothers were the first to produce newspapers successfully without specific authority from the government in the 1720s. Ben Franklin's *Pennsylvania Gazette* was probably the first modern newspaper to be commercially viable.

The market for modern mass circulation newspapers can be traced to social and economic developments beginning in the 1830s. Changes in the following decades in demographics, political institutions, technology, communications, literacy and living standards were necessary prerequisites for a take-off of the newspaper industry in Britain and America. These changes dramatically increased potential demand and reduced supply costs.

On the supply side technical improvements after 1850 included the linotype and the rotary press to speed production. The use of telegraphs, telephones and typewriters improved the collection and processing of news. The use of wood pulp lowered costs, after severe shortages of rags-derived paper had created bottlenecks to growth in the 1860s. Wire services essential for the dissemination of news, had begun in 1840. The building of railroad networks in Europe and America which began in the 1840s helped distribution.

By the latter half of the nineteenth century the patterns of the first industrial revolution of England had been or were being repeated in much of Europe. With the rise of the nation state and imperialism, made possible by the ability to communicate, sizeable numbers of Westerners settled in all corners of the world. Many were literate and affluent. To meet their demand, English-language newspapers were established on all five continents. In 1824 the *Australian* was launched in Sydney.[8] In 1833 the *Daily Advertiser* was launched in Montreal. In 1838 the *Times of India* began publication, and in 1845 both the Malaysia *Strait Times* and Hong Kong *China Mail* were started. In China the first modern newspapers were weeklies and monthlies established by British missionaries such as the *Eastern Western Monthly Magazine*. In Japan, also, the first newspapers were English-language papers. In Japan *Herald* began in 1861 and a dozen more English papers appeared during the decade. In 1865 the independent Japanese language *Kaigai Shimbun* was launched.

To summarise, urbanisation, economic growth, rising income and compulsory education were important factors creating market demand from both advertisers and readers for mass circulation newspapers throughout Europe and America in the late nineteenth century. Imperialism spread English-language newspapers worldwide. Technological advances in newspaper production and communications improvements created production efficiencies and lowered supply costs. The removal of government impediments such as the Stamp Tax (the tax on knowledge) in Britain in 1852 further facilitated newspaper industry growth. The rise of nation states, increased international trade and imperialism created enclaves of Westerners around the world and their demand for newspapers, either imported from England or local English-language papers, exerted a demonstration effect. Around the world local newspapers in the vernacular were then started, though often the prerequisites for commercial success were not there since the literate and affluent usually spoke English.

The heyday for newspapers in terms of influence lasted from about 1880 to 1930. Circulations rose. Substitutes were few. Sensationalism was used to expand circulation. Newspapers enjoyed, in the words of Prime Minister Stanley Baldwin, 'the prerogative of the harlot', power without responsibility. In America, Randolph Hearst's papers were alleged to have pressured President McKinley into starting the Spanish American War. Economies of scale and the inevitable concentration of ownership that accompanies a maturing industry led to the rise of press barons including Lords Beaverbrook and Northcliffe in Britain, and Joseph Pulitzer, Randolph Hearst and E.W. Scripps in the USA. Tabloids with an emphasis on sensation were started in the last years of the nineteenth century in England by Lord Northcliffe with *Titbits* and in America by Joseph Pulitzer with *New York World*.

It was not therefore until the early twentieth century that the familiar modern newspaper industry structure with mass circulation tabloids and broadsheets, populars and qualities and with chain ownership was established, even in the West. The mass circulation newspaper is largely a twentieth-century Western phenomenon.[9]

Between 1900 and 1960 there were changes in the industry but they were not dramatic ones. There were no major changes in production methods. Radio and television were introduced and provided competitive media. Competition between the media then reduced the number of dailies in most countries. Chain ownership expanded. But the most important changes in both the functions of newspapers and the structure of the industry had occurred in the years following the industrial revolution. Then, in the 1960s, with the information revolution, the industry began a transformation. The basic conditions of supply and demand, industry structure, its conduct and performance were all affected by that transformation. That transformation is not yet completed and the final outcome is impossible to assess.

In most of the Western world in the 1980s the newspaper industry, therefore, is a mature industry in a process of transition. In much of the Third World, development of the newspaper industry has been slow, and often stunted, aborted, frustrated and pre-empted. In the Communist world the newspaper has been converted to a weapon of propaganda and control.

THE NATURE OF THE NEWSPAPER MARKET

Newspapers in the developed world are traditionally thought to serve two separate markets: readers and advertisers. Readers buy a mix of information, opinion, analysis, persuasion and entertainment. Advertisers buy the attention of potential customers. Newspapers act as intermediaries between readers and advertisers bringing them together. For any particular newspaper nearly all the services it offers, in both markets, are subject to competition either from other newspapers or from other media.

In the last decade there has been enormous public concern in many of the Western democracies concerning so-called newspaper monopolies.[10] The concern is that if only one newspaper is available in a given market then the problem arises of market power and the curtailment of freedom of speech. This view is not without foundation but, given the complex nature of a newspaper and the communications industry in the 1980s, it can be misleading. Figure 1.3 therefore attempts to provide a schematic presentation of the different dimensions in which newspapers, if examined alone, may compete with each other.[11] Figure 1.4 then shows how newspapers compete with the other media. The figures attempt to illustrate the broad array of actual and, most importantly, potential competition, facing all newspapers, including 'monopoly' newspapers, for readers and advertisers.

[In other words, newspapers are a medium. They deliver a message. The competition is more between the messages than between the mediums, so the same medium (newspapers) carrying different messages ('quality' versus 'popular') may not compete, whilst different mediums (newspapers and television) carrying similar messages (hard news) do compete.]

Competing media information products can also act as complements to the newspaper. For in-depth coverage of the television news, viewers may be induced to become readers and buy a newspaper having had their appetite initially whetted by the broadcast medium. A newspaper item may encourage readers to buy a magazine for further comment, or turn to the radio for the latest updates. Increasingly in the future newspapers will interact with the electronic media, using information services for inputs, contributing to electronic data

Figure 1.3: Inter-newspaper competition

Dimension of Competition

Category of Competition

GEOGRAPHICAL
International → National → Regional → Metro → Local

TIMING
Weekly ----→ All Day ----→ Morning ----→ Evening

QUALITY
"Quality" ----→ Middle Brow ----→ "Popular"

GENERALITY
General ----→ Speciality

POLITICS
Leftwing ----→ Non-Partisan ----→ Rightwing

Note: To compete head to head two newspapers must generally share the same category in all five dimensions.

Figure 1.4: Intra-media competition

Dimension of Competition	Print Medium	Broadcast Medium	Electronic Medium
Hard News	Magazines – NEWSPAPERS –	Radio –	Television – Data Banks
Advertising	Billboards, Magazines NEWSPAPERS Flyers, Freesheets	} – Radio – Television	
Soft Content[a]	Books – Magazines – NEWSPAPERS –	Radio –	Television – Video

Note: a. Any leisure activity, sports, gardening and so on, competes for the time required to read a newspaper.

bases, and encouraging readers to follow up newspaper articles by exploiting information services to answer any questions raised by the print media.

At the same time that the electronic media poses a possible threat to the newspapers' audience, electronic technology has also permitted an expansion of the newspaper's role. In Australia, Canada and the United States the satellite has made national newspapers, long familiar in geographically compact Japan and Britain, feasible. Satellites in the 1980s have enabled *The Financial Times, The Wall Street Journal, The International Times Tribune* and *USA Today* to develop into international newspapers. Electronics have also enabled newspapers like the *Los Angeles Times* and the *Asahi Shimbun* of Japan to expand their area of coverage, to offer more editions and to offer zoned editions. In 1986, *Asahi Shimbun* launched a French-language edition.

As yet, the electronic media is still relatively small. A.C. Nielsen reported that in 1983 computerised information deliveries brought in revenues of $3.2 billion in the United States compared to $42 billion for print-delivered information (newspapers, books, magazines).[12] But the former enjoyed a growth rate of 25 per cent per annum versus 11 per cent for print, with predicted revenues of $60 million in 1990. Still the appetite for information appears virtually insatiable so that electronic media growth need not replace newspapers.

Finally, although print is a 500-year-old means of conveying information it still has some advantages over broadcasting and the electronic media. It is cheap, it can be clipped and kept as a record, it has the advantage of habit and familiarity, it requires no hardware and it can be used at any time. It is easy to carry around. Rather than replace print, broadcasting and now electronics often supplement and complement print, though this is not guaranteed into perpetuity. A viable newspaper industry requires circulation revenues, but also national, local and classified advertising revenues. Should alternative media undermine any of these four key revenue foundations, then the future of cheap mass circulation newspapers would be in jeopardy. It is as an insurance against this possibility that many newspapers have expanded into the other media, a process examined in chapter 3 when conglomerate media chains are discussed.

THE FUTURE: THE ELECTRONIC THREAT

We're in a new era . . . We've all traditionally thought of amassing a volume of data and putting it on a printing press . . .

information is the business we're about. While the method of distributing that information is important it should not be the controlling (factor).[13]

This statement, made in 1985 by the chief executive of one of America's largest and most innovative newspaper corporations, clearly recognises that newspaper companies collect information, process it and distribute it. They are information providers. It recognises that they collect data which is not just traditional 'news', but also includes advertising messages, opinion, advice, commentary, analysis, entertainment and any other form of message that makes up information. Newspapers then decide what, where and how to distribute that information. In the 1980s the vast bulk of the words collected daily by the news agencies was junked. The public never saw it. The information was never used.

The term 'newspaper', therefore, is a misleading misnomer for the real business of most newspaper firms. It understates their activities as distributors of all sorts of information, including traditional hard news. It overstates their commitment to paper. They handle much more than 'hard' news and they can and do distribute by means other than paper.

The huge potential demand for electronically delivered information has attracted not only newspaper companies but banks, retailers, finance companies, computer companies, broadcasters and book publishers. Such big name corporations as Citicorp, Sears, Merrill Lynch, RCA, IBM, ATT, CBC, McGraw-Hill and Lockheed are all involved. To what extent electronic publishing will replace the familiar paper is unclear in the mid-1980s. Forecasts of change are most unreliable. For example, in 1978 UK forecasts for Prestel videotext terminals in use in 1981 were for one million. In fact in 1981 13,000 were in use.

One major difference between the publishing and electronic media is the financial requirements. Even for major media companies electronic costs can be prohibitive and the uncertainties considerable. For these reasons the New York Times Company abandoned its electronic New York Times Information Service in 1983. From 1979 to 1984 Knight-Ridder invested $30m in Venture home information services to reach just 6,000 homes. In 1986 having lost $60m they abandoned Venture. In 1983, on the other hand, the Reuters news agency was an electronic success and 90 per cent of Reuters' $344m revenues came from electronically delivered products. In France an experiment with an electronic delivery system in 1986, called Minitel, met with overwhelming success.

11

One major problem for electronic publishing is that it competes with heavily subsidised media alternatives. The advertisers or state usually pay totally for broadcast media. Likewise advertisers or governments pay the bulk of the costs of daily newspapers. Advertisers pay all the costs of freesheets. In the mid-1980s it is not clear which of the electronic products can cover their costs and therefore what the *commercially* viable substitutes for the newspaper in the future will be. To state the obvious: just because something is technologically feasible it does not necessarily mean that it is commercially viable.

Any electronic product must attract sufficient revenues, be it from advertisers, users or elsewhere. For this governments may have to play a special enabling role just as they did with newspapers in the nineteenth century, which required government-provided education and transportation systems. In France, in 1986, it was the free government-provided terminals which largely made Minitel videotext successful.

Table 1.1: Newsprint consumption, selected years, selected countries[a] (in metric tons, and kilos per thousand of population), 1970, 1982

Rank	Country	1970 (in tons)	1982 (in tons)	1982 (kilos per thousand)
1	USA	8,924,000	10,218,000	44,051
2	Japan	1,973,000	2,858,000	23,961
3	UK	1,544,000	1,345,000	23,904
4	West Germany	1,077,000	1,322,000	21,458
5	USSR	928,000	1,224,000	4,536
6	China	392,000	1,040,000	1,234
7	Canada	656,700	1,039,000	42,193
8	Australia	448,500	605,500	40,829
9	France	605,500	554,400	10,225
10	Mexico	158,800	475,700	6,435
11	Italy	282,300	316,000	5,509
12	Brazil	251,800	311,500	2,431
13	India	181,500	278,900	392
14	Sweden	343,400	292,200	35,086
15	Spain	193,800	232,000	6,128
16	Venezuela	84,300	140,000	8,382
17	South Africa[b]	212,500	120,500	3,886
18	Nigeria[b]	17,100	36,000	437

Notes: a. Includes all major consumers (top 17 in 1982).
    b. Largest two in Africa.
Source: UNESCO, *Statistical Year Book*, 1985.

Table 1.2: Distribution of radios and television by major world areas, in percentages, 1965, 1975, 1982

	1965		1975		1982	
	Radio	TV	Radio	TV	Radio	TV
North America	47.9	40.9	45.5	33.8	38.0	28.5
Latin America	6.5	4.3	8.7	6.7	9.2	7.6
Europe, USSR	35.1	40.3	29.8	43.0	26.8	42.4
Oceania	0.6	1.3	1.4	1.4	1.6	1.3
Africa	1.2	0.1	1.8	0.2	2.4	0.7
Arab States	1.1	0.5	1.8	0.9	2.1	1.8
Asia	7.6	12.6	11.0	14.0	19.9	17.7
	100	100	100	100	100	100

Source: UNESCO, *Statistical Year Book*, 1985.

Table 1.3: World distribution of large circulation daily newspapers, by nation, 1985

	Number with circulation over 1,000,000	Number with circulation 500,000– 999,999	Number with circulation 250,000– 499,999	Number with circulation 100,000– 249,999
Japan	15	12	15	84
USSR	10	2	5	2
China	9	11	2	1
UK	5	1	6	22
USA	3	12	20	84
Germany	1	3	11	57
France	0	3	17	18
Australia	0	2	6	8
Italy	0	2	4	14
Canada	0	1	2	13
Sweden	0	1	3	5
Africa (all)	0	0	4	9
Spain	0	0	2	4
Argentina	0	0	2	4
Mexico	0	0	1	9
Chile	0	0	1	3
Brazil	0	0	0	0

Source: Editor and Publisher Year Book, 1985.

Table 1.4: Distribution of newsprint consumption by major areas: 1965, 1975, 1982 (percentages)

	1965	1975	1982
North America	47.9	41.6	42.0[b]
Latin America	4.7	5.1	6.3
Europe, USSR	32.0	29.9	27.5[c]
Oceania	3.0	2.8	3.0
Africa[a]	0.6	1.2	0.7
Arab States	0.6	0.5	0.4
Asia[a]	11.2	18.9	20.1[d]
	100.0	100.0	100.0

Notes: a. excludes Arab States.
b. of which Canada represents 4%.
c. of which USSR represents 5%, UK 5%, Germany 5%, France 2%.
d. of which Japan represents 11%, China 5%, India 1%.
Source: UNESCO, *Statistical Year Book*, 1985.

Table 1.5: Distribution of daily general interest newspaper circulation by major areas, 1965, 1975, 1982 (percentages)

	1965	1975	1982
North America	18.9	16.2	13.2[b]
Latin America	5.4	5.6	6.4
Europe, USSR	51.2	53.0	45.6[c]
Oceania	1.6	1.7	1.2
Africa[a]	0.6	1.0	1.0
Arab States	0.5	0.7	1.2
Asia[a]	21.8	21.8	31.4[d]
	100.0	100.0	100.0

Notes: a. excludes Arab States.
b. of which Canada represents 1%.
c. of which USSR represents 13%, West Germany 4%, UK 4%, France 2%.
d. of which Japan represents 13%.
Source: UNESCO, *Statistical Year Book*, 1985.

NOTES

1. *Sunday Times*, 19 January 1986.
2. The method of analysis used in this book is one frequently used in industrial organisation studies. Industry conduct and performance is largely determined by the basic conditions of supply and demand and industry

structure. By examining changes in supply and demand, changes in structure can be explained. Structure determines conduct. Conduct in turn determines performance. See F.M. Scherer, *Industrial Market Structure and Economic Performance* (Rand McNally, Chicago, 1976), p. 4.

3. From 1981 to 1986 the number of television sets in China increased from three million to 60 million. It meant 600 million had access to television in China. Meanwhile in India, the satellite Insat 18 launched in 1983 increased the number with access to television to 400 million.

4. Marshall McLuhan, *Understanding the Media* (McGraw Hill, New York, 1964), p. 155.

5. McLuhan, *Understanding the Media*, p. 11.

6. The exclusion of countries such as Brazil, Mexico, Egypt, Indonesia and Pakistan with large populations, and of countries like Sweden and Israel with high circulations and interesting state subsidies is justified on the pragmatic grounds that the book had to be kept to a manageable size.

7. Court papers such as *Chin Pao* (Capital Paper) and *Ti Pao* (Court Gazette) appeared in China in the mid-seventeenth century.

8. No relation to *The Australian* launched in 1964.

9. In 1880 *The Times* had 80 per cent of the London market.

10. See the preambles to both the 1977 British Royal Commission and the 1980 Canadian Royal Commission on the press.

11. Figure 1.3 is explained in terms of specific examples to show that not all newspapers compete for the same reader. (i) In the geographical dimension in Britain, the venerable world-renowned newspaper *The Times* of London is one of several quality national newspapers which compete with each other. It also competes very marginally with the *International Herald Tribune* for international readers and the reputable regional *Yorkshire Post* in Yorkshire for readers there. It does not compete at all with a local paper like the *Darlington and Stockton Times*. (ii) In the time dimension *The Times*, a morning paper, competes only slightly with London's evening *The Standard*. (iii) In the quality dimension, *The Times* is a quality paper and so does not compete with Fleet Street's popular tabloid daily *Sun*, also owned by News International. (iv) In the generality dimension, *The Times* is a general newspaper so competes only marginally with the specialist *Sporting Pink* or even the *Financial Times* despite its extensive sports and business coverage. (v) In the political dimension, *The Times* is slightly right of centre so competes to some extent with the more left-wing quality national the *Guardian* and the right-wing middle-brow *Daily Telegraph*.

Often in fact a newspaper's most intense competition comes not from newspapers but from another medium. Turning to the other media in Figure 1.4 *The Times* competes with, but also complements, more serious television shows, documentaries and serious radio like BBC Radio 4, and such serious weekly magazines as *The Economist* and *The Sunday Times*, for readers' attention.

The Times therefore competes to some extent with the other media for the same advertising expenditures. Those 'top people' who read *The Times* may also watch national news, and read quality magazines such as *Home and Gardens, Punch* and the *Illustrated London News*. The 'top people' also see billboards and have letter boxes into which freesheets and flyers may be placed, and sometimes even read. All these media products compete for

The Times readers' attention, and therefore *The Times'* actual and potential advertising revenues. Readers of *The Times* may also have home computers and access to electronic data banks, which again compete with *The Times*. Finally, readers of *The Times* have only limited time and funds. To the extent that *The Times* offers entertainment, and some observers and owners such as Murdoch place newspapers in the entertainment industry, *The Times* even competes with a good novel, a game of golf or the latest movie.

To illustrate the case of the United States, the quality metropolitan, the *Washington Post*, competes with the national *Wall Street Journal* but not the national *USA Today*. Because of the distances and different time zones of the USA it barely competes with the quality metropolitan *Los Angeles Times*. The *Washington Post* competes marginally with local papers from Washington suburban areas but not at all with California locals. The magazines *US News and World Report*, *Business Week* and *Atlantic* provide some competition in terms of hard news, as do quality radio and television programmes such as CBS' '60 Minutes' and PBS' 'Washington Week in Review'. Information Services such as the Dow Jones News/Retrieval Service likewise compete with the *Washington Post* as a source of data.

12. *Editor and Publisher*, 4 April 1984.
13. *Business Week*, 2 February 1985.

2

Basic Conditions of the Newspaper Industry

The basic conditions under which newspapers are produced are the subject of this chapter. It begins with a discussion of the different ideological and political systems under which newspaper production takes place and their implications for the nature of the product. It then discusses the newspaper market and the three different groups who buy newspapers: the advertisers, the readers and the influence-seekers. It stresses the importance of advertisers and influence-seekers. The nature of newspaper competition with the other media and the problems of defining the newspaper industry are examined.

IDEOLOGICAL THEORIES OF THE PRESS

Press analysts attempting to explain the press have traditionally identified four overlapping ideological patterns.[1] The first two are the similar (1) authoritarian and (2) Communist patterns, the second two types of press system are the related (3) libertarian and (4) social responsibility theories. Recently a different pattern more appropriate to Third World countries and a variant of the first two has appeared. Clearly the economic behaviour and performance of a newspaper depends upon the philosophical environment in which it operates. A brief review of the four traditional theories of the press emphasising the economic implications follow. The evolving philosophy of the role of newspapers in the developing world is also examined.

The authoritarian pattern

This has its history embedded in the mercantilist philosophy of the sixteenth century in England. The role of the press, as of trade, was to support the government in its efforts to build up the strength of the nation. The press existed only under tolerance of the government. It therefore had an obligation to put forward the government's view and avoid undue criticism of the government, even though it operated as a private enterprise. In the twentieth century many countries endure such an authoritarian or neo-mercantilist system in which privately owned newspapers have no more press freedom than the state interprets as beneficial to the state. Hence within authoritarian systems wide variations in the extent of press freedom may be found but newspaper firms are typically privately owned and profit motivated.

The Communist system

This is a derivative of the authoritarian system since the function of the press is to serve state interests and support world socialism. However, the press is owned by the state. It is an integral and vital part of the state propaganda machine. It is a vehicle to control the people, not to entertain and inform them. Enhancing and strengthening socialism, not profits, motivates the press in the USSR, China and the other Communist countries. The state not only controls all aspects of newspaper production but also distribution. The state decides who should, and who should not, receive particular newspapers.

The libertarian state

This can be traced back to the Enlightenment and the rise of rationalist thought. Philosophers such as John Locke propagated the view that man had inherent natural rights including the right to pursue truth. Enshrined most clearly in the Declaration of Independence of the United States in 1776, these views claim individuals should be free to pursue these liberties without interference, particularly without government interference. Indeed the state is seen as the major threat to these rights. From the economic point of view this philosophy emphasises a free market permitting: (a) anybody to act as a supplier of information and pursue the truth, and (b) everybody to be free to choose who is to supply information to them. From the social and political point of view the press becomes the 'fourth estate' informing the public about the activities of the state, and acting as watchdog over it.

The social responsibility theory

This evolved in the second half of the twentieth century out of the libertarian theory. It claims that the newspaper has a social responsibility that goes beyond the truth-seeking and informing role of the libertarian press to that of carrying out these activities in a socially responsible way. This implies a public service role and social and moral obligations, which then necessitate some sort of control, preferably self control and Press Councils. This view may open the door to some form of government interference.

New information order

The traditional ideologies discussed above focus largely on how the press operates within a country's own boundaries. Whilst the 158 members of the United Nations (UN) have pledged support to the UN Universal Declaration of Human Rights and its goal of press freedom, the 1980s saw a controversy develop centred at the UN Educational, Scientific and Cultural Organisation (UNESCO) which has its headquarters in Paris. The issue involved the so-called 'new information order' and the desire of many Third World countries, supported by the USSR, to control what is reported about them to the outside world. Concerned that much coverage of Third World countries is inadequate and negative, a majority of UNESCO members, mostly developing countries, have proposed a new information order. This new order would include government licensing of journalists, government enforced codes of conduct for news agencies, government restriction on news sources and government protection of journalists. Such government supervision of the media is anathema to the Jeffersonian concept of a free press, its role as the Fourth Estate and watchdog on the government, and to the free flow of information.

The economics of the new information order include both practical and political factors. At the purely practical level news

19

collection in the developed world is cheaper and easier than in most Third World countries. The developed world has the social overhead capital in place — transport and communications — to facilitate news collection, the literate readers to consume it, the advertising markets to make news collection commercially viable, and the trained and educated personnel capable of editing, processing and distributing it. Those purely practical economic prerequisites are not available in much of the Third World. Problems of news collection in the Third World are often compounded by political uncertainties and bureaucratic road-blocks. These obstacles to a worldwide balanced collection of information support the Third World's contention that the world's news agenda is biased in favour of items about the West. The flow of news is grossly uneven and the result is 'information imperialism'. Many smaller developed countries sympathise as they find their media dominated by US and Western news and entertainment. The Western nations in general, however, do not accept the 'new information order' with its curbs on reporting as the solution to the acknowledged problem. Whilst the smaller Western countries have pledged themselves to work within UNESCO to enable the communications revolution to continue without government control, the USA and Britain have withdrawn from the organisation.

THE READER MARKET

In the 1980s newspapers are just one in an ever increasing number of means by which citizens can receive news, opinion, analysis, information, entertainment and advertising. Prior to World War I newspapers had a virtual but not absolute monopoly of mass communication. There were few good substitutes, but even then there were telegraphs, word of mouth, letters, billboards, books and periodicals. Since the turn of the century more efficient alternatives have been developed. Films appeared in 1910, radio in the 1920s, television in the 1930s. The electronic media in the 1970s based on the microchip has created an information revolution.

As new means of mass communication have evolved the traditional methods have not in general been replaced but have adjusted and modified their role to meet the new condition. Radio reduced the importance of the newspaper 'scoop' and the impact of the 'extra' whilst television eliminated demand for such radio content as 'soaps' and 'situation comedies'. Television came to dominate much entertainment, radio to dominate the latest news, and newspapers to specialise in more in-depth coverage and analysis of news and entertainment than could be provided by broadcast media. Clearly the newspaper market for readers is 'soft edged', and other media industries provide keen competition for the reader's time, attention and money.

Accompanying the rising competition from newer media many analysts of the newspaper industry have perceived increased emphasis of what has been called 'commercialism' or the pursuit of profit.[2] Frequently, without proof, this has been regarded as a retrograde step.[3] As a result, it has been said, newspapers have de-emphasised their traditional role of creating and leading public opinion and instead become followers of public opinion supplying what the public demands. Thus the product is different. Quality is different. Whether it is worse is moot.[4]

In the developed countries of northern Europe, North America, Japan and Australia there is an established press and established newspaper reading tradition which developed before the rise of close message-delivery substitutes in the form of radio and television. There exists in these countries an engrained newspaper habit, even an addiction. Though their markets are mature in terms of readership with circulation per household in most of the developed countries showing little or even negative growth in recent decades, it is still a constantly changing market.

The potential reader market depends upon:

Literacy

Literacy and an 'adequate' income are prerequisites for mass circulation newspapers. In general, where the newspaper habit was already established newspaper demand survived the introduction of radio and television. But where the radio preceded general literacy and adequate incomes, as in many developing countries, radio provided a powerful alternative and barrier to entry. Furthermore, in the late twentieth century many other consumer goods which did not exist 80 years ago compete for the limited discretionary income of consumers in developing countries.

Demographics

World population growth suggests a large potential market for newspapers, although Europe, North America and Japan which account for three-quarters of world newsprint consumption, have slow population growth. Within any given population the propensity to purchase newspapers is affected by the structure of the population. The young and the old are known to have a lower propensity to consumer newspapers. The aging of the Western world on its own implies that circulation per 1,000 will drop in the future. Likewise, faster than average growth rates for minority and immigrant populations in the developed countries, who typically have lower propensities to buy newspapers, implies falling circulation per 1,000.

Lifestyles

Changing lifestyles influence the propensity to consume newspapers and some generalisations can be made. Several recent developments in the West have worked against newspaper consumption. (a) As more people abandon public transport to drive their own car to work so their opportunity to buy newspapers on the street and their ability to read them in transit diminishes. (b) In North America particularly, the movement away from the city centres to the suburbs has had negative effects on demand for big city newspapers as commuters' sense of identity with the city centre has declined. (c) Whilst increased female participation in the workforce in many countries has increased family incomes, it has also meant less time available to adult family members to read the newspaper. (d) The additional family income from higher female participation has also enabled family members to pursue more expensive leisure activities in their available, and now often scarce, leisure time. Consequently increased female participation in the labour force has been associated with a negative effect on newspaper demand. It has also altered the nature of demand with increased demand for working women magazines, and in newspapers living sections and material for the working woman.

Mobility

A further social development working to decrease newspaper demand is increased mobility. Particularly in geographically large countries where national newspapers are few, such as Canada, USA and Australia, and where regional newspapers have traditionally

22

predominated, increased mobility implies decreased attachment to a particular locality. On average Americans move once every five years. Since newspapers are, amongst other things, a recorder of local activities, increased mobility is correlated with decreased demand for this particular function of newspapers. At the same time, the mobile society creates a more homogeneous society with broader interests. This factor has meant increased demand for mass-circulation national newspapers in the United States, sufficient to support in the 1980s such newcomers as *USA Today*. Greater mobility has also meant decreased demand for local news and increased demand for syndicated material of a more general interest.[5]

The cover price of the newspaper to the reader in the Western world would appear to make it a magnificent bargain since the typical price for a daily newspaper covers little more than the cost of ink and newsprint.[6] The newspaper is one of the few items available to the customer from the private sector for less than its variable cost. However, since most of the alternative sources of media information and entertainment are provided at zero price, once the consumer has bought the receiver, the price of a newspaper is a consideration to the reader.[7]

In the reader market, therefore, the newspaper generally faces a downward sloping demand curve (Figure 2.1). As price increases, quantity demanded will decrease despite the apparently inconsequential price and small income effect. For example, some subscribers in two-newspaper households can opt to buy just one newspaper; regular household subscribers may decide to go without regular delivery and buy on the street as required or only on those days important to them (for example, on the day food stores advertise, TV guides are issued, or weekend supplements added); irregular buyers may buy even less regularly. In other words, for many functions of the newspaper the reader does not have to buy daily and can use the newspaper less intensively by not buying every day and substituting more of the broadcast media for his total information input. Pass-along use can also increase.

In the developing world, prices to readers make the paper less of a bargain. In India, a newspaper subscription for one year for a school teacher in 1985 could absorb up to one month's income. Such a price for a newspaper, in a world where transistor radios are cheaply available to provide free information and news, is a formidable obstacle to circulation growth. The tradition or habit of newspaper reading is not widely engrained and not likely to be

Figure 2.1: Reader demand

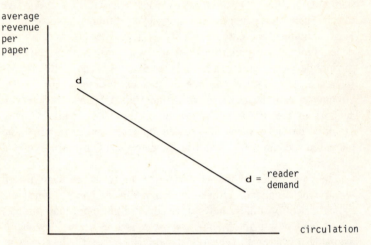

adopted. The explanation is as follows. Since newspapers in the Third World reach only a small proportion of the population, many of whose incomes are low by Western standards, the newspaper has little appeal to advertisers as a medium to sell their products and services. Furthermore, advertising budgets for all media are small in the Third World. Circulation revenues must cover the bulk of costs. Consequently newspapers are frequently caught in a vicious circle in developing countries: low incomes lead to low circulation; which leads to low advertising revenues and so inadequate total revenues; this necessitates low editorial budgets, usually poor quality and therefore low circulation, even in relation to the potential market. The potential of the reader market in many developing countries can be compared to the pre-popular press, pre-general education newspaper market of nineteenth-century Britain and America but with additional handicaps, in particular the competition of cheap broadcast media substitutes.

ADVERTISING DEMAND

Advertising and related promotion expenditures in 1985 amounted to about $150 billion worldwide.[8] The United States alone had estimated advertising and related promotional expenditures of $96 billion for 1985. Table 2.1 gives the share of total world advertising

Table 2.1: World advertising expenditures, 1985

Country	% of world advertising expenditure	% of GNP
United States	51.1	1.4
Japan	12.2	1.0
Britain	6.4	1.3
W. Germany	4.8	0.6
Brazil	3.7	0.3
Canada	3.2	1.0
France	2.9	0.5
Australia	2.7	1.5
Italy	1.8	0.3
Spain	1.5	0.4
Holland	1.4	0.9
Other Europe	3.4	—
Other Latin America	3.0	—
Other	1.5	—

Sources: The Economist; Europa Year Book, 1985.

expenditures by country.

For the newspaper industry the major market is the advertising market. Most newspapers in the developed world get the majority of revenues from advertisements and advertising is essential to them. As much as 80 per cent of revenues at *The Times* of London, the *Wall Street Journal* and *Le Monde* come from advertisements. Advertisers are not merely interested in a newspaper's circulation but rather in its ability to reach those readers who have a high propensity to purchase their products. For these reasons newspapers which reach a very specific identifiable affluent market, for example *The Times* or the *Wall Street Journal*, can charge much higher advertising rates per 1,000 readers than down-market papers. In 1985, it cost $100,000 per page, at the *Wall Street Journal* to reach less than one per cent of the US population; but a very rich one per cent.

The percentage of national income spent on advertising over the years varies by country and according to the business cycle. Governments, large corporations, small businesses and individuals all buy advertising space basically to provide information, to persuade and to create image. Over the years the general trend worldwide has been for newspapers to receive a declining proportion of a growing advertising pie. With more and more television channels and stations it was inevitable newspapers would lose some market share, but so long as the pie grew their advertising revenues could be maintained.

25

Advertising trends

Since 1945 advertisers have become much more sophisticated in the allocation of their advertising budget and much more specific in their requirements from the media. There has been increased use of statistics, market research, market surveys and quantitative methods. Furthermore, the industrial structure of many economies and the nature of the industry of many important advertisers has changed in recent years. The information and service sectors have grown, whilst primary and secondary industries have declined. In 1986, also, the world of consumer products was becoming increasingly homogeneous as more and more products were sold on a global basis. Large chains of department stores and supermarkets have evolved in North America and western Europe. There has been an accompanying move of advertising decision-making away from the local level, at which most newspapers operate. In addition, for purposes such as broad image, other media, particularly network television, claim to be more successful. Consequently in some areas newspapers' share of total advertising expenditures has declined more significantly than in others. Recent developments, particularly in North America where the three major television networks have declined as television diversifies, the use of videos, television commercial 'zapping' and increased satellite communication both for broadcasting and for producing newspapers will further change the pattern of newspaper advertising.[9]

These developments have created a bias in favour of newspaper chains for national advertisements. Chains can offer space across the chain's products. Thomson International and News International have the capacity to offer newspaper advertising space worldwide as well as in other media. In 1984 only six per cent of national brand advertising expenditures appeared as newspaper advertisements in the USA, in part because of the difficulty of placing advertisements in 1,700 separate daily publications.

Advertising classifications

Newspaper advertising can be characterised in different ways but a breakdown by national, local and classified is often made. For each of the categories of national, local and retail, classified and non-run-of-the-press (ROP) advertising there are different actual and potential alternatives. At the national level the aim of advertising is mainly to bring the name of the company before the consumer and to project a certain image. Up to 1986 this was the forte of network and national television with its broad reach, reflected in the high rates charged during Princess Diana's wedding, the 1984 Olympic Games and the US National Football League Superbowls. For example, at the 1986 Superbowl, it cost $1.1 million per minute.[10]

At the local level, radio and local television provide close substitutes for the newspaper as a means of sending out specific informative advertising messages. If the message is of a very detailed nature however, then hard copy, newspaper, has a clear advantage. For weekly grocery prices, entertainment details, information about houses or new cars, newspapers are still favoured.

For most classified advertisements in the mid-1980s television and radio are unsatisfactory alternatives. Hard copy enables the consumer to browse, select, clip, back-reference and compare. But newspapers do not have a monopoly of hard copy, and an increasing number of non-run-of-the-press (non-ROP) 'shoppers', flyers and similar free newspaper products provided stiff competition in the 1980s. In addition videotext (electronic classifieds), could provide a powerful competitor in the near future, allowing the consumer to scan constantly updated data on a home VDT.

A recent source of revenues for many newspapers has been non-ROP advertisements. To a considerable extent competition for the newspaper's advertising dollar, flyers and inserts are frequently distributed with the daily newspaper and sometimes printed by it too. As a result the newspaper, by exploiting its existing circulation and distribution network, has been able to turn this new competition to advantage. In the future, they could well expand this delivery service to distribute magazines and other material currently carried by the increasingly expensive and inefficient mails.

Nevertheless, the newspaper industry depends upon all categories of advertising and, should an economically superior means of supplying any one of these advertising classifications evolve, the total economic viability of cheap subsidised mass-circulation newspapers could be undermined. To defend their advertising market, newspaper firms have produced freesheets, introduced colour, changed format, advertised, modified product content and introduced new products.

New products

In 1982 the Gannett Company introduced a new sort of newspaper for the North American market called *USA Today*. In Britain in 1986 *Today* was launched with a similar format. Made possible by the use of satellites to distribute copy, *USA Today* had, by 1984, created the third-largest daily circulation in the United States. Independent market research showed that many *USA Today* readers were 'young, male, professional, educated and affluent', typically the sort of consumer advertisers wish to reach.

Analysis of *USA Today* provides some insight into the demand for newspaper advertising. In 1983 this market in the USA was worth $25 billion. Advertisers wished to reach specific audiences and this was part of *USA Today*'s problem. Its sales were spread nation-wide. This excluded *USA Today* from the 57 per cent of the market provided by retail advertisers, since it could carry no local advertising. Secondly, 69 per cent of its readers were anonymous in the sense that they bought from newsstands and vending machines. In fact many readers were probably occasional readers, typically travellers. Consequently, *USA Today* failed to achieve either the deep penetration of a particular local market, as does a local daily, or of a specific market, as do specialist newspapers like the *Wall Street Journal*, or of a huge well-defined mass market, as do the news-weekly magazines like *Time, Newsweek, US News and World Report* with a total circulation of over ten million. Thus even though a full page advertisement in *USA Today* cost $28,000 in 1984, versus $100,000 for a full page in the *Wall Street Journal*, analysts estimated that by 1986 *USA Today* had lost $300 million.[11]

USA Today illustrates that to advertisers readers are not all equal. At *USA Today*, despite reader circulation exceeding expectations and forecasts, advertising demand did not meet Gannett's goals and ran about 20 per cent below projections. The problem at *USA Today* was an affluent but unidentified audience. Similar cases of advertisers shunning either high circulation or increased circulation have been recorded in the past. *Life* magazine folded despite high circulation. In London *The Times* twice increased circulation only to find advertisers were uninterested in reaching the students and lower income intellectuals who made up the bulk of the new readers.

Advertising and the monopoly dailies

Where two dailies compete the second newspaper often propagates the message that a monopoly newspaper would have the power to boost advertising rates to newspaper advertisers. They argue that it is in the interest of merchants who advertise to support the underdog newspaper in order to prevent high advertising rates from the monopoly survivor newspaper in the future. Even without the option of alternative advertising media such as radio, television, flyers and billboards, the argument is not compelling. It is based on a fallacy of composition. The argument for an advertiser *not* to support the second newspaper is as follows: if all merchants support the second newspaper in proportion to its circulation the second newspaper might be viable, but since first newspapers have proved themselves the better advertising medium in reach per dollar (that is usually why they are the first newspaper), it is in the self-interest of each merchant individually to place all his advertisements in the first newspaper. Then, if all other merchants support the second paper he enjoys a permanent advantage over them in reach per dollar. In other words he enjoys a free ride, a costless advertising advantage. If he supports the second paper then he permits rival merchants to enjoy a costless advantage over him. And if they all pursue their own individual self-interest, advertise only in the first paper, and allow the second to fail, then all merchants will pay any higher advertising rates in the future. No merchant will enjoy a competitive advantage. Finally there is little evidence that higher advertising rates per 1,000 readers do follow the decline of the second paper.

The surviving paper usually enjoys additional circulation within its own area without significantly increased editorial and distribution costs. In terms of advertising reach, costs may even fall as first copy costs and distribution costs are spread over more readers. Average cost per reader reached falls. Given the availability of non-newspaper advertising alternatives and some countervailing power on behalf of the bigger merchants, the survivor newspaper needs them as customers as much as the merchants need the newspaper. Hence it is unlikely rates will be increased appreciably. There is little advantage, either in the short run or the long run, for merchants individually or even collectively to support the second paper. This natural tendency to one monopoly daily in all cities is called the Jackal effect.[12]

Advertising in perspective

To put world advertising demand into perspective, the United States accounted for more than half of all advertising expenditures in the 1980s. Britain, Australia, Canada and Japan account for nearly one-quarter more. Africa, Asia (less Japan) and Latin America together account for less than 15 per cent. The USA, Britain, Canada, Australia and Japan therefore absorb 75 per cent of world advertising expenditures but represent just 10 per cent of world population. Advertising expenditures are biased towards affluent countries. Within any country advertising expenditures are also skewed towards the more affluent. Whilst this is not surprising it is important. Since advertising underwrites the free press it means that both internationally and intranationally the affluent are better served than the poor.

Up until 1985 governments, particularly in Europe, regulated broadcast advertising. In Sweden television advertising is totally banned. In West Germany it is limited to one 20 minute block daily. In Italy it is 80 minutes per day. In both Britain and France the number of channels was limited to three commercial channels in 1985 but with more to come. In Italy, television advertising grew fifteen-fold to $720 million between 1982 and 1984 when regulations on commercial broadcasting were relaxed. In 1983 the EEC recommended relaxing many broadcasting restrictions. To some extent this recognises the inevitable, as satellites and new technology make it increasingly difficult to exclude broadcasting from outside national boundaries. The implications for print advertising's share of advertising expenditures in Europe is that it must decline with further broadcasting deregulation. As Table 2.1 shows, the share of GNP spent on advertising in Europe is low compared to other developed countries. In absolute amounts therefore newspapers may not suffer if deregulation encourages increased expenditures to the levels of North America, Japan and Australia.

In theory, so long as additional advertising expenditures generate even greater additional total revenues there will be advertising growth. Consequently, the new techniques need not necessarily draw expenditures from traditional methods such as newspapers, but rather may increase total advertising expenditures. The newspaper advertising base is not necessarily threatened.[13]

The press in 1985 continued to dominate advertising. In Britain in 1983 regional newspapers took 23 per cent, nationals 16 per cent and locals, freesheets and magazines another 23 per cent of the total.

In the USA in 1984 daily newspaper advertising was about one-third of the US total. In France in 1984 newspapers still took 49 per cent of the total.

Advertising is a mixed blessing. Controversial as it is, it provides the essential foundation of mass circulation newspapers in the developed world in the 1980s. Equally, an inadequate demand for newspaper advertising jeopardises the future of the newspaper industry in the developing world.

PROPAGANDA DEMAND

In addition to the demand of the readers and the advertisers there is the demand of owners to propagate their point of view and to influence the reader. In the Communist countries, and most of the Third World, political propaganda is the chief *raison d'être* for newspapers. Propaganda is also important in the West.

The demand for power and influence or to propagate is most apparent in the developed world in the national papers, particularly the high prestige papers, such as *The Times* of London, *El Corriere della Sera*, the *Washington Post* and other big city, and particularly capital city, papers. Many of the most famous papers have been run at a loss for years with little prospects of a turn-around and have been owned by groups who do not throw money away elsewhere. The reason they will sustain losses for long periods of time is that the influence that those papers exert makes them valuable. Their economic pay-off can be considerable.[14]

Demand for propaganda is unlike the demand of readers and advertisers which is reaffirmed and renewed daily. Purchasers of influential loss-making newspapers have to evaluate the likelihood of being able to turn the paper around and make it profitable, along with the ability to influence those people who might be able to help the owner of the paper in other activities at some time in the future. For example, conglomerates such as ARCO, News International, Fiat, Thomson and Lonrho have bought newspapers which have been able to help and influence politicians, including Mrs Thatcher, Mayor Koch of New York and President Carter. In Italy a group of businessmen bought *El Corriere della Sera* in 1986 to prevent it falling into the hands of those who might use it to pursue ends costly and unacceptable to them. Putting a value on the ability to support those who, later on, may have a say in the granting of television licences, oil drilling rights, loans, in the decision to approve mergers

31

or thwart them, to decide what is in the public interest, and also to punish those who obstruct the owners' plans, is exceedingly difficult. But it provides the rationale for otherwise thrifty owners to subsidise small elite papers for prolonged periods. They represent investment in lobbying, insurance and personal relations. It is like a stock of goodwill to a conglomerate and represents an asset even if, like goodwill, it does not appear explicitly on a conglomerate's balance sheet.

Finally, there is Communist propaganda demand outside the Communist world. In 1985 the USSR's International Department spent three billion dollars to provide disinformation to the Western media.[15] The KGB set up newspapers throughout the West. These were non-Communist papers, often apparently conservative, whose purpose was to be disruptive to the NATO alliance. In 1981 a millionaire businessman set up *Ethnos* in Greece. *Ethnos* soon had the largest circulation in Athens. Apparently conservative and sensationalist, *Ethnos* supported the USSR when a Korean commercial aeroplane was shot down in 1982. It claimed USA involvement in the assassination of Indira Gandhi in India. Not until 1983 was the KGB identified as the true backer of *Ethnos*. In the early 1980s, the financial manager at *Sankei Shimbun*, Japan's huge circulation financial daily, was identified as a KGB agent.[16]

DEFINING THE NEWSPAPER MARKET

A central issue of competition policy throughout the Western economy has been a concern with maximum social and economic welfare. To this end a number of Royal Commissions in Britain, Sweden and Canada, and similar public bodies in the US and elsewhere, have examined their newspaper industries out of concerns that industry structure, behaviour and performance were sub-optimal. In other words, there were grounds to believe that newspapers could be made to serve the public interest better.[17] Defining the newspaper industry from the supply side, in general terms of products made from newsprint used to convey news and opinion, is not always an appropriate grouping for the examination of firms' and industries' conduct. Nevertheless, it was the approach largely taken by all these bodies and merits discussion.

The conduct of firms actually in the newspaper industry as well as of potential new newspaper suppliers is much influenced by the availability of non-newspaper substitutes able to meet the demands of readers and advertisers. Producers of non-newspaper substitutes for newspaper readers and advertisers create significant competition and will influence newspaper conduct even if they are not newspapers, but rather radio or television or magazines (see Figure 1.3).[18]

In this book the central concern is the structure, conduct and performance of the newspaper industry. In terms of firms' behaviour the demand side of the economic process may also be very important. Goods with similar raw materials and productive methods of supply, in other words from the same SIC (national standard industrial classification), may not be closely competing goods in the market, for example the British *The Times* and the sensational tabloid *Daily Mirror*.

Nevertheless, substitution can and does take place on the supply side. Firms have to take account of the ability of other firms to respond to a rise in the price or quality of their good, that is firms with a similar production capacity which already produce substitutes might produce additional quantities whilst potential rivals in the same SIC might enter their market. Whilst Gannett's *USA Today* in 1986 still had a monopoly of the daily national tabloid market, Gannett had to take account of the possible introduction of, say, a Knight-Ridder or Newhouse equivalent.

Furthermore, different supply groupings may be required for studying different aspects of newspaper firms' conduct. When account is taken of geographical and qualitative sub-markets, the majority of newspapers are monopolies and national SICs underestimate the market power; but in terms of meeting demand for newspapers as bundles of characteristics, many close substitutes and potential substitutes exist and national SICs overestimate market power. Often the SIC supply side grouping is inappropriate and can lead to misleading conclusions about monopoly and market power.[19]

To examine market conduct economic theory suggests defining an industry to include those firms which produce goods and services seen as close substitutes by either buyers or sellers. For newspapers, buyers include both advertisers and readers. For both advertisers and readers non-newspaper vehicles are available to meet the demand.[20]

Using all these criteria can lead to a different viewpoint on the newspaper industry, one which is frequently more relevant as regards firms' conduct and performance than that derived from a simple SIC supply side characteristic.

In the reader market any given newspaper provides the reader with a number of product characteristics, for example: news, information, opinion, analysis, comment, entertainment and advertising. Frequently the newspaper has an apparent monopoly in the sense of there being no close substitute in the form of another newspaper. In Britain in 1985 no city had two evening newspapers and in the United States in 1985 only 27 cities had competing dailies. Most local newspapers have a geographic monopoly. Yet if the newspaper price goes too high or quality falls too low the reader can obtain news, information, opinion and analysis from a mix of radio, television, magazines, national newspapers and other sources. Substitutes on the reader demand side exist.

For advertisers too there are frequently satisfactory alternatives available from other SICs. Radio, television, billboards and magazines can provide image; yellow pages, flyers, catalogues, freesheets and inserts can provide detail. Competition for the advertising dollar across the media is intense in the developed countries. Clearly therefore, even where a SIC newspaper monopoly exists either by virtue of geography or quality, alternatives to both the reader and the advertiser are available and influence newspaper firms' conduct.

Finally, newspapers are perishable products. This affects market power. When a strike occurs in industries, such as the motor industry or textile industry, producers can build up inventories beforehand and firms can then run down their inventories to protect market shares. But in the newspaper industry stocks cannot be built up. Nothing is more obsolete than yesterday's news. When a strike occurs the advertisers and readers who make up demand immediately look for both newspaper and non-newspaper substitutes.

In summary many newspapers have an apparent monopoly but those monopolies are generally vulnerable to existing or potential competition from newspapers and, very importantly, to non-newspaper competition. The last decade has seen dramatic technological change, making it easier for new competitors to enter the media market and, at the same time, making existing newspapers more competitive.

MOTIVES

This section examines the question of what motivates newspaper owners to produce newspapers. Elementary economic theory assumes that profits are the carrot that drives the capitalist system.

Some newspaper industry observers have suggested that such a simplistic approach as the profit motive may be a useful and practical working assumption to analyse industries producing most consumer goods and services, but not for newspapers with their important role in the democratic system and their ability to influence. In 1982 the former head of a Canadian Royal Commission on the press attacked certain newspaper firms on the very grounds that they were profit motivated.[21] The implication was that owners of newspapers should be above profits, rather as church ministers are supposed to be above a decent salary and poorly-paid nurses in Britain and doctors in Italy above going on strike.

Adam Smith, in discussing the market system and the invisible hand, said, 'Man is led to promote an end which was no part of his intention.'[22] In other words, even if businesses, including newspapers, are motivated solely by self-interest, the final outcome can be in the public interest. The results of human designs are not necessarily those intended, but equally important, neither are they necessarily the opposite of those planned. Sometimes the results are those planned but in addition have favourable externalities or outcomes for others not considered at the planning stage. This is Adam Smith's reason for advocating the market system, 'it is not from the benevolence of the butcher, the brewer or, baker that we expect our dinner, but from their regard to their own interest'.[23] On the other hand the external effects, the effects on others, of pursuing our own self-interest may not be in the public interest. Furthermore, individual human designs may not achieve their intended outcomes, nor may group plans be fulfilled. The important point is that approval of motives does not necessarily mean approval of outcomes and vice versa. Pursuing our own self-interest may lead to socially desirable outcomes.

The special roles of the newspaper in many societies, both democratic and authoritarian, in the twentieth century include those of informer, educator, opinion-maker, persuader and commentator. What motivates the controllers of the newspaper industry and what goals they plan to achieve is clearly of great concern. However, it is the consequences of their plans on the rest of society which are important for this study where newspapers are assessed in terms of performance not owners' intentions, whilst stressing that the two are obviously inter-independent.

Religious motives

Some newspapers are produced for non-economic reasons. In a secular era in northern Europe when only a small minority of the population are active churchgoers, claims of biblical righteousness in 1986 were rare. In American where 40 per cent of the population attend church, Christian papers produced as a vehicle of ministry still flourished. The recently revitalised *Christian Science Monitor* was perhaps the best known example. It lost money but making money was not its prime objective. President Reagan's first read, so it was reported, was the *Washington Times*, not the world-famous *Post* (just as Winston Churchill's reportedly was the *Daily Mirror* not *The Times* of London). The *Washington Times* cost its owners $100 million per year to produce in 1985 and lost $50 million.[24] Started in 1982 after the *Washington Star* folded, it had several Pulitzer Prize winners on its staff and spent lavishly on international reporting. In 1985 it began distribution across America. Yet advertisers particularly, but readers too, ignored it. The reason appeared to be that the paper was owned by the Unification Church, better known as the Moonies, and headed by the controversial Rev. Sun Myung Moon.

Conglomerates' motives

Large newspaper chains are often publicly-owned corporations. Driven neither by egomania nor religious fervour they probably most closely approximate the profit maximisers of traditional theory. In 1984 John Quinn of Gannett claimed: '. . . our policy is not to have a policy'.[25] Such a philosophy implies their papers are followers of public opinion, not leaders, with potentially detrimental effects on product quality. Traditionally newspapers have led opinion but the stockmarket treadmill compels public corporations to pursue commercial success measured by profits.[26]

Recent contributions to the theory of the firm have paid attention to the difficulties involved in co-ordinating the individual career ambitions of all levels of a corporation bureaucracy with the corporation's goals.[27] Few of Thomson's or Gannett's editorial staff, for example, would put corporation profits before a good salary, a good expense account, a good story, their own professional reputation, promotion, an injustice rectified, good working conditions, journalistic excellence and a host of other personal and worthy considerations. Similar non-profit objectives of managers and personnel also affect firms' conducts when newspapers are employee-owned, employee-controlled, trusts or run by political parties. By and large each case must be examined on an *ad hoc* basis as to motivation.

All newspapers have to meet some sort of budget constraint. Even the Moonies must have an upper loss figure above which they will close down or modify their product strategy. However, the influence potential of a major newspaper can make long-term accounting losses acceptable for managers of conglomerates. Owning a loss-making daily can bring publicity, recognition, power, honours and a capitive public forum. One successful government contract, a grant of an oil drilling licence, a television station licence, a knighthood or an indebted politician who can oil wheels at an opportune moment, can make up for years of tax deductible losses. These things may not appear as the balance sheet but are a form, albeit non-pecuniary, of revenue.

Many newspaper conglomerates are publicly owned but are dominated by one shareholder or one family. Their ability to pursue other goals than profits is broader but not without constraints. Firstly, as Rupert Murdoch has pointed out, banks who lend money exert a discipline on newspaper firms. Secondly, a firm that fails to maximise profits but instead pursues other goals will see its stock value fall and attract takeover bids. Third generation or disenchanted family members are then prone to sell.

Where newspapers are a small part of a larger publicly owned non-media conglomerate, for example *The Observer* which was owned by ARCO until 1981 and Lonrho since then, their goal will be to maximise the group profit of ARCO or Lonrho. This may justify newspaper losses, as at *The Observer*, if they generate power and influence to improve the profitability of other enterprises within the group. In such cases the newspaper becomes a non-revenue department much like public relations or advertising within the conglomerate whole, but subject to the conglomerate's own internal accounting procedures and the conglomerate's overall stockmarket constraint.

Editors and journalists' motives

In an ideal world journalists might be free to report, investigate, inform and educate as they felt inclined. In the days of partisan press, as in much of the Third World today, poorly-paid financially insecure journalists wrote to please their publishers and keep their jobs.

In the 1980s groups owning as many as 200 newspapers amongst other interests are largely profit motivated. Within broad limits editors are free as to the content of their newspapers so long as they meet budget objectives. There may be some explicit overall policy but for practical business reasons editors must be free as to day-to-day operations. For the most part, owners' policy goals are met by hiring editors and journalists with like views. Those hired are consequently likely to feel free and claim to be free.[28]

Journalistic standards in the West affect newspaper format and product quality. For example, fabricating facts violates professional ethics. Opinions can be made in editorials, but altering facts to achieve dramatic effect or serve some supposed greater purpose is, ethically, unacceptable. The economic incentive, however, for journalists to 'sweeten' material to 'improve' copy is considerable. Whenever it is identified there is enormous peer pressure to expose it. In 1983 a Pulitzer Prize was awarded to the *Washington Post* for an article on an eight-year-old heroin addict and drug abuse. It turned out the story was fabricated. The journalist was fired and the prestigious *Washington Post* was humiliated. In 1984 the Hitler diaries hoax in *Stern*, also published in *The Sunday Times*, even led to prison sentences for its perpetrators in Germany.

To distinguish fact from fiction, newspapers in the West make a clear distinction between editorial and advertisements. Newspapers carry feature supplements, for example on automobiles or tourism, to attract advertisers. They will also allow a country, region or industry to pay for and insert a complete special section with sponsored editorials and advertisements in the newspaper's format, except that across the top of each page is a heading 'advertisement feature'. But advertorials which mix editorial and advertising, whatever their individual merit, conflict with accepted journalistic standards. Advertisers in the West cannot buy the editorial news hole, the space available for non-advertising content.

NOTES

1. Fred S. Siebert, T. Peterson and W. Schramm, *Four Theories of the Press* (University of Illinois Press, Urbana, 1956), p. 14.
2. D.H. Simpson, *Commercialisation of the Regional Press* (Gower,

Hants, 1981), p. 41.

3. T. Kent, *Policy Options*, January 1982, pp. 15–21.

4. Biographies of press lords such as Randolph Hearst and Lord Beaverbrook show they were capable of trying to lead their public in questionable directions.

5. Syndicated material is usually cheaper than in-house generated editorial.

6. Firms which cannot cover variable costs usually close down.

7. A full cost-to-the-reader general newspaper free of advertisements would not be commercially viable. Without advertisements newspapers would cost perhaps five times their current price after taking account of the accompanying decrease in demand, decrease in quantity demanded and cost savings.

8. *The Economist*, 9 March 1985.

9. International advertising agencies in 1985 handled 20 per cent of the world's advertising, up seven per cent in a decade. The eight biggest agencies handled one-fifth of all advertising. Multinational companies are using fewer agencies, Kodak used three in 1986, as opposed to 35 in 1980, whilst by 1985, Proctor and Gamble had created a single European marketing division.

10. Nobody gives up market share lightly and in 1986 television advertisers used a split screen to show advertisements around a box on the screen as World Cup soccer action continued. This tied viewers to the advertisement.

11. *New York Times*, 5 August 1985.

On the supply side *USA Today* demonstrated how a newspaper can aggressively seek out advertisers. Initially Gannett offered free advertisements to some advertisers. It later introduced packages of advertising in which advertisements in *USA Today* were also carried in Gannett's over 100 local newspapers and on their system of billboards. It has also emphasised the 'advertorial', a four page insert mixing both sports information and advertising. Gannett's losses of over $1m per week in 1986 on *USA Today* are charged to the group's pre-tax profits so that 50¢ of each dollar is in effect subsidised by the taxpayer.

12. *Time*, 14 September 1981.

13. Advertising has become increasingly sophisticated. Data on who buys what, when and where can now be gathered from credit cards, point of sale terminals, bar coding and market research. Audiences can be targeted with increasing accuracy. Cable television, magazines and FM stations all serve special-interest groups. Direct response advertising, where readers and viewers phone in for retail goods and catalogues in response to television advertisements has expanded rapidly since 1983. Demassification has made advertising more efficient.

The real efficiency of advertising is hard to estimate and much debated. There are those who think advertisers prey upon consumers' weaknesses, dictating purchases. However the failure of the Edsel car in the 1950s was not unique and puts the lie to such claims. IBM's IBM Junior Personal Computer bombed in 1984. Advertising does not always increase sales. Researchers report most adults do not even believe advertisements and rely on consumer reports, salesmen and friends for information. What advertising does do successfully is remind consumers about the product. Research reveals in fact that a rise in sales leads to a rise in advertising, not vice versa.

14. Press baron Rupert Murdoch, head of News International, is a case in point. He also owns the largest Australian private airline, Ansett. In 1979, Ansett was updating its fleet of aeroplanes and was in the process of deciding between the European Airbus and the new Boeing 767. In the same week that Murdoch met President Carter, his *New York Post* came out in support of Carter in the New York primary. That same week Ansett was granted loans from the government Export-Import Bank at favourable rates of interest. Murdoch obtained eight per cent loans at a time when other banks loans were about 8.5 per cent and commercial rates as high as 17 per cent. Each one per cent cut in the rate was worth about $6 million per year on the deal. A *New York Times* investigation found no evidence of impropriety. Indeed, Murdoch had asked for more favourable terms. It seems likely that there was no wrongdoing, but that Carter aides had, in good conscience, merely interpreted the rules as favourably as they could. Carter is unlikely to go down in history as a great president but his personal integrity has rarely been questioned. Perhaps in this case owning the *New York Post* had no influence. It certainly did Murdoch no harm.

In 1981, Murdoch's own *Village Voice* ran a story suggesting that a tax reduction on the *New York Post*'s buildings in New York had been made as a reward for supporting Ed Koch in his mayoral campaign. As in so many of these allegations it is impossible to ascertain the relationship between political suport and the apparent commercial benefit. Perhaps the taxes would have been the same whatever the *Post*'s position had been on Koch. The point, once again, was that the support was not harmful.

15. *Los Angeles Times*, 15 December 1984.

16. CBC Radio, 'As It Happens', 12 April 1986.

17. Newspapers can create external economies if they contribute to a more knowledgeable, informed and cultured society.

18. Most countries have classified their economies on the supply side into a number of industrial classifications for the purposes of producing official statistics. For example, United Nations Standard Industrial Classification (UNSIC) consists of ten divisions for economic activities, each division then being divided into nine major groups and each major group into nine groups.

19. This criticism can be levelled at both the Canadian and British Royal Commissions on the press in 1980 and 1977 respectively.

20. The extent to which goods are close substitutes and compete on the demand side can be shown using the concept of the cross elasticity of demand. This says that, if other things being unchanged, a given positive percentage change in the price of good Y leads to a significant positive proportionate change in the quantity demanded of good X, then there is a strong positive cross elasticity of demand. For example, if a price increase in the *Daily Mirror* leads to a significant increase in the quantity of the *Sun* demanded (with no change in price of the *Sun*) then the cross elasticity of demand is significantly positive. The goods are substitutes. If a rise in the price of television commercials leads to an increase in demand for advertising space in the *Daily Mirror* the goods are substitutes, even though on the supply side they come from different SICs.

Cross-elasticity concepts can help identify those newspapers which are affected by another's pricing behaviour for advertising or the newspaper itself. It helps identify which firms take account of each other in deciding their own individual firm's policies, that is, which firms they see as actual or potential competitors whatever that firm's product. Although complicated by measurement difficulties, the cross-elasticity concept is useful, and an important complement to the SIC supply-side approach to assessing competitiveness. The logic of the cross-elasticity concept is helpful in analysing the newspaper industry and provides a different perspective of newspaper monopoly.

21. T. Kent, *Policy Options*, January 1982, p. 17.

22. Amartya Sen, 'The Profit Motive', *Lloyds Bank Review*, January 1983, p. 3.

23. Ibid.

24. *Columbia Journalism Review*, December 1984, pp. 23–30.

25. *Business Week*, 30 September 1985.

26. *Fortune*, 20 February 1984.

27. A. Koutsoyiannis, *Non-Price Decisions: The Firm in a Modern Context* (The Macmillan Press, London, 1982), p. 211.

28. In this sense chain newspapers are similar to organisations such as hospitals and universities. Academic and hospital training, accreditation and hiring procedures sift out those who do not fit mainstream views in medicine and academia. Professional 'standards' and regulations limit those who are able to practise 'academic freedom' by becoming academics. Those who do not accept current paradigms are not hired. Marxist economists are not hired by major US universities. Practitioners of hypnotism, acupuncture and homeopathic medicine are shunned by hospitals. Radical journalists get passed over.

3

Structure and Conduct

This chapter provides an overview of the structure of the newspaper industry. It examines the nature of suppliers in the industry and their form of organisation. It makes an analysis of the nature of the costs facing firms in the industry. It examines the trend to conglomerate ownership throughout the industry. It discusses entry requirements to the industry and barriers to entry. Finally the all pervading influences of the government are surveyed.

FIRM ORGANISATIONS

Newspaper firms in the West are organised as proprietorships, partnerships, private corporations, public corporations, trusts, co-operatives and public agencies. Many newspaper firms in the West have become subsidiaries of large conglomerations. In addition, political parties and religious institutions, as well as traditional businesses run newspapers. The question arises as to whether, and if so how, the form of organisation affects the economic conduct of a newspaper firm.

The available evidence would suggest that the *form* of the firms' organisation is not particular important.[1] The decision-makers in all cases face similar objectives and constraints. All must produce a paper as efficiently as possible and attract revenues. Revenues will come from sales to readers, sales to advertisers and from subsidies. Subsidies are made by religious institutions, individual proprietors, public corporations, political parties and governments.[2]

Those who subsidise papers can be viewed as buying something in return. Governments buy the means to propagate, as do political parties and religious groups. Individuals and conglomerates buy power and influence. Controlling a news medium guarantees a public forum. It can be good insurance in adversity. Decision-makers in newspapers, whatever the organisation, are still faced with a budget constraint. Some receive no subsidy and must make profits, for example, most small independent newspaper chains. In the highly competitive newspaper market of Hong Kong, the *Far Eastern Review* claimed in 1984 that most small newspapers there were produced solely as business propositions.[3] Some must survive on their own efforts and break even, for example, *Le Monde* in Paris, and until 1985 London's *Daily Telegraph*. When in 1985 the *Daily Telegraph* was sold by the Berry family to Conrad Black it was because they could no longer afford to finance what they felt was a public trust. Finally some can assume a certain level of subsidy or accounting loss, but as *The Times* of London sale demonstrated in 1980, even Thomson International's subsidies from oil had an upper limit.

The key point is that a firm's organisation is not necessarily a major factor in how a firm will behave or perform. In 1985 the quality capitalistic *New York Times* was highly profitable providing a generally acclaimed service, whilst the titillating capitalistic *New York Post* lost money; in the 1970s the worker-controlled *Le Monde* made profits and provided quality service, as did the trust-owned *Guardian* of London in 1985. In the USSR the government-owned *Izvestiya* has even claimed to cover its costs. Economic conduct and performance in the newspaper industry does not appear to be closely identifiable with the form of a firm's organisation. In terms of conduct, the non-economic objective of educating, influencing and propagandising certain viewpoints can be discerned in all forms of organisation.

COST STRUCTURE OF THE INDUSTRY

The Canadian Royal Commission in 1980 stated categorically, 'The newspaper industry is characterised by economies of scale.'[4] Certainly the cost per circulated *page* in Canada was lower in 1980 for higher circulation newspapers than for lower circulation newspapers. However, larger circulation newspapers contained more pages and the Kent Commission concluded, 'economies of scale disappear [sic] into making the newspaper larger' so that 'costs per copy increase marginally as circulation increases'.[5]

The statement that 'economies of scale disappear into making the newspaper larger' is misleading. Cause and effect run both ways. Editorial costs, circulation and advertising demand are interdependent. Larger copies and higher costs are prerequisites for larger circulation and so greater advertising revenue. Costs per page are the inappropriate unit of measurement of output. Customers want the whole paper, not one page, just as they want a whole book. And costs and prices, as with books, vary with size and quality. Larger size, larger circulation, higher quality papers generally charge their advertisers more per page than do smaller newspapers, even if there is little variation in cover prices. The unit of measurement of output for the industry is the newspaper. There are accordingly few economies of scale in the publication of newspapers. Whilst some costs fall as circulation increases, others inevitably rise.

Costs can be broken into (i) newsprint costs, (ii) production costs, (iii) advertising sales costs, (iv) circulation and distribution costs and (v) administration costs. These are examined in turn. Labour costs are part of each of the categories and make up close to half of total costs for all newspapers, regardless of size. The newspaper is a labour-intensive product even in the computer age.[6]

Newsprint

Both technical and pecuniary economies of scale are found in newspaper production on a per page basis. Large newspapers are able to get more pages per ton of newsprint (technical economies of scale). Also large newspaper chains get purchase discounts (pecuniary economies of scale). However, on a per copy basis larger circulation newspapers require more newsprint to carry the larger volume of advertisements created by larger circulation. Furthermore, with more advertisements large circulation newspapers usually have a larger editorial news hole since most newspapers maintain a stable advertisement/editorial ratio.[7] The additional editorial of larger circulation newspapers further increases newsprint required per copy. Frequently on a per copy basis the additional newsprint requirements more than offset any efficiency or pecuniary savings achieved on a per page basis.

Table 3.1 shows how newprint costs have risen in recent years. The average size of newspapers in many countries has also risen in the past decade.[8] Despite increasing efficiency in the use of newsprint as a result of changing page size, changing the numbers of columns, moving to lighter paper and less wastage, so that

Table 3.1: Wholesale newsprint prices (US $/tonne in country of origin)

	1975	1977	1979	1981	1982	1983	1984	1985
Canada	270	300	350	450	520	500	520	530
Sweden	360	380	430	470	440	380	370	370
USA	280	330	380	480	490	480	500	530

Source: Bank of Montreal, *Business Review*, December 1985.

newspapers get more pages per ton, often as high as 150,000 pages per ton, newsprint costs as a share of total costs have been rising since 1973. At 1986 world prices this worked out to 300 pages per US dollar.[9] The rise in newsprint costs per copy, therefore, is explained by higher costs per ton and higher per copy newsprint requirements as newspapers have increased in size.

Production costs

Recent dramatic changes in newspaper technologies have made it almost impossible to determine the current extent of economies of scale in production. The last decade has seen a major change in how newspapers are produced. Based on computers, lasers and satellites, the whole process of newspaper production from initial reporting to final delivery has changed.

Journalists were amongst the first major users of laptop portable computers. Telephone modems enabled them to convert words to sound and to input directly to a computer at their newspaper head offices from anywhere around the world using telephones. Software now exists enabling all reporting, writing, editing and checking to be done quickly and efficiently on VDTs. There are imaging systems such as Vista which by 1985 were capable of designing and creating full page layouts. Colour photographs can be digitalised and transmitted over the telephone. In 1985 *Time* magazine claimed a colour photograph could be taken anywhere in the world, edited into completed page proof, and transmitted to a printing plant anywhere in North America in 90 minutes.[10]

At any one time engineering estimates can be made concerning the most efficient plant size. When economies of scale were found in large plants with long life expectancy, as was the case in the early 1970s, firms setting up large plants were then locked into that technology.[11] When in the following years technological advances took place, as in the late 1970s and early 1980s, smaller newspapers using shorter lifetime systems were able to exploit more rapidly the new technology and so enjoy cost advantages. For these reasons smaller newspapers in North America and Europe were able to switch to offset printing more rapidly than larger newspapers and so, for a time, enjoyed a cost advantage.

The adoption of potential cost savings in production by large newspapers can be inhibited by labour relations. Trade unions tend to have a greater presence in large newspapers in all countries and have used that presence to resist modernisation of production. Together, fixity of capital and more powerful trade union opposition and restrictive practices, have often offset the potential ability of large newspapers to enjoy production economies and may even have created diseconomies. London's Fleet Street, until 1986, was the most dramatic example of this.

There are three costs of production: pre-press costs, printing costs, and building and depreciation. Pre-press costs refer to composition, photo-engraving and platemaking, and make up nearly one-half of production expenses. Printing costs refer to press room expenses, production supplies, inks, other supplies and electricity costs. Depreciation costs refer to the assumed wearing down of plant and buildings. Newspapers in most countries have wide discretion in how they estimate depreciation costs which can affect reported profits and losses and intrafirm comparisons.[12]

The Canadian Kent Commission in 1980 found pre-press costs showed diseconomies of scale even on a per page basis, so that on a per copy basis diseconomies of scale were significant.[13] It found printing costs tended to decrease on a per page basis, but rise on a per copy basis as circulation increased.[14] Building and depreciation costs were approximately constant but very hard to estimate because of different historic costs, depreciation procedures, allocation or joint costs by conglomerates, contracting out by some newspapers and the joint use of facilities by others. In conclusion, on a per page basis unit production costs rise as circulation rises.

Editorial costs

Editorial material comes from three sources: (a) material generated by the newspaper's own staff, (b) material purchased from news services and syndicates, and (c) other material — material from letters and free-lancers and purchased supplements, such as magazines, comics and television guides. Editorial costs are first copy costs incurred whatever the level of that day's circulation. The size of the editorial hole is usually determined by the volume of advertising for the day. To some extent editorial is an investment. Good editorial today helps sales in the future, though for accounting purposes it is treated as a current expenditure. Generally, larger newspapers spend or invest more per page of editorial than do smaller newspapers, and therefore more per copy. This reflects either underemployment (X-inefficiency) or higher quality or both. At papers like *Asahi Shimbun* in Japan and the *Daily Mirror* in Britain huge highly qualified staff produce relatively few stories compared to smaller newspapers. To maintain circulation and market share lower editorial costs might be acceptable by the public in the short run, but the newspaper will frequently incur higher costs to protect future circulations and to achieve other non-economic and long-term objectives.

The costs of news services, news bought from agencies like Associated Press (AP), United Press International (UPI), Agence France Presse and Reuters, are determined in general by the circulation of the newspaper.

In conclusion, no significant economies of scale are to be found in editorial costs.[15]

Advertising sales expenditure

Large circulation newspapers spend more on attracting advertising than small newspapers. This translates into higher costs for selling advertising on both a per page basis and on a per copy basis for larger newspapers. In Canada small daily newspapers (250,000 per week) had costs of $56 per million copies run-of-the-press (ROP) whilst large newspapers had costs of $275 per million ROP. All newspaper groups in Canada spent slightly more than ten per cent of total advertising revenues on advertising expenditures.[16] In Britain, national newspapers spend heavily to advertise (see Table 5.4).[17] In conclusion, there are diseconomies of scale in advertising sales expenditures. Large newspapers spend more per copy on advertising.

Circulation and distribution expenses

Circulation and distribution expenses are high for newspapers representing up to 75 per cent of circulation revenues for large newspapers, and about 15 per cent on average of total newspaper expenses. The process is labour intensive and is one area of production which has changed little in decades. It still requires physically carrying a perishable, large size, low priced item promptly from factory to the individual consumer. In Japan distribution employs 400,000 people, in North America over one million, many part time, female or minors.[18] Distribution may well be the Achilles' heel of the newspaper industry. Should a commercially viable means of electronic transmission acceptable to the consumer ever be developed, the newspaper as it is currently known could disappear. Ultimately the newspaper industry in the major newspaper producing countries depends on hundreds of thousands of young people getting up before dawn in all weathers to work for below average wages.

Large circulation newspapers experience diseconomies of scale in circulation and distribution costs. Covering larger areas involves a more than proportional increase in costs per copy, often compounded in large metropolitcan areas by problems of traffic congestion, urban crime, wear and tear on delivery vans and labour problems. In Canada, distribution costs per thousand copies in 1980 rose from $32 to $63 as circulation rose from 250,000 to one million.[19]

Administration costs

There is some evidence that there are administrative economies of scale. As size increases the proportion of administrative staff falls. The problem of joint costs arises in that in the 1980s many newspapers are owned by media conglomerates. Their allocation of overheads between divisions allows for considerable discretion.

Conclusion

In conclusion, based largely on Canadian data but supported by observations, studies and comparisons elsewhere, there is little evidence for either significant economies of scale or diseconomies of scale when based on a per copy basis in the newspaper industry.

CONGLOMERATES AND NEWSPAPERS AS CASH COWS

The decline of family newspapers is a worldwide phenomenon explained by the fact that the external benefits of owning a newspaper are greater to conglomerates than to independent families or individuals.

The demise of independently owned family newspapers has characterised most of the Western world in the decades since World War II. The demise of the newspaper itself has been anticipated since the nineteenth century. A shortage of rags for newsprint in the 1870s, the introduction of films after the turn of the century, of radio in the 1920s, of mass television in the 1950s, and in the 1980s the rise of the electronic media have all been identified as the apocalyptic horseman.

For many firms in the developed world, newspapers have in fact been prodigious cash cows which have generated considerable profits over long periods of time.[20] The cash generated has sometimes been used to finance new newspapers but also to diversify into other seemingly less-mature industries. Many of the big newspaper firms have grown to become conglomerates hedging their bets on the long-term survival of newspapers. The Hearst family moved heavily into real estate, the Beaverbrook family to finance, the Thomson family to oil and gas, Rupert Murdoch to broadcasting, entertainment and films. These, and other interests, absorbed the flow from their cash cows so that eventually newspapers typically became a small part of the conglomerate.

Monopoly or potentially monopoly newspapers are highly desirable cash cows. Even then there is pressure to minimise costs. A newspaper that spends more than it has to on editorial in the name of quality or social responsibility earns less profit than it could do. Therefore its share value is less than it would be under a cost-cutting ownership. Therefore, it's ability to survive independently must be short-lived.[21] Any profit motivated cost-cutting conglomerate will wish to buy the paper, cut costs and so drive up profits and share prices. Merger mania in the media in the mid-1980s led to many examples of this. In 1986, the *Detroit Free Press* in the USA was sold to Gannett. Conrad Black bought the *Daily Telegraph* in Britain saying it was worse run than a nickle and dime store. Robert Hersant in France bought the Delaroche chain.

To conglomerates, newspapers also have a special value since they can yield huge returns which do not show up immediately on the balance sheet. They can earn political friends and therefore favours of an economic nature. Examples include television franchises and oil leases in Britain for Thomson International from 1955 to 1980, financial assistance for News International from President Carter in 1979, and the likelihood of television stations for Mr Hersant in France in 1986 following the Socialists' loss. In the end all important newspapers are likely to be owned by conglomerates for three reasons: (i) political favours mean papers are worth more to conglomerates since they have more opportunities to exploit those friendships; (ii) complementary of inputs including management skills with other media and (iii) risk spreading and ability to cross-subsidise during recessions and circulation wars.[22]

Newspaper conglomerates often have fairly long time horizons and deep pockets, and are willing and able to sustain losses for long periods. At Gannett, in the United States, losses of over $100 million from the launch of *USA Today* from 1982 to 1986 were anticipated. By 1986, they were twice as much. In New York Murdoch boasted that he would bleed the rival *Daily News* to death in five years. To that end he lowered the price of his *Post* to 25 cents, introduced morning printing and introduced bingo games. This reflected his long-term view of sacrificing current profits for the chance of earning monopoly profits in the long run. From 1982 to 1986 his *Post* lost $40 million.

Whenever major newspapers are threatened with closure, mention of co-operative ownership by the employees is suggested. At the *Sunday Times*, the editor Harold Evans devised a scheme in 1980 in which journalists would buy shares at $1,000 each and the owner of the *Philadelphia Sun*, Charter Oil would provide additional financing. The editor of *The Times*, William Rees-Mogg, also attempted to form a workers' co-operative at that time. Whilst intellectually attractive, trusts and co-operatives such as *Le Monde* and *The Guardian* have shallow pockets and are financially vulnerable, particularly to predator conglomerates like Robert Hersant in France and Rupert Murdoch's News International in Britain and the USA.

BARRIERS TO ENTRY

Entry barriers into the newspaper industry are still high even if entry requirements are low and thanks to computers, getting lower. It is easy to start a new paper in the sense of physical production, but identifying, capturing and then maintaining a market niche for a new daily is difficult.

Newspapers act as intermediaries enabling exchanges of messages and information. Home computers linked by telephones can provide a similar service. In 1985 there were 75 computer bulletin boards in Los Angeles alone. The largest, CompuServe had over a quarter of a million subscribers in 1985. Until the 1980s sending information to millions of people required considerable capital requirements, for printing presses or broadcasting transmitters. Home computers linked by telephones are changing the capital requirements and challenging traditional publishers and broadcasters. For a few thousand dollars an individual in 1986 can effectively have a printing press in his home with an instantaneous distribution system of potentially global proportions. It is a new age in that virtually everyone who wishes to can became a pamphleteer.[23]

In France *Libération*, started in 1973, still lost money in 1986 after a reorganisation, circulation increases and trade union concessions. By 1986 *USA Today* still lost after four years, as did the *Mail on Sunday*, also after four years, in Britain. In Italy *La Republica*, started in 1976, despite sensational sales growth was also not profitable for a decade.

Strikes create a market vacuum and new daily papers almost inevitably rush in to meet the deprived advertisers and readers. In addition, fringe market newspapers either up or down market or from neighbouring localities, such as suburbans, attempt to meet the market vacuum created by a strike. To prevent such parasitical tactics and maintain market shares during the 1978 New York city newspaper strike when there were strikes at all three major papers, the emergent papers were financed by the very papers hit. The *New York Times* helped the *City News*, the *New York Post* helped the *Daily Metro* and the *New York Daily News* helped the *Daily Press*. Their motives were clear. The emergent papers helped repel the inroads made by the established suburbans, and once the strike was over would be persuaded to close so opening up the market again for the established city papers. The requirements for entry to the newspaper industry are not great, the high entry barriers to the industry result from the loyalty and habits of both readers and advertisers to established papers. To protect their markets established newspapers will go to considerable lengths and endure significant short-term losses.

GOVERNMENT ROLE

Many constraints on newspaper firms' conduct result from government policies which over the years have created the economic, political and institutional environment in which newspapers operate. These include the whole range of laws that make up the various national legal systems, and include such legislation as copyright laws, libel laws, education acts, transport regulations, labour laws and secrecy of information acts, all of which have a general impact on the newspaper industry. This section examines the wide variety of legislation which has recently influenced the structure and conduct of the world newspaper industry.

Ultimately all press systems exist to some degree on sufferance. Governments have a formidable arsenal with which to control the press even within countries which have a libertarian press. Important legal and political restraints are outlined below before surveying the array of essentially economic policies used to influence press structure, behaviour and performance.

Legal pressures

Within the free world there exists a wide range of constitutional traditions which guarantee press fredom. All claim exceptions to press freedom and in some cases these severely limit the press. In general these restraints cover protection (i) for individuals against libel, (ii) for society from obscenity and (iii) for the state from internal and external threats. They vary widely in their interpretation from country to country as to what constitutes libel, obscenity and internal and external threats.

Since newspapers are the medium of record and legislation may be retroactive, newspaper conduct can be affected not only by current legislation but also by potential legislation. This is particularly relevant for firms' conduct in countries which have a recent history involving political instability, dictatorship and military rule.

Secrecy

The vastly increased size of the government sector, and its wide involvement in the life of every citizen of the Western world since World War II, has meant that the government itself has become a major source of information for the press. Even in the free world the government, therefore, has considerable control over what information is made available, and without free access to information the freedom to disseminate information is obviously curtailed. In the United States, for example, it was the limited ability of the state to protect secrets which enabled the Watergate and Pentagon Papers affairs to be uncovered.

Political censorship

Censorship can take many forms. In authoritarian countries the press knows what it cannot publish. In Communist countries the press is told what it may publish. In countries which claim some form of libertarian creed, censorship may involve instructions and warnings or more direct action such as harassment and violence.

There is a spectrum of censorship ranging from complete government control and government-owned and -issued newspapers, as in China, to a theoretically completely free press, most closely approached by the USA. Censorship has definite economic repercussions on the industry. It is often insidious, leading to self-censorship which may be mild or extreme. Such self-censorship may take the form of British newspapers which at the request of the Royal Family adopted a policy of 'bloody well leaving the Princess of Wales alone' even though pictures of her sold newspapers. In the USA, newspapers at the request of the Carter administration held back on the Iran hostages incident in 1980 but contrary to administration requests fully covered covert US military support for Central America in 1984. In Japan, the major newspapers failed to report the 1974 Tanaka-Lockheed bribes scandal out of misplaced loyalty and fear of being excluded from future news sources. In Britain, during the Falkland War of 1982 there was self-censorship at government request, which when combined with government-supplied misinformation led to the embarrassment and loss of credibility of the British press.

Economic constraints

Economic factors provide a subtle and powerful tool for government influence over the press. A political event such as the house arrest in South Africa of top newspaper editor David Woods made world

Table 3.2: Summary of government economic policies affecting the viability of newspapers

Area of policy	Comments
Advertising	Restrictions on broadcast advertising.
Government Advertising	Awarded to favoured newspapers.
Newsprint	Subsidies support newspapers. Licences, quotas, exchange controls can inhibit newspapers.
News Agencies	Grants and subsidies lower costs to newspapers.
Banks	Through banks government can allocate capital to newspapers or deprive them of capital.
Labour	Compulsory arbitration, closed shops, redundancy payments all affect newspaper costs.
Distribution	Exemptions from minimum age laws for juveniles (US), from Sunday observation laws (UK), cheap postal rates and subsidised freight rates (Italy).
Taxation	Exemptions from sales taxes (US advertising), income tax concessions (Italy and France).
Anti-Trust	Restrain monopoly, ownership.
Foreign investment	Restricts ownership.
Education	Governments underwrite the costs of training journalists. In the Third World, literacy is a prerequisite to newspaper growth.
Monetary and fiscal policy	Wide-ranging effects on input costs and advertising demand.

headline news. In contrast, less sensational and apparently dull news such as removal of a newsprint subsidy, as in Turkey in 1981, or a cutback in the advertisements placed by the French government in *Le Monde* might well not make the front page. Nevertheless, whilst arresting courageous editors might have some effect on editorial content, courageous replacements can often be found; removing advertisements and subsidies can undermine the commercial viability of the newspapers involved as in Turkey and cause their eventual closure. This emphasises a vital fact. For many newspapers in the Western world economic and commercial viability and survival depends critically upon a wide array of direct and indirect government supports. These are summarised in Table 3.2.

Purists might wish that the press was truly free and that these economic realities did not exist. In fact, as the Western newspaper industry is structured in the late twentieth century, a newspaper's commercial success is a prerequisite for the vital 'fourth estate' function in a democratic society. Eventually, a newspaper that is not a commercial venture will fold as its owners run out of funds or it runs out of people prepared to underwrite its losses. Without the government suports outlined in Table 3.2, few newspapers could survive.

The relevant legislation embraces both general policies and a considerable amount of specific media-related policies. In view of the soft-edged nature of the newspaper market, legislation which affects close media substitutes such as cable, television, magazines and telecommunication is also important. The environment in which newspapers operate, and therefore how they behave, is changing dramatically under the influence of rapid technological change. How government responds to that change is critical. Governments continue to have a pervasive influence on the whole media so enhancing in some cases, but also inhibiting in others, the conduct of both newspapers and those media which act as substitutes for newspapers. For example, in 1986 the French government decided to slow the rate of expansion of the number of new television channels partly in order to protect newspapers.

For a free press to be commercially viable, in the absence of either explicit government or private subsidies, certain prerequisites are required. These include reasonable affluence, a literate audience and a transport system capable of distributing the newspaper. These are necessary, not sufficient, conditions which can generally only be met as a result of government policy and economic development. A lack of these requirements has meant few successful newspapers in most parts of the Third World (see Table 1.3). High literacy rates require public education. Reasonable affluence requires peace, order and property rights. A transport system requires heavy investment in social overhead capital, which history generally shows had to be undertaken or underwritten by governments, even in laissez-faire North America.

Where governments have met these requirements, as they have in most of North America, East and West Europe, Japan and Australia, recent fiscal and monetary policy has also been important to the survival of newspapers. For example, advertising expenditures are cyclically sensitive. This major revenue source for newspapers is vulnerable to recession when advertising budgets are an easy target for cost-cutting managers, and to favourable economic conditions when growth-oriented companies invest in advertising for

Table 3.3: World newsprint flow, 1985

Exporters:	Canada, Norway, Finland, USSR, Sweden, South Africa
Self-sufficient:	Japan, China
Producing importers:	Mexico, Argentina, Brazil, France, West Germany, Australia, USA
Importers:	all others

Source: UNESCO data.

their products and employment advertisements. In the early 1980s tight money policies and high interest rates caused some newspapers in the West to cut back on investing in new newspaper technology and even fail.[24] Again, during the 1970s when wage and price controls were implemented in many developed countries in an attempt to control inflation, newspapers reported profits were squeezed and even eliminated.

Legislation and government policies which affect the newspaper industry are grouped, for exposition, into a number of headings. All countries, rich and poor, planned and free enterprise have policies falling into each category.

Economics of legal issues

Libel laws are critical to the operation of newspapers. In the late 1970s and 1980s in the USA, for example, there was considerable concern over the rising number of libel cases, court judgements and court awards. Punitive awards encourage newspapers to be cautious and exert self-censorship to the detriment of the 'fourth estate' role and product quality.

The ability of a newspaper to inform, comment and educate is also influenced by contempt laws and freedom of information acts. To the extent that investigative journalism sells newspapers, freedom of information is important to the economic welfare of the newspaper even if the political outcomes are socially more important. Scandals such as Watergate, the Marcos corruption and the Lockheed bribes, all exposed by the US press, helped newspaper sales as well as dethroning the US President, the Filipino President and the Japanese Premier. Likewise, contempt laws and the ability to protect sources influence content, product quality and ultimately sales. Contempt laws help restrain sensationalism. Shield laws as in the US, by contrast, protect journalists and encourage the pursuit of truth.

At the national level, government legal constraints on pricing frequently exist.[25] In Britain, newspapers had to list price increases before the Prices Commission in the 1970s, whilst in the USA the *Los Angeles Times* in 1981 appeared before the Supreme Court on the issue of price discounts, hence unfair competition, to large advertisers. For many newspapers severance pay legislation requiring sizeable payments to redundant workers has inhibited the speed with which new technology has been introduced and has even been a factor in the decision not to close a failing newspaper, for example, *The Times* of London in 1980, and the New York *Post* and *The Observer* in 1983.

Competition policies in many countries have paid special attention to the media structure and to newspapers in particular. Three Royal Commissions in Britain in 1948, 1961 and 1977; two Royal Commissions in Canada in 1970 and 1980; Senate inquiries, Joint Operating Arrangements legislation in 1970, and relaxations on media cross-ownership restrictions in 1985 in the United States; and legislation to limit market share in France in 1985 all reflect this concern. There is special legislation dealing with foreign ownership in Australia, France, India, Zimbabwe and Canada. Attitudes have varied by country.

In many countries the government owns all the press or much of the press, as in the USSR, China and the Eastern Bloc. Nevertheless, even in these countries papers are put out by both recognised groups, such as trade unions and scholars and also by clandestine groups, like Solidarity in Poland or the Jews in the USSR.

In other countries the government determines who can own a newspaper and on what conditions. These conditions change. In the 1980s Canada passed laws restricting foreign content in the media. Spain demolished the Franco-inspired government-owned newspaper framework and privatised 27 newspapers. The Peruvian military government also privatised state newspapers. In Zimbabwe the government took over the press, previously owned by South African companies. Most countries with a so-called free press have laws restricting ownership and cross-ownership with the other media is generally viewed with suspicion so that laws exist in many countries to limit it.

Alternative media regulations

The conditions under which the broadcast media operate have been closely controlled in all countries, with important repercussions, often favourable, for newspapers. For example, where there is no commercial radio there is no radio competition for the advertising dollar. This was the case in Britain until 1973, in France until 1982, and still is the case in India. In West Germany television advertising is limited to 20 minutes per day. Morning television was introduced on commercial television in Britain only in 1983 and competes for the time of the morning newspaper reader as well as the newspapers' traditional advertising revenues. Clearly when much television and radio is government-owned and -controlled, is financed by licences, and carries few or no commercials, newspapers are at an advantage for the advertising dollar. Sometimes governments go even further. Specifically to protect the press, until 1939 the British radio monopoly, the BBC, used to give out no news until 6 p.m. Taking a different approach in the USA, until 1983 when the Federal Trade Commission (FTC) relaxed the requirements, all radio stations carried advertisements thus competing with newspapers, but no more than 18 minutes of advertising per hour was permitted, possibly helping newspapers. In Wales, the government decreed that one of the four television channels be carried in Welsh so unintentionally but marginally limiting competition for the press.

Governments determine the structure of the broadcast media by granting radio and television franchises, and by setting the conditions under which they operate. The rationale is not always clear. In Britain Canadians own much of the commercial radio which has developed since the mid-1970s and Canadian-born Lord Thomson, a naturalised British citizen, owned commercial Scottish Television. But because he was a foreigner, Australian Holmes La Courte was not allowed to purchase ABC TV from Lord Grade. Canada and Australia limit foreign ownership of all their media even though their own citizens own huge chunks of the international media. The USA allows foreigners to own newspapers but not television stations. Murdoch had to become an American in 1985 so that he could operate broadcasting there. No longer an Australian, he therefore had to sell his Australian television stations.

As cable television, satellite and Direct Broadcast Satellite (DBS) and the whole information revolution have developed, governments have been called upon to regulate the new means of communication in terms of ownership and content. Questions about who owns the news and who carries it have yet to be satisfactorily answered. The nature of essential forthcoming media regulations about the ownership of information will be critical for newspapers.

Economic censorship

Censorship and control using economic measures to influence content are widespread as the following examples illustrate. In Egypt and India governments have used alleged newsprint shortages to punish opposition newspapers forcing them to close down. Such policies encourage self-censorship by other newspapers for fear of similar action. Where political action, jail, deprivation of livelihood and similar measures are used, the incentive for self-censorship is very powerful.[26]

Governments can influence newspaper content both directly and indirectly. In Taiwan newspapers are limited to twelve pages; in Japan incentives in the form of postal subsidies kept advertisements at less than 50 per cent of content. In the United States newspapers are required to turn down information-advertisements or advertorials. In 1981 the United Nations gave prestigious newspapers such as *Le Monde* and *Asahi Shimbun* subsidies to finance content dealing with the Third World. In Britain newspapers are prevented from publishing more than two days' concurrent television and radio schedules under the copyright law which says they belong to the BBC's weekly, *Radio Times* and to the IBA's weekly *TV Times*. The 1980 Kent Commission in Canada recommended legal editor contracts to prevent owners from influencing content. In France and Japan the banks work closely with the government and serve as a means by which the government can influence investment in the industry. Government can limit foreign ownership and hence entrepreneurship, as in Canada, license journalists, as in Spain and Italy, and set the terms on which editors operate, as in Britain. Governments influence the prices, quality and character of inputs to the newspaper industry.

Taxes and subsidies

Structure, conduct and performance in the newspaper industry are profoundly affected by taxes and state subsidies. Many newpapers would not survive without the subsidies they receive on newsprint, rail transportation, postal rates and job training programmes, or the tax benefits and tax breaks granted to them through capital allowances and the corporation tax structure. Sweden has one of the most extensive systems of taxes and subsidies, but special tax privileges to the press or certain segments of the press exist in all

Western countries and Japan. In Turkey, ending newspaper subsidies in 1981 created severe financial problems throughout the press, as did the imposition of import duties on newsprint in India in 1981. In Britain it has been argued that the survival of *The Times* occurred partly because owners could write off their losses against the taxes on profits from profitable newspapers and other ventures. Again, in the USA the highly reputable *Christian Science Monitor* as a religious institution gets special tax status, so does the *Washington Times*. Corporation taxes and depreciation regulations affect the rate at which newspaper firms invest in the new technology, in new newspapers, in take-overs and in diversification into other areas of the media. For example, cross subsidies to losing cable and satellite television ventures in the 1980s were government-subsidised because their losses offset profits, subject to taxation, from newspapers. Treating newspaper advertising as a tax deductible business expense is vital to a viable press.

In Sweden, Britain and Canada governments have examined the way in which subsidies might be used to slow the rate of increase in concentration of their respective newspaper industries.[27] In Canada and Britain the suggestions of Royal Commissions were not implemented but in Sweden in 1970 a unique system of press subsidies was introduced. In each case the objective of the government was to encourage a wide range of opinions in the press without the government directly interfereing in the running of the press.

In Sweden the method adopted gave subsidies to the press based on market shares, thus newspapers are not discouraged from attempting to minimise cost nor from seeking after profits. Instead subsidies are based on the amount spent on editorial and the proportion of the market captured. The effect is to subsidise newspapers with smaller circulations and high editorial costs enabling them to survive, and so avoid the inevitable process of the Jackal effect that would otherwise inevitably occur.[28] However, it also has the effect of freezing the structure of the Swedish industry in that new entrants face greater competition in the form of more existing newspapers, whilst newspapers that would otherwise have folded continue in production. It is also expensive, costing $40 million in 1983 on a circulation of eight million.

In Canada, the proposal of the Kent Commission was that firms that spent more than the industry average over a three-year period on editorial would receive a tax credit whilst newspapers that spent less would incur a special surtax. Obviously the net cost to the government of such a scheme is zero, it simply redistributes monies

Figure 3.1: The effects of a progressive levy on newspaper output

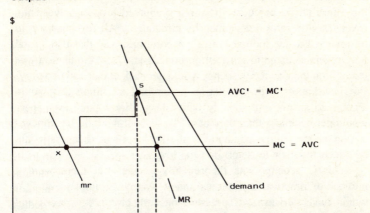

Notes: a. Assumes average variable costs (AVC) = marginal costs (MC).
b. AVC' = MC' = average and marginal costs *after* levy.
c. MR = marginal revenue large circulation paper; mr = marginal revenue small circulation paper.
d. After levy large newspaper cuts newspaper output from r to s; small newspaper holds production at x, though rise in price of large newspaper may cause the demand curve of the small newspaper to shift right. Small paper may continue to produce despite losing money if the prospect of a rebate is sufficient to offset losses.

from low editorial spenders to high spenders. The intention of the proposal was to encourage increased editorial expenditures overall and so the quality of Canadian papers, particularly the quality and quantity of Canadian content. It would also have encouraged wasteful editorial expenditures and penalised efficient news coverage.[29]

In Britain, Lord Kaldor proposed to the 1961 Royal Commission that a levy be used to increase the cost to a publisher of increasing production beyond a certain level.[30] The example used by Kaldor to illustrate the scheme proposed that newspapers with circulations under half a million would pay no levy on their gross advertising revenues, papers with circulations between half a million and one million would pay 7½ per cent, between one and two million would pay 20 per cent, between two and three million, 40 per cent and over three million 60 per cent. It was a graduated levy on advertising revenues with rates determined by circulation. All revenues would be returned to the industry on a per copy basis, so that if the total levy revenues came to ten million pounds and total circulation was ten million then each newspaper would get back one pound per copy. For newspapers with circulation under half a million this would amount to an outright subsidy whilst large circulation newspapers would get back less than they paid. To discourage industry concentration the sum of the circulations of all a chain's newspapers would be added together to determine the levy due.

Kaldor's scheme was theoretically elegant but there were a number of practical difficulties and it was never implemented. It would have put upwards pressure on both circulation prices and advertising rates, increased profits in an already highly profitable industry, frozen industry structure, and tended to subsidise the low quantity quality papers of the rich by the high circulation populars of the poor and middle classes. It would have penalised proven winners and have hit the chains particularly hard.

The justification for Kaldor's proposals was that newspapers are a special product. The resultant standardisation and reduced choice with many products that results from industry concentration and the ability to exploit economics of scale, is not acceptable in the area of 'intellectual goods'. Further, the Jackal effect is unique to newspapers. It exaggerates the advantages and disadvantages of marginal success and marginal failure in the newspaper industry. Figure 3.1 shows how the levy puts upwards pressure on prices and advertising rates. A firm with a circulation of over two million cuts production from a to b.

Favours and punishments

Finally governments can 'favour their friends, and punish their enemies' in a multitude of ways. By the 1980s governments themselves had become the major source of news on a regular daily basis as well as being the major newspaper advertiser in many countries. Withholding information and advertisements can hurt, even destroy, a newspaper, whilst leaks and advertisements can help both circulation and revenues. Blatant use of government influence is more likely to be found in Third World countries.[31] In India the *India*

Express was refused permission to close down its Bombay edition in 1981. At the *Express* in Bombay labour problems were allegedly government-inspired. In Uruguay and Nicaragua, the government punished newspapers in 1981 by closing them down for periods ranging from two days to four weeks with consequent financial hardships. In the developed world, in France the socialist *Le Monde* in 1980 was harassed by the D'Estang government because of its prominent reporting about gifts he had received from the Central African Republic. In 1984 the Mitterand Socialist government passed a monopoly law specifically to punish Robert Hersant's conservative newspaper chain. In Britain Murdoch has enjoyed favour from Mrs Thatcher, in the USA from Reagan and Carter and in Australia from Prime Minister Fraser.

NOTES

1. See Table 4.7.
2. *The Washington Times* in Washington DC is subsidised by the Unification Church better known as the Moonies; *Libération* in Paris by the French government; *Le Devoir* in Quebec by an individual businessman Pierre Péladeau; the *Observer* in London by the conglomerate Lonrho; and *L'Unità* in Italy by the Communist party.
3. *Far Eastern Review*, 25 October 1984.
4. Canada, *Royal Commission on Newspapers* (Supply and Services, Ottawa, 1980), p. 67.
5. Ibid.
6. Tony Griffin, 'Technological Change and Craft Control', *Cambridge Journal of Economics*, 1984(8), pp. 41–61.
7. A typical Thomson ratio is 60/40 advertisements to editorial.
8. An examination of Tables 1.1 and 1.4 shows the rise in the newsprint/circulation ratio.
9. Bank of Montreal, *Business News*, December 1985.
10. Transmission of the photograph was by fibre optics to an earth station and then via Telstar satellite 22,300 miles above the earth to regional printing plants. Input scanners converted transparent images into digital information for transmission. After transmission the printing plants converted the compressed digital data with a decompressor and then used a laser to convert to film, which could be made into plates.
11. A. Smith, *Newspapers and Democracy* (MIT Press, Cambridge, 1980), p. 37.
12. See Table 8.6, p. 208 which contrasts News International results in US and Australia.
13. By 1986 computer systems such as Atix had radically altered pre-press methods and lowered costs at some large newspapers.
14. Canada, *Royal Commission*, p. 73.

15. Ibid., p. 76.

16. Ibid.

17. *The Economist*, 16 March 1985.

18. Special laws allow minors to deliver newspapers in many developed countries.

19. Canada, *Royal Commission, 1980*, p. 77.

20. Cash cows are firms which generate healthy cash flows over prolonged periods of time. Dogs are money losers. Stars are rising firms with potential to make profits.

21. Share prices are usually positively influenced by higher earnings.

22. The sale of the last family-owned and -run British national, the *Observer* of London, in 1975 to Arco Corporation of the USA reflected the nature of demand for newspapers from conglomerates. The sale of the *Observer* had created interest amongst such potential owners as Associated News, Tiny Rowland of Lonrho, who would later buy the paper in 1983 from Arco, and Murdoch, who made the revealing comment that 'The third world doesn't sell newspapers' when informed that the *Observer* had the best Third World coverage of perhaps any newspaper published in the developed world. For all the potential buyers the *Observer* would have complemented their other activities. Arco appeared as a buyer at the last minute and decided to buy the paper within a matter of days. The reasons were clear. For a huge oil company the price of the paper, £15 million, appeared relatively trivial, about the cost of sinking half a dozen wells, but the political leverage and insurance were considerable. First, they saved the paper from otherwise undesirable owners which in itself was good public relations; second, it gave Arco an inside edge in the pursuit of oil licences in the North Sea; third, any losses incurred would be tax deductible.

23. *Los Angeles Times*, 12 December 1985.

24. These included the *Washington Star* and *Philadephia Journal*.

25. In the 1970s Britain, Canada, Australia, Italy, France and the USA all controlled newspaper prices.

26. In much of South America, Asia and Africa such incentives were familiar in the early 1980s and are powerful economic incentives for self-censure.

27. Canada supports her national press by making advertisements in foreign publications subject to taxation.

28. See p. 29 for discussion of Jackal effect.

29. The proposal was not adopted.

30. Great Britain, *Royal Commission on Newspapers, 1960–61*, Vol. VI, (HMSO, London), pp. 55–8.

31. *Far Eastern Review*, 18 March 1983.

4

United States

The US newspaper industry has been by far the largest and most influential in the free world since 1945. In 1986 it was arguably the most free, the most analysed, the most copied, the most admired and also the most despised and the most controversial. This lengthy chapter examines it in some detail, particularly recent changes and trends in structure and conduct. The US industry will be used in subsequent chapters as a benchmark against which to examine and compare other national newspaper industries.

BASIC CONDITIONS

The 1,688 dailies of the USA in 1986 far outnumbered the 125 of Japan, 93 of Britain and the 91 of France. United States dailies had circulations which were relatively small by international standards. The largest and most profitable, the *Wall Street Journal*, had a circulation of approximately two million per day in 1986. This was less than half that of the *Sun* in Britain and *Bild-Zeitung* in Germany, or one-sixth of *Yomiuri Shimbun* in Japan. By the mid-1980s new production technology had created the ability to overcome the geographical constraint, but in 1986 satellite-transmitted national dailies such as *USA Today* and the *Wall Street Journal* were exceptions.[1] The US press was still a regional press in 1986.

With its large, highly educated and affluent population imbued with the traditions of a free press and free speech, the USA reader market for newspapers in 1986 was enormous. Nevertheless the many large minority groups with different cultural backgrounds, added to a profusion of media alternatives, pulled down the US per capita consumption of newspapers to levels below those of Scandinavia, Britain or

Table 4.1: Circulation of major US dailies, by rank, 1984

Over one million	N.Y. Wall Street Journal	1,959,000
	N.Y. Daily News	1,347,000
	U.S.A. Today	1,247,000
	L.A. Times	1,047,000
500,000–1,000,000	N.Y. Times	935,000
	N.Y. Post	930,000
	Chicago Tribune	776,000
	Washington Post	729,000
	Detroit News	656,000
	Chicago Sun-Times	650,000
	Detroit Free Press	647,000
	Long Island (NY) Newsday	539,000
	San Francisco Chronicle	536,000
	Philadelphia Inquirer	526,000
	Boston Globe	520,000

Source: Editor and Publisher Year Book, 1985.

Japan, although newsprint consumption per capita is much higher since the average US daily is a much bigger product than its European or Asian counterparts.

The United States press as a whole dominated the world press and world media in terms of volume, newsprint content and influence. US newspapers were the major suppliers of news to UPI and AP news wire services which in turn dominated the dissemination of news around the world.

Table 4.2: Weekly pay scales for reporters at selected major US dailies

	Amount (in $)	Year	Union Affiliation
N.Y. Times	926	1986	Newspaper Guild
Washington Post	664	1985	Graphical and Commercial International Union (GCIU)
San Jose Mercury News	711	1985	Newspaper Guild
Wall Street Journal	785	1986	Independent Union
Los Angeles Herald-Examiner	516	1986	GCIU

Source: Editor and Publisher Year Book, 1985.

Table 4.3: Circulation and distribution profiles of US newspapers, 1985 (circulation in millions)

	Number of titles				Total daily circulation	Total Sunday circulation
	AM	PM	Total^a	Sunday		
Over 500,000	14	4	15	19	13.04m	16.2m
250,000–500,000	18	8	20	34	6.65	11.9
100,000–249,999	52	39	84	73	12.86	11.5
50,000– 99,999	85	54	134	105	8.93	7.4
25,000– 49,999	98	177	270	168	9.56	6.1
10,000– 24,999	100	414	513	210	8.09	3.4
5,000– 9,999	52	371	423	134	3.10	1.0
0– 4,999	39	190	229	40	0.85	0.1
Total	458	1257	1688	783	63.08	57.6

Note: a. Includes 27 all-day newspapers as both a.m. and p.m. editions.
Source: Editor and Publisher Year Book, 1985.

Even though it ranked as the United States tenth-largest industry in terms of sales and third-largest in employment, the social and political importance of the US press outweighs its economic significance as an industry. Together the press and the wire news service had enormous influence not only in the US, but worldwide, in setting the daily agenda of what was considered 'news'. However in 1985 much of the public, especially in developing countries, collected that 'news' from other media, particularly broadcasting, and so generated no revenues for US newspapers.

Advertising demand

Advertising demand and the business cycle

Newspapers depend upon advertising and it has been the growth of the advertising industry in recent years which has underpinned the survival and continued success of the US newspaper industry. Newspapers are vulnerable to the business cycle. In 1982 during the recession ten US daily newspapers closed. In the USA expenditures on advertising tripled from 1975 to 1985 growing at 12.3 per cent annually from 1980 to 1985. In the same decade the cost of a television commercial on the major networks jumped three-fold to $100,000 so that although in 1984 the Federal Communications Commission (FCC) eliminated all restrictions on the number of commercials that television could carry, network sales in 1986

Table 4.4: US nominal advertising expenditures growth and business cycle activity, 1975–85

Year	1975	1976	1977	1978	1979	1980	1981	1982	1983	1984	1985
per cent change GNP	8.0	10.8	10.9	12.0	11.5	8.2	12.1	3.4	7.2	10.3	6.7
per cent change advertising	4.8	19.2	12.4	15.7	12.7	9.8	12.6	9.8	13.6	15.7	9.6

Source: McCann-Erickson, Commerce Dept.

virtually stagnated. From 1981 to 1985 the cost of a prime-time television advertisement rose by 40 per cent to $250,000, twice the rate of increase of the Consumer Price Index. The cost of making commercials also rose significantly over the same period, doubling from $50,000 on average.[2] Fragmentation of the broadcasting market causing a decline in market share for the big three television networks from 93 per cent in 1979 to 76 per cent in 1985 also worked in favour of US newspapers. Local advertising expenditures in newspapers increased strongly, particularly in the areas of local retailers' inserts and classified advertising.

The dependence of US advertising on the state of the economy is shown in Table 4.4 where the cyclical nature of the industry is illustrated. Whilst advertising has outperformed the economy in every year, the pattern of growth follows the economy closely. The relationship is clear. Prosperous, and therefore editorially free, newspapers depend on advertising. Advertising depends upon the state of the economy. Classified advertisements in particular respond to the cycle, and given their high price per line and low marginal cost have a substantial effect on newspaper profits. For example, during the economic recovery from March 1983 to March 1984 help wanted, homes and automobile classifieds rose by 40 per cent at the *Los Angeles Times*. The parent Times Mirror Co. reported a 32 per cent increase in classified advertisements for all its seven daily papers over the same period.

US demand for newsprint is so large that it is a major influence on world prices.[3] An increase in US advertising demand puts upward pressure on world newsprint prices.[4] Increased circulation, advertising and consequently editorial, caused newsprint consumption to rise 14 per cent in 1983 and newsprint prices which had fallen 4 per cent in the recession, rose 7 per cent to $475 a metric ton on

Table 4.5: Sales, profits and assets of major US media corporations, 1985 ($m)

	Sales	Profits	1984 Assets
CBS	4,756	203[a]	3,100
Time	3,403	200	2,381
Times-Mirror	2,959	237	2,436
Dun & Broadstreet	2,772	295	2,260
Gannett	2,209	253	1,711
Tribune	1,938	124	1,676
Knight-Ridder	1,730	133	1,274
McGraw-Hill	1,491	147	1,091
New York Times	1,393	116	850
Washington Post	1,078	114	590
Dow Jones	1,039	139	750
Capital Cities/ABC	1,020	142	1,164
News International[b]	455	24	n/a
Thomson International	£1,735m	£98m	£1,308m

Notes: a. Poor profits at CBS reflected weak magazine performance.
 b. US operations only.
Source: Business Week, various issues; *Financial Times*, 3 August 1985.

Table 4.6: Sales, profits and assets of selected major US non-media corporations ($m)

	1985		1984
	Sales	Profits	Assets $m
Ford	52,774	2,515	27,088
General Motors	96,372	4,000	49,576
Dow Chemical	11,537	58	11,778
RCA	8,972	244	8,121
Proctor & Gamble	14,162	690	10,054
Sears Roebuck	40,715	1,303	53,174

Source: Business Week, various issues.

on the west coast and $535 on the east coast.[5]

The stock market, which has proved itself a good predictor of firms' fortunes, recognises the cyclical sensitivity of US newspaper firms. Standard and Poor's index of newspaper stocks more than doubled from late 1982 to the start of 1984 during the economic recovery. This was an important development because it reflected a general optimism about the ability of US newspaper firms to survive long term, to develop new media products and to make profits.

Newspaper advertising effectiveness

Despite the vast amounts spent, little is known about the effectiveness of advertising. Proctor and Gamble was the largest advertiser in the world in 1985 buying over $1 billion of advertisements, an amount equivalent to one-half total advertising expenditures in Italy or one-third total advertising expenditures in France.

New research techniques have enabled companies like Proctor and Gamble to lower the costs of promoting new products, to identify efficient promotional techniques and to isolate the age and income profile of consumers. The techniques create a threat to newspapers. For example, computers have been used to monitor every television programme watched by volunteer families and every commercial. Over cable each family was delivered a selected array of commercials. The computer was programmed with all the family's tastes and family economic profile. All purchases made by the family at the supermarket were then monitored using a special card. By giving different groups different commercials it was possible to identify the effectiveness of each commercial as well as which new products were bought by each age, income and sex group. For so-called blunt-edged instruments like newspapers, the inability to deliver a similar measured response for advertisers will increasingly prove a competitive disadvantage in the future.

Advertising demand and monopoly dailies

The Jackal effect describes the market forces which in the United States have led to the closure of most second daily newspapers. In 1986 fewer than two dozen survived. All other markets had become monopolies. The forces leading to monopoly stem from the nature of advertising demand and US advertisers' preference for the leading daily.

Advertisers' preference for the leading daily in a city with competing dailies is illustrated by a case study of Cleveland, Ohio.[6] Cleveland in the early 1980s was the twelfth largest newspaper market in the United States. The highly-regarded *Cleveland Press* (circulation 304,000) enjoyed 43 per cent of total daily circulation in 1981 but received only 26 per cent of the total advertising revenues collected by Cleveland's two dailies, the *Press* and its rival the *Cleveland Plain Dealer*. The *Dealer* enjoyed the remainder, 74 per cent.

For many advertisers the leading daily reached a sufficient proportion of the population. Furthermore, the advertising director of the trailing *Press* newspaper observed that the electronic and other media tended to work harder to attract advertisers from the number two paper.[7] The economic consequences for the *Press* of its failure to attract advertising include the following. At a big New York fashion show the prospering *Dealer* paid for its reporter to stay in an expensive hotel whilst the *Press* reporter lodged with a former college roommate. The food editor at the *Dealer* had the use of a test kitchen whilst her *Press* counterpart tested recipes at home. Working conditions at the *Press* newroom were stark, whilst at the *Dealer* they were modern and comfortable. Even without higher salaries, therefore, the *Dealer* was a more attractive workplace. It was also more secure. As advertising revenues declined the size of the *Press* news hole diminished. Fewer staff were needed. As the *Dealer* locked up the major wire and feature services such as the *New York Times* and the *Los Angeles Times*, the *Press* had to rely on less prestigious services. As the stature of the *Press* declined, news sources tended to favour the *Dealer* as a better place to air their stories. As with all failing firms, the best staff moved on. The *Press* became smaller and of lower quality, more advertisers withdrew and the outcome was inevitable.

In 1878, E.W. Scripps had opened the *Cleveland Press* and established what became the Scripps-Howard chain upon it, but by 1980 the Jackal effect had made the group's flagship paper lose unacceptable amounts of money. In 1980, E.W. Scripps Co., unable to sell the paper to other major chains, threatened to close the paper. In 1980, a diversified manufacturing corporation, Cole National Corporation, headed by Joseph Cole purchased the *Cleveland Press* determined, he said, to keep Cleveland a two-newspaper city.[8]

The comeback strategy at the *Press* involved some changes, but E.W. Scripps managed many successful dailies across the USA, so inevitably most of the obvious remedial measures had been considered. By 1982 an unlikely but successful comeback appeared to be underway at the *Press*. Then, in June 1982, claiming losses running at $6 million annually, the paper was suddenly closed. A month later the *Press* plant had been made inoperative with facilities and equipment dismantled and destroyed. This made it unsaleable despite the appearance of potential buyers.

Cole later admitted selling the *Press* subscription list to the rival Newhouse *Plain-Dealer* though the privately-owned publisher did not disclose the price. At a grand jury inquiry in 1985 however, it transpired that $14.5 million had been paid for the list which was of 'negligible or non-existent' value and $8 million for a shoppers' guide created for $500 earlier that year by Cole. Cole and Newhouse were indicted for conspiracy in restraint of trade. The point was clear. Second newspapers may not be viable as commercial operations because advertisers avoid them but their market share is highly valuable to the potential monopoly first paper.[9]

Advertising demand and newspaper collusion

In 1985 the largest privately-owned publishing company in the United States, Advance Publications Inc., owned by the Newhouse family, became involved in a number of other legal cases emanating from the Jackal effect. In addition to owning 27 daily newspapers, the Newhouse family produced such prestigious publications as *Vogue, The New Yorker* and *House and Garden*. As a private company it had been able legitimately to hide many of its activities from public scrutiny. Some of these involved trying to convert losing newspaper duopolies into profitable monopolies.

The organisation's strategy in New Orleans and Portland, Oregon had been predatory pricing to drive out rivals. In St Louis it had been a scheme, disclosed in 1983, to close its own *Globe-Democrat*, and then share profits from the rival, *Post-Despatch*. In Cleveland it was a conspiracy with the competing *Cleveland Press* to close that paper. In all these instances anti-trust suits were instigated.

The background to the St Louis closure is noteworthy in terms of the firms' strategy and US anti-trust legislation. In St Louis unlike Cleveland, the opposing newspaper was owned by a large newspaper group, Pulitzer, whose community-minded family used the *Post-Despatch* to propagate their liberal views. Though an afternoon paper with a smaller circulation than the morning *Globe-Democrat*, Pulizter was strongly averse to closure. In the circumstances, and as an unintended consequence of US anti-trust laws, the dominant *Globe-Democrat* was worth more to Newhouse closed than operating.

The pertinent legislation in St Louis was a 1961 joint operating agreement (JOA). The two papers had been granted a JOA by the US Justice Department under the special failing newspaper anti-trust provisions of 1971.[10] JOAs had proliferated rapidly in the 1950s and 1960s amongst metropolitan newspapers as television attracted advertisers and the suburbs attracted readers. In 1953, 90 per cent of US cities had had genuinely competing dailies. Since then, by merging their advertising efforts and revenues, sharing printing plants and distribution networks and having one morning and one afternoon paper, many newspapers found joint profitability could be improved. For example, since 1965 Hearst's *San Francisco*

Examiner and the *San Francisco Chronicle* had operated profitably together. In 1969 the Supreme Court concluded that such agreements breached anti-trust laws. Consequently, to give them immunity, newspapers were granted special treatment in the 1971 Newspaper Preservation Act. Editorially separate, papers shared advertising, circulation and management personnel as well as their usually non-existent profits. Most importantly, in St. Louis, under the JOA if one paper closed it would share the profits of the survivor for 50 years. The incentive for Newhouse to close the *Globe Democrat* and share profits, created by the JOA's profit-sharing provision, was overwhelming and evidently legal, but clearly contrary to the spirit and intent of anti-trust legislation.

Joint operating agreements have led to legal tangles elsewhere. The 1971 Act states that JOAs are legal only if one of the parties to the agreement is in financial trouble and is unlikely to become 'financially sound'. In San Francisco both advertisers and the suburban newspaper owners of the *Pacific Sun* and the *Berkeley Barb*, claimed the San Francisco papers were financially sound. They demanded damages for unfair competition from Hearst and the *San Francisco Examiner* in a case which dragged on for six years from 1975 to 1981.

Hearst ran into similar difficulties in Seattle. Hearst claimed losses from 1971 to 1981 of $14 million on the *Seattle Post-Intelligencer* and planned a JOA with the profitable *Seattle Times*. The two traditionally Republican newspapers were granted an agreement by President Reagan's Attorney-General, William French Smith. The central problem with a JOA arises from the difficulty of identifying failing newspapers and monopoly newspapers. In Seattle the suburban newspapers subsequently brought court action claiming that they could provide competition to the *Seattle Times*, should the *Seattle Post-Intelligencer* close, and that Hearst's conglomerate accounting methods overestimated the Hearst paper's losses.[11]

US advertising demand and countervailing power

Large chains claim that one advantage they offer the public is independence from advertiser blackmail. They are able to resist editorial pressures from large advertisers who threaten to withdraw advertising. The *Christian Science Monitor* has rejected Mobil Oil Corp. advertisements for not meeting their ethical standards.[12] In 1984 the *Wall Street Journal* ignored Mobil Oil Corp.'s threat to remove its $500,000 annual advertising account after the *Journal* disclosed that the Mobil chairman's family would benefit financially from a new $300 million Mobil office block in Chicago. The *Journal* had revealed similar questions about in-family deals at Mobil in 1983 involving shipping purchases. Mobil claimed there was a vendetta against Mobil but other corporations, for example Chrysler, have also been unhappy with unfavourable *Journal* comments. In broadcasting the two large US television networks, CBS and ABC, had so outraged all the heavy advertisement-spending Detroit motor manufacturers by 1983 as to be boycotted from interviews. *Forbes* magazine after reviewing such incidents observed that 'corporate government by tantrum' does not work.[13] There is countervailing power. The ability of corporate officers to bully the press for economic advantage is curtailed when the press has size. US corporate organisations need the press, just as the press needs them.

Propaganda demand

The *Christian Science Monitor* was founded in response to and to counter the low standards of yellow journalism in the US early this century. It is a propaganda vehicle. The founder, Mary Baker Eddy, set the paper the task: 'To injury no man but to bless all mankind'. The *Monitor*'s high moral tone was supported by high journalistic standards which brought five Pulitzer prizes between 1950 and 1985 but disappointing circulation, only 170,000 in 1984.[14]

Since 1974, the *Monitor*'s circulation had been static. The paper lost $10 million in 1984. As a commercial venture, as opposed to a Christian mission, the paper faced several obstacles. First, it censored advertisements. All liquor and tobacco advertisements were rejected and in the 1980s it refused advocacy advertisements. Second, the median reader age was 60 and the typical reader was perceived as a poor sales prospect by advertisers. So, despite low advertisement rates, about $6,000 per page versus $100,000 on the *Wall Street Journal*, advertising demand was poor and two-thirds of revenues was from circulation. Third, the paper relied heavily on the poor US postal service for delivery creating frustration for readers.[15]

In 1985 the paper began a revival. The First Church of Christ Scientist had both the will and the deep pockets to continue the *Monitor*'s service of Christian ministry. In America, where a sizeable part of the population regularly attended church, there was a market for such a quality moral newspaper. New technology would make national distribution by satellite easier. New market-oriented staff were hired. Diversification into the recently deregulated broadcasting medium was undertaken to complement the *Monitor*'s service of ministry.

A comparison in 1986 could be made between the *Monitor* and the Communist press. The First Church wished to propagate its Christian message. Like the Chinese press it would carry suitable advertisements, sharing its medium in order to subsidise its own costs of advocacy. However, in the more competitive media market of the USA the *Monitor*'s editorial had to attract readers even if advertising revenues and circulation revenues were secondary to the Church's desire to minister.

Legal issues

Influence and conflicts of interest

Newspapers can themselves affect the economy. Commercial news has for long been subject to special publishing legislation. The 1940 Investment Advisory Act gave the Securities and Exchange Commission (SEC) control over adviser publications. Up until 1982 they brought few insider trading cases. In 1984 however they brought six cases against investment/advisory publications. The most sensational case involved the *Wall Street Journal*, the United States' largest general circulation newspaper. At the highly respected *Journal*, R. Foster Winams wrote for the influential stock-tip column 'Heard on the Street'. He failed to let readers know that he had himself taken a position in some of the stocks he wrote about, and passed on information to others enabling them to make considerable profits. The SEC has a mandate to act as a watchdog and prevent stock market illegal insider trading and so brought a case against the *Journal*. Winams' position was one in which he had the power to make news and move the market. He abused that position.[16]

At his trial in 1985 Winams claimed an important distinction. He knew that what he did was journalistically unethical but not that it was illegal. The prosecution's successful case was not therefore based on the effects of other investors and the market as might be expected, but that Winams took confidential information owned (sic) by his employer, the *Journal*, and used it for his own purposes. This verdict portends considerable media problems in future over who owns information.

Litigation and self-censorship

In 1985 the United States was wracked by a series of spy cases and leakages of classified information to the press. The US has no legislation equivalent to the British Official Secrets Act. The 1917 Espionage Act had been used in US spy cases, but never until 1985 had it been used for leakages to the press as opposed to other countries. In 1985 a critical test case was instigated against a civilian research analyst at the Naval Intelligence Support Center for leaking pictures to the British press.[17] His financial reward was small and his undisputed if misplaced patriotic motive was to alert the US public to USSR military strength. The analyst was convicted, though not the British publication owned by Thomson International.

The economic as well as the political implications of such espionage are very considerable. The government rightfully claims the need to protect military secrets and the benefits of the approximately $50 billion annual expenditure for military research and development. In 1986 the administration believed new laws were neccessary to curb the press and safeguard US defence. Leakages and espionage, particularly to the USSR, cost untold billions to the American public. The information was often sold for a small fraction of US economic cost or public worth. There was a very real dilemma in such cases for all the media concerning press freedom versus national security. The public has the right to information with which to judge defence policies.[18] The public also has the right to have its expensive tax-financed defences protected.

Should journalists be prosecuted and newspapers become involved in expensive litigation over investigative reporting, caution and self-censorship detrimental to product quality and so the public will ensue. A reluctant response of self-censorship by the media as regards such investigative reporting was hinted at following two successful, but very expensive, media defences, by Time and CBS in 1985.

The libel case General Westmoreland brought against CBS, following a CBS '60 Minutes' television documentary, asked for $120 million damages. Westmoreland lost and a settlement was reached, but the costs, both financial and non-financial, to CBS were high. At *Time*, litigation followed a 1983 story about the Israeli Defence Minister which claimed his indirect responsibility for the massacre of 700 Palestinian refugees. Ariel Sharon asked for $50 million damages. Sharon was also unsuccessful, but once again the financial and non-financial costs were considerable.

The outcomes upheld a 1964 Supreme Court decision. In the

1964 *New York Times* vs *Sullivan* case, journalists were allowed to write almost anything about public officials as long as it was not false or written with 'reckless disregard' for the truth. The purpose of the decision was to ensure that public discussion be 'uninhibited, robust and wide-open'.[19] In 1986 the United States still had the least-inhibited press in the world but legal opinion and public opinion were working against open public debate. The Libel Defense Center reported in 1984 that before 1980 only one libel suit against the media for over $1 million had been lost. Between 1980 and 1984 20 such cases were lost.[20] Typical of such cases was one launched in 1984 for $250 million by a Republican Senator against a small California paper, the *Sacramento Bee*. Unfavourable verdicts involved a multi-million dollar award to the president of Mobil Oil Corporation against the *Washington Post* and $1 million to the genetics theorist William B. Shockley against the *Atlanta Constitution*.[21] Although the majority (62 per cent) of jury trials in libel cases against the press were eventually reversed on appeal, the legal and public mood in 1985 was clearly against the press. Lawyers and judges saw the media as being powerful profitable corporations able to afford expensive court cases and settlements.[22]

The long-term economic and social effects of all the litigation were critical. The direct legal costs to a newspaper of court cases ignore the costs of time and energy diverted to the case and the effects on morale, ambition, and commitment to the media's 'fourth estate' responsibility. Such cases greatly increase the risk of investigative journalism and therefore its costs. Since investigative journalism sells few additional papers — *Washington Post* circulation actually fell during Watergate — the likely outcome is self-censorship. Public debate and criticism will not be uninhibited and robust.[23]

Pressure for US newspapers to be censored or censor themselves has come from other quarters. Recently the US press has come under considerable criticism outside the US, notably from the Third World. In 1945 UNESCO was established for 'the unrestricted pursuit of objectives and the free exchange of ideas and knowledge'. The US provided 25 per cent of its annual budget of $187 million in 1983. In 1984, the world's 24 most industrialised nations requested changes in UNESCO be made by the current director-general, Amadon Malitar McBow. The United States gave notice of her intention to withdraw from UNESCO. The 24 nations' protest was against UNESCO's Third World bias, politicisation of the organisation and the New World Information and Communications

Order. The London *Sunday Times* called the director-general a 'fanatical Moslem' with 'a profound anti-Western bias' and a 'dictator'. The division between the 24 nations and the Third World and Communist countries was over many issues but highlights were (i) the emphasis of the West on human rights, the Third World on collective rights (New World Information and Communications Order [NWICO]); (ii) concern by the Third World countries that 90 per cent of the information about their own countries came from the Western media; and (iii) a rejection of the very concept of a free press by Third World countries, most of which control their own media.

STRUCTURE

Concentration and chains

Concentration of the newspaper industry in the United States in 1986 was lower than in most other democracies. The large, affluent, literate market enabled more large newspaper groups to exist. Since 1970 the industry had attracted foreign entrants, such as Thomson of Canada (and in 1986 the second largest US chain), Pergamon PLC of Britain, Birkmann of Germany and Rupert Murdoch's News International of Australia. All had exhausted their growth potential in their own countries. Despite this entry of foreign companies into the US industry, the US trend was still to higher concentration, group ownership and cross-media ownership.

Monopoly control and chain ownership in the newspaper industry are both controversial issues in the United States and elsewhere. Neither is good nor bad of itself from either the economic or the public-trust viewpoint. On the one hand, the benefits which *newspapers* with a local monopoly generally enjoy are: (i) economic stability allowing higher expenditures on editorial inputs; (ii) freedom from advertisers' influence and other local pressure groups; (iii) the poential for impartiality, balance, leadership and social responsibility, rather than following what their market niche compels; (iv) economies to advertisers. On the other hand local monopolies may (i) lack incentives to produce a quality product; (ii) increase advertising rates; (iii) demonstrate apathy over local issues and (iv) exercise information control. These are potential evils, but because of the plethora of the other competing media such as magazines, radio, television, as well as the threat of new newspaper entrants, they were not general characteristics of American newspapers in the mid-1980s. Each case of newspaper monopoly has to be examined on its own merits, in the context of the soft-edged nature of the industry.

The arguments in favour of newspaper *chains* which may have local monopolies are: (i) the market has selected the survivors of competition as the most efficient providers of information; (ii) the chain's success gives them economic strength with which to improve further the quality of inputs — new capital, more investigation, more and better journalists, greater use of wire services, additional sections and zoned additions; (iii) chain owners are less partisan and grant editorial independence; (iv) chains can afford to enter each others' market, so inceasing competition. The arguments against chains are that (i) they produce blenderised newspapers; (ii) they are often imitative rather than innovative; (iii) they are mere profit centres and (iv) they ignore local issues.[24]

Compared to other countries' newspaper industries, large newspaper companies in the United States in 1986 were small in relation to the size of the market. Whilst in 1985 Murdoch enjoyed 41 per cent of Australian circulation revenues and 39 per cent of British circulation, Thomson International had 29 per cent of Canadian circulation and Hersant 40 per cent of French circulation, the largest US group, Times Mirror Co., enjoyed under 10 per cent of US circulation. In 1984 the Times Mirror group earned $2.8 billion and profits of $421 million from its diversified interests which included the *Los Angeles Times* (1,047,000 circulation) and six other newspapers. This made it the largest US newspaper company although Gannett with 121 papers and 85 dailies owned more newspapers. Gannett's revenues in 1985 from papers, broadcast and advertising were $2.21 million. All the large US newspaper companies had invested heavily by 1986 in non-traditional but related areas to become media conglomerates.

Until the Reagan administration, the presumption in the United States had been that horizontal mergers were against the public interest. Despite legislation passed in 1970, 1972 and 1979 which attempted to maintain newspaper competition, by 1980 groups which had controlled 63 per cent of weekly circulation and 65 per cent of Sunday circulation in 1970 had acquired 75 per cent and 80 per cent respectively. By 1980 the 20 largest groups held over 50 per cent of total daily circulation.[25]

These concentration trends reflect the dynamics of the market throughout the Western world. Successful newspapers have traditionally made good profits. US tax laws encourage investment in the same or related industries, as does management specialisation. Recognising that US newspapers are a regional product and that regional media monopolies can threaten diversity of views regionally, United States anti-trust legislation has encouraged geographical diversification and so the emergence of national newspaper chains. It is preferable competitively to have 50 chains each with a newspaper in every state to 50 chains each with a monopoly in a single state. Gannett, with newspapers in 36 states, was the most widely-diversified geographically in 1986. In fact, chains can and do provide good papers. When in 1984 *Time* magazine selected the ten best US newspapers, a selection made every ten years, all the major chains were represented.[26]

In 1945 the US was still dominated by independently-owned newspapers. By 1983 the number of independents had fallen from 1,381 to 531; those group-owned had risen from 368 to 1,169.[27] The process continued in 1985 and 1986. In 1985 Gannett added the prestigious *Des Moines Register* and three other Cowles family papers to its roll and also the Detroit *Daily News* from Evening News Association.

The years 1983 to 1986 saw the sale of the flagship papers of such famous newspaper families as the Cowles, the Scripps, the Burnheims and the Fields. The explanation for such sales are similar. Estate taxes, dispersion of stock within the family, lack of capable and inspired third- and fourth-generation management, family squabbles and finally the stock market treadmill effect all encouraged family sell-outs to chains.

The treadmill effect refers to the relationship between stock value and performance. If a chain feels it can improve the financial performance of any paper then it will be prepared to bid more for that paper than the current stock market value. In Detroit the Evening News Association's *Evening News* owned by the Scripps family, for years fought a money-losing battle with Knight-Ridder, publisher of the *Detroit Free Press*. The Detroit paper was the Scripps flagship and for reasons of pride they were determined to remain independent even though a joint operating agreement with the *Detroit Free Press* could have brought the two companies profits of as much as $27 million per year. In 1985 a number of bids for Evening News Association topped by Gannett drove the price of the privately-held company's shares from $150 to $1,300.[28] Commenting on the bids, one fifth-generation shareholder in the 112-year-old Scripps company said, 'The end of a dynasty? I'd rather have the cash.'[29]

Whilst trusts and family pride may be able to resist bids in some cases, in many cases generous offers more than offset the regrets associated with the end of dynasties to whom a dispersed progeny have limited loyalties.

Whilst the sale of family newspapers has often occurred because chains have a record of improving financial performance, the effects on product quality have been ambiguous. Only on an individual paper-by-paper basis can the welfare effects of the sale of an independent to a chain be determined. After several generations family newspapers can lose their ability to lead, inspire, investigate and cover the community. They may not. Chains can bring expertise, capital and quality without loss of contact with local needs. They may not. On a cumulative basis however, even if each individual sale has merit, increased chain ownership may rise to levels of concentration which create anti-trust problems. In 1986 the United States had not reached that stage, given the standards for concentration set in Canada, Germany, France and other countries as acceptable.[30]

Concentration and product quality

Time magazine's selection of the ten best US newspapers in 1984 was illuminating. Despite the decline of local daily competition and the closure of one 1964 selection, the *Cleveland Press* in 1982, *Time* found overall quality had not suffered. Gannett has 'shifted emphasis from moneymaking boosterism to enterprising reporting',[31] and editions had 'a broader range of syndicated news and features to choose from'.[32] *Time* found that, 'some local papers might qualify for national influence if they were not overshadowed by even better nearby competitors'. It found that in Dallas local daily competition between the *Morning News* and *Times Herald* and in Detroit between the *Free Press* and *News* had had 'happy results', as these newspapers fought to be the survivor in the local market.[33] Indirectly it gave some support to chain ownerships by noting the case of the weekly *Georgia Gazette*. This local paper broke a succession of local stories and in the process antagonised a prominent local family, in a story exposing that a missing son had been kidnapped. As a result advertising and circulation suffered and the paper nearly failed. *Time* also reported that papers with circulations of less than 40,000 were handicapped and found it hard to be enterprising because financial resources were spread so thinly. Reporters might

Table 4.7: The ten best newspapers in the USA, 1984

Paper	Owner	Mono-poly	Daily circ.	Sunday circ.
Boston Globe[a]	Affiliated Publications	Yes	515,000	782,000
Chicago Tribune	Tribune	No	770,000	1,138,000
Des Moines Register[b]	Cowles Foundation	Yes	239,000	381,000
Los Angeles Times	Times Mirror	No	1,038,000	1,294,000
Miami Herald	Knight-Ridder	Yes	407,000	495,000
New York Times[a]	New York Times Co.	No	911,000	1,523,000
The Philadelphia Inquirer	Knight-Ridder	Yes	533,000	995,000
St Petersburg Times[a]	Andrew Barnes	Yes	243,000	310,000
Wall Street Journal[a]	Dow Jones	Yes	2,020,000	—
The Washington Post[a]	Bancroft Family	Yes	719,000	997,000

Notes: a. Family owned.
      b. Sold to Evening News Association, 1985.
Sources: Time, 30 April 1984; *Editor and Publisher Year Book*, 1985.

write 15 stories per day. Still many local newspapers were socially responsible and continued to crusade on important issues, to make enemies if necessary and to fulfil the watchdog function at the local level.

The generally healthy state of much of the US newspaper industry was discernable in Los Angeles. The *Los Angeles Times* was widely acknowledged in 1986 to be one of the finest newspapers published in the world. Despite that, quality surburbans like the *Bee* and *Daily News* had successfully rebuffed its efforts to take over suburban markets around Los Angeles. In Orange County (pop. 2 million) where a local edition of the *Los Angeles Times* sold 164,000 copies in 1985, the local suburban, the *Register*, owned by a smaller 32-newspaper chain called Freedom Newspapers even increased its lead from 38,000 in 1979 to 110,000 in 1985.[34] To do this it invested heavily in new staff and state-of-the-art colour technology printing presses. Despite comparable bulk, around 200 pages daily, the *Register* sold for less than the *Times* yet still earned $25 million profits in 1985.[35]

Table 4.8: Revenues of major US media conglomerates, 1984

	1984 Revenues ($b)
CBS	4.93
ABC*	3.71
Time Inc.	3.07
Times Mirror Co.	2.80
Dun & Bradstreet	2.40
Gannett Co.	1.96
Tribune Co.	1.79
Knight-Ridder Newspapers	1.66
New York Times Co.	1.23
Dow Jones & Co.	0.98
Capital Cities*	0.97
	0.94

Source: *Business Week*.

Structure and product differentiation

In terms of influence, information carried, revenues, circulation, employment, assets employed and newsprint consumed, the 1,700 metropolitan daily newspapers dominated the US newspaper industry. Increasingly important were suburban newspapers and tabloid newspapers which enjoyed 10 per cent growth in the 1970s. It was to meet this competition that US metropolitan dailies added increasing quantities of zoned additions, special sections and colour supplements.[36]

In addition to the dailies, the US consumer market was flooded with over 7,500 paid weekly newspapers and 6,000 non-paid weeklies. Free newspapers' circulation by 1985 exceeded 60 million though many were basically 'shoppers' or 'flyers' filled with advertising.[37] In 1985 such newspapers attracted $3 billion of advertising revenues. To meet this threat many traditional US newspapers joined the new competition. They began using their own distribution systems to deliver flyers produced and printed elsewhere, whilst others started their own flyers.

Numerous specialist newspapers are produced in the United States. Many have small circulations of just a few thousand but their total circulation exceeds five million. Their start up and production have been facilitated by technological advances, particularly offset printing, so that their numbers are likely to increase further in the 1980s. Specialised newspapers in the United States in 1985 included some 2,000 student newspapers, 400 foreign-language newspapers for ethnic minorities, 300 black newspapers, 400 regional business newspapers and many trade newspapers, military newspapers including the daily *Stars and Stripes*, sports papers and other special interest papers.[38]

Minority press

The US has a long tradition of a press to serve immigrants and minorities. America's first foreign-language paper was *Zeitung* published by Benjamin Franklin in 1732. In 1985 many of the 300 foreign-language papers served Asians and Hispanics in contrast to some 1,300 newspapers at the turn of the century which served a largely European audience.

The huge US immigrant population has always created a large market for information about the mother country as well as news about ethnic happenings in the new country. Most Americans are aware of the large Jewish population in New York, Chinese in San Francisco and Hispanics in Los Angeles. But in 1984 there were also 150,000 Koreans living in New York, the *Philippine News* sold 73,000 copies to Filipinos living in California, and California alone supported 24 Vietnamese papers.[39] In New York, 45,000 copies of the *Haiti Observer* were sold to Haitians who had fled 'Papa Doc' Duvalier. Total foreign-language newspaper circulation in the US in 1985 exceeded three million per day. The opportunity, affluence and freedom of the US have created the incentive for the minority press whose size exceeded that of most national press systems (see Table 1.4).

Entry into the US minority press is often easy. *Nguoi Vet* was started in 1984 for $5,000. It relied mostly on local community-minded Vietnamese merchants for advertising revenues. In New York in 1984 over 1,000 Koreans ran produce stands and supported the *Korean Times* totally with their advertisements. Concentrated close-knit populations made news collection and distribution reasonably inexpensive, and the market easily identifiable.

Many speciality newspapers have short life-spans. This reflects that entry to the US market is easy and start-up costs low. The number of entries and exits points to the difference between freedom of speech and the freedom to be heard. The decline of the underground press movement in the 1970s reflected changing market tastes and an increasing reluctance of the public to listen to those particular messages. Instead, in the 1980s the public has been increasingly willing to listen to health, fitness and lifestyle information leading to a plethora of running, diet, cycling, fitness and similar topic newspapers and magazines.

Structure and diversification

In 1934 the Communications Act took the view that the airways were a limited resource and should therefore be controlled. In 1953 there were 3,000 radio stations, 199 television stations and 1,700 dailies. A 7-7-7 rule was implemented limiting media companies to seven television stations, seven AM stations and seven FM stations. Cross-ownership of broadcasting and newspapers in the same area was prohibited. By 1984 there were 9,000 radio stations and 1,169 television stations but still 1,700 dailies. The Federal Communications Commission (FCC) concluded that a 12-12-12 rule should be implemented and all regulations eliminated in 1990. The FCC chairman, Mark Fowler, likened regulations to censors who, he said, had no place in a democratic society. Deregulation would lead to 'the elimination of pervasive government control over the lives and commerce of the American people'.[40] In addition the restrictions on station owners reselling stations which they had held for less than three years were removed.

Deregulation led to a feverish restricting of the US media industry as a whole in 1984 and 1985. In 1984 media mergers worth $3 billion occurred, in 1985 another $10 billion. Many of the major players had wide newspaper interests, most notably Ruper Murdoch and Tribune Co., but also Gannett and Times Mirror.[41] The most sensational moves were the Capital Cities friendly take-over of ABC, Ted Turner's unsuccessful hostile $5.4 million bid for CBS, Rupert Murdoch's friendly $2 billion take-over of Metromedia and Tribune Co.'s take-over of KLTA-TV in Los Angeles for $510,000.

The Capital Cities/ABC merger was for $3.5 billion. The resulting company owned 100 publications including the *Kansas City Times*, 24 radio stations, 12 television stations and 50 cable networks.[42]

In 1984 Rupert Murdoch paid $250 million for half Twentieth Century Fox Film Corporation and $320 for the other half in 1985. In 1985 he paid $2 billion for Metromedia's seven independent television stations. To avoid cross-ownership in Boston where Murdoch owned the *Boston Herald* a Metromedia ABC-TV affiliate was sold off to the Hearst Newspaper Corporation for $450 million. With these moves Murdoch put together a three-continent media empire.[43]

Murdoch's arch-rival in the New York and Chicago newspaper markets, Tribune Co., likewise became a media giant in 1985. Tribune paid $510 million for KTLA-TV in Los Angeles. To meet FCC requirements it sold the *Daily News* in Los Angeles in 1986. As a result Tribune owned eight daily newspapers, four radio stations and six television stations. These six stations reached 19.6 per cent of US households in 1985. Tribune also produced television so, like Murdoch, had the potential in 1985 to create another US television network.[44]

Structure and foreign investment

The unique nature of the newspaper has made the United States newspaper market a target for foreign investment. Both push and pull factors have been at work over the past decade, pushing foreign investors out of their own domestic newspaper markets and pulling them to the US.

In Britain, Canada and Australia there are special regulations and threats of regulation dealing with newspaper industry concentration. These have pushed successful native press barons into new markets. The pull factors of the US market were its huge size (50 per cent of world advertising expenditures), potential profitability and relatively few restrictions on foreign investment. These made it particularly attractive to English-speaking firms, but Koreans, Japanese, German, Chinese and many others have also been attracted to the US market.

The Byzantine operations of Rupert Murdoch have made him the best-known foreign media investor in the US. Prior to 1984 Murdoch had paid $30 million for the *New York Post* (1976), $1 million for the troubled *Boston Herald* (1982), $90 million for the Chicago *Sun-Times* (1983) and $35 million for the *Village Voice* (1977) which he sold for $50 million in 1985. His first acquisition was the San Antonio *News and Express* in 1973. In 1974 he founded *The Star*, a sensational supermarket weekly.[45]

In Boston Murdoch appeared as a white knight in 1982 to save the failing *Boston Herald*. After losing $25 million in four years, Hearst Newspaper Group had planned to close the *Herald*. By 1985, under Murdoch, circulation had risen 39 per cent to 268,000 whilst the rival up-market *Globe*'s circulation stagnated. The Murdoch strategy was as usual to cut costs, in this case to move up-market reducing sensationalism, to adopt a conservative viewpoint and to offer cheap advertising. Profits were anticipated for 1987.[46]

In Chicago the independent Field Enterprises company operated the prestigious but number two paper the *Sun-Times*. The rival *Chicago Tribune* had a higher circulation when Field decided to sell in 1983. No major American media company was interested in the marginally profitable paper and Murdoch's high $90 million bid deterred the also interested Canadian Toronto Sun Publishing Company and a local group.[47] In the deal Murdoch also took over the profitable Field Newspaper Syndicate wire service with exclusive rights to the very popular Ann Landers personal advice column read by 37 million every day.[48]

In Houston, the Toronto Sun Publishing Company having failed to get the *Sun-Times*, paid $100 million in 1985 for the *Post*, another second paper, though still the seventeenth largest newspaper in the US. Founded only in 1972, Sun Publishing had started successful tabloids in the major English-speaking Canadian cities but had already outgrown the limited Canadian tabloid market by 1985. The Canadian broadsheet market was dominated by Southam, Thomson and other powerful local monopolies. These factors pushed Sun into foreign investment in the US.[49]

In 1985 the British conglomerate, Pearson PLC decided to launch the *Financial Times* of London via satellite to the USA. They anticipated it would become a complement, rather than a challenge, to the *Wall Street Journal*. In 1985 Pearson had had US revenues of $300 million from its successful Penguin paperbacks, Longman hardcover books and *The Economist* weekly magazine (US circ. 100,000). Pearson's success with the weekly *The Economist* in the USA persuaded them that corporations, business professionals, and six-figure income earners would pay $400 per year (usually tax deductible), for an additional financial paper emphasising European and international views.

Not all foreign investors have been successful in the United States. Canada's most successful French-Canadian press baron, Pierre Péladeau of Quebecour, lost $12 million in a competitive struggle in Philadelphia from 1977 to 1981. In 1981 he closed the Philadelphia *Journal*. In 1985 claiming 'There are simply no good markets left in Canada' the print and publishing baron felt impelled to try the US market once again. His first step was to buy a majority of Pendall Publishing Inc. of Midland, Michigan but reportedly Péladeau sought the prestige and potential profit from owning a US daily.[50]

Canada's major foreign investor in the US is Thomson International. For Thomson the small Canadian market had become confining in the 1950s. In 1952 he bought his first newspaper in the United States, *The Independent* of St Petersburg in Florida, a favourite wintering spot of winter-weary Canadians. Thomson's success has been based on small newspapers. By 1985, Thomson had acquired over 140 newspapers in North America, more than half in the USA, but over one hundred had circulations of under 20,000. In the United States only Gannett with 130 newspapers in 1985 owned more newspapers. For Thomson small-town monopoly news-papers have been highly profitable in North America.

Structure and collaboration

The variety of special legislation dealing with the US press reflects its uniqueness as an industry, particularly the protection afforded the press by the First Amendment to the Constitution. Journalists are regarded as professionals with an established code of ethics. For exam-ple, the 1985 *Wall Street Journal* 'Heard on the Street' affair was clearly a breach of ethics, even had the case been dismissed in the courts. There are other industry issues involving ethics and influence.

Those who own and control major US dailies and newspaper chains exert enormous potential economic influence. Their relation-ships and associations with other powerful groups in society are of concern. It is inevitable, and arguably essential to the smooth run-ning of any country, that personal and informal communication systems develop between the military, the civil service, the legislature, industry, the universities and the professions.[51]

Research shows that in fact all the major US press chains have links to the government, major universities and industry. Amongst the 24 largest newspaper chains' 290 directors in 1981 there were the following links: 196 with *Fortune* top 500 companies, 24 with the twelve major universities, 34 with top-level federal government positions and 15 with major business policy groups while 130 were members of elite social clubs. Most represented in 1982 were the Dow Jones Company, the Washington Post Company and the Times-Mirror Co.

These affiliations are not necessarily sinister. They enable papers to lobby, campaign and influence in their own interests and on what they perceive as the public interest. They give the papers access to the gossip, leaks and ideas that currently influence decision-makers. Affiliations are a two-way process by which papers can both influence and be influenced. Such influence may be economic.

CONDUCT

Market dynamics

As with most consumer products in a mature market, producers of newspapers must constantly adapt to a changing market. As some products become 'dogs', for example many second metropolitan dailies in the United States, new products have the appearance of 'stars', for example suburbans. Whilst commentators have lamented the decline of second or competing metropolitan dailies over the last 30 years as a weakening of democracy, new newspapers and other mediums have arisen to create new voices and new outlets for opinion. In the United States newspaper circulation declines and newspaper closures have characterised the north-east and midwest, whilst the south and west have seen growth. Metropolitan dailies have faced a stagnant market whereas nationals and suburbans have grown. And whilst total metropolitan daily circulation has shown little growth since 1970, those newspapers that have survived and become local monopolies have often enjoyed circulation growth, improved quality and good profits.

In 1983 ten more metropolitan second newspapers closed their doors leaving 27 survivors. The closure of the *Washington Star* in 1983 meant that the capital city was served by one daily newspaper, *The Washington Post*, and a daily, *The Washington Times*, funded by the Moonies religious group. Closure of the Philadelphia *Bulletin* left a single daily there. However, a battle in Detroit epitomised the best of the Jackal effect in action and how it can affect conduct. In 1982 the two Detroit daily newspapers together lost over $20 million. Respectively the all-day *News* (643,000 circulation) and the morning *Free Press* (632,000) were the ninth- and tenth-largest newspapers in the USA. Rivalry took many forms. The *News* offered discounts on advertising and circulation rates. There was price competition. The *News* sold for 15¢ and the *Free Press* from Knight-Ridder for 20¢ at a time when most Knight-Ridder dailies and most dailies sold for 25¢. The *News* placed greater emphasis on hard news, whilst the *Free Press* offered more zoned editions and local news. Both papers paid high salaries and encouraged the best talent of the opposing paper to jump ship. The results of this intense competition was favourable for the readers and advertisers and the quality of the papers was generally high. Both won Pulitzer prices during the 1980s.[52] Knight-Ridder Newspapers which owned the *Free Press* had resources which far outweighed those of the privately-owned Evening News Association. It seemed like one more potential victory for the chain newspaper. Then, reflecting that the most likely new competition for a monopoly newspaper is another chain, Gannett bought the Evening News Association in 1985.[53] In 1986 a joint operating agreement was instituted.

Rupert Murdoch has introduced the same methods successfully used in Australia and Britain into the USA. His strategy has been to try to reverse the Jackal effect. He buys a number two daily newspaper, adds sports, sensationalism, shocking headlines, partisan politics and then promotes the paper aggressively. His *New York Post* doubled circulation from 1977 to 1984 to nearly one million and the *Boston Herald* increased 40 per cent from 1981 to 1985. But US advertisers tend to shy away from associating with sensational daily papers.[54] In New York the *Post* took 11.3 per cent of advertising expenditures in 1977 yet just 7.6 per cent in 1983.[55] So unless, as happened with Murdoch's *Sun* in Britain, readers can be burdened with most of the costs, racy tabloids are not commercially viable in the US. The traditional wisdom in the 1980s was that American readers would not pay for such products on a daily basis, though they would pay for sensational tabloid weeklies sold at supermarkets where products such as *The Star* and *National Enquirer* carry little advertising. Up to 1986 the *New York Post* had cost Murdoch $50 million. In fact, the *Post*'s competitor the *Daily News*, owned until 1983 by Tribune Company of Chicago, until the 1960s made excellent profits using the sex, sports, scandal formula used by Murdoch. The *Daily News* moved up market in the wake of demographic and social change which had reduced New York's blue-collar commuter audience and had brought them losses.[56] From 1977 to 1983 advertisement revenues at Tribune's *Daily News* rose 30 per cent as the paper became more middle class. Nevertheless from 1981 to 1986 Murdoch's aggressive strategy had slowed the Jackal effect wherever he entered the market.

National editions

In general the development of US national newspapers had been hindered until the 1980s by distance, though the *Wall Street Journal* (two million circulation) had served the national business market for years. The *Christian Science Monitor* had likewise served a section of the intellectual market on a national basis. Launched in 1963, a west-coast version of the *New York Times* had sold a highly respectable 100,000 copies, but failed to attract sufficient advertisers and was folded in 1977. Such nationals as there had been before 1980 appealed to a narrow market of up-market readers and up-market advertisers.

In 1984 *USA Today* extended its grasp. At any time there are some three million Americans overseas, including 600,000 service-men. To serve them, a 16-page international version of the paper selling for 75¢ was introduced. Gannett perceived that *The International Herald Tribune* and *Wall Street Journal Europe* did not meet the demand of many tourists and Americans living in Europe for soft news.

JOAs and conduct

Public concern in the United States over the tendency of the Jackal effect to eliminate competition amongst metropolitan dailies led to the passage of the 1971 Newspaper Act. By 1983, 24 cities had joint operating agreements under which two newspapers were allowed by the Justice Department to combine their business operations and printing operations, but had to maintain separate editorial divisions. To qualify for a JOA one newspaper had to demonstrate that it was failing and that the alternative to a joint operating agreement was a monopoly. Whilst it was felt that one and one-half metropolitans was better than one, there was considerable controversy about specific JOAs. Allocating costs to individual newspapers by conglomerates is somewhat arbitrary. When Hearst newspapers sought a joint operating agreement between its *Seattle Post-Intelligencer* and the profitable rival *Seattle Times* objections were raised by the other media and particularly suburban and local newspapers. They claimed Hearst's losses were overestimated and that the agreement eroded their market. In other words, metropolitan daily monopolies face competition from suburban dailies, national newspapers and the other media.

Surviving monopoly newspapers, once the second newspaper has folded, frequently adopt a new product strategy. They wish to attract as many of the defunct newspaper's readers as possible. They therefore expand; they offer more pages, more colour and hire more staff. With more potential readers, more potential advertisers and higher potential advertising rates it becomes profitable to expand. Arguably the customer gets a bigger and better newspaper for the same price, although the temptation to appeal to the lowest common denominator also exists. The closure of the *Memphis Press-Sentinel* in 1983 illustrated firm conduct by a survivor. Within days the Scripps-Howard-owned *Commercial Appeal* raised advertising rates, introduced colour, increased its number of pages and moved down market to tap the blue collar market previously dominated by the *Press-Sentinel*.[57]

Product diversification trends for the future

Newspaper companies are really information providers. Firms in the information industry worldwide provide information in response to market demand, and changes in market demand require constant adaptation. Preparation to meet market change in the 1980s led to heavy, sometimes high-risk investment by US newspaper firms in new newspaper and newspaper-related products. These included national newspapers, zoned newspapers, newspaper magazine supplements, freesheets, teletext, videotext, cable and satellites. Newspaper firms in the 1980s faced uncertainty about what new directions technology would take and which innovations would be commercially viable. The only certainty was that there would be change and product diversification would be needed to meet that change. Meeting that change in the USA, the newspaper firms increasingly ran into competition with other media monoliths.

As federal regulations were relaxed, a period of media consolidation and vertical integration began. The US experience in 1985 was a portent of developments that either were occurring or were likely to occur in the rest of the Western media.

Magazines

The widely respected *New York Times* newspaper has been accused of becoming a daily magazine as the proportion of hard news content has declined and features and advertising have increased. Newspapers in terms of content have infringed on the magazine market. On Sundays many newspapers carry Sunday supplements which are magazines. *Parade* magazine is owned by the Newhouse newspaper chain and is included as part of some 500 Sunday newspapers. In 1985 with a circulation of 23 million it had the largest magazine circulation in the United States.[58] In 1984 *Parade* earned $156 million in advertising revenue. The second largest Sunday supplement in 1984 was *Family Week*. In 1980 CBS Inc. bought *Family Week* (circulation 12.8m) for $50 million. In 1985, as part of the CBS restructuring against a hostile takeover from Ted Turner, the magazine was sold to the Gannett newspaper chain for around $35 million. Gannett renamed it *USA Weekly* in 1985 to complement *USA Today*.[59]

Rising circulations and falling advertising revenues at *Parade* and *Family Week* epitomised the changing nature of advertising demand as advertisers became infatuated with target audience. In fact by 1985 Sunday supplements had become highly dependent on tobacco advertisements banned from television.

Sunday magazine supplements' advertisements were also challenged by increased use of so-called free standing inserts (FSI). By 1985 the majority of US Sunday newspapers were filled with a mix of individual and combined coupon advertisements. FSIs had expanded the role of the newspaper as a simple distribution vehicle, but had undermined their Sunday magazine supplement advertising market. The problem for advertisers with Sunday supplements was that people actually read them. In contrast they picked up FSIs specifically to clip the advertisements. Though 4.5 per cent of coupons in FSIs were redeemed in 1985, only 2.5 per cent of magazine coupons were redeemed.

Special interest magazines with targeted audiences attractive to advertisers prospered in the 1980s, though not all were successful. Newhouse newspapers, through Conde Nast Publications which it owned, bought *The New Yorker*. Rupert Murdoch's News America Publishing paid $350 million for the half of Ziff-Davis Corporation which published business magazines. CBS paid $362 million for the other half which produced consumer magazines like *Road & Truck, Flying, Boating, Skiing* and *Stereo Review*. Murdoch added twelve titles to his five magazines, CBS twelve to their eight. Time Mirror, Time Inc., Hearst, New York Times Co. and ABC had all expressed interest in Ziff-Davis, reflecting the general desire of both newspaper and television companies to diversify into well-proven magazines.[60]

In 1985 Ziff-Davis introduced a novel new daily newspaper, *Computer Industry Daily*. It carried no advertisements and cost $1,000 per year. It was distributed both electronically to computer terminals and on paper. It closed within a year. Its closest competition came from products like Gannett's *USA Today Update*. Derived from *USA Today* this product was delivered electronically but was not available on paper. It included a daily executive news summary of the most important computer industry developments which Gannett has obtained from 200 publications. To get *USA Today*

Update the consumer connected to a communications network such at CompuServe at a cost of $12.50 per hour.

The fickle nature of demand for magazines was reflected in the special interest field of computer publications which had grown dramatically on the back of the booming computer industry. In 1984 that industry began a shake-out and so did computer publications whose 600 journals and newsletters had quickly built a total circulation of 12 million. By 1985 many had folded in the face of advertisement cutbacks. Meanwhile, accompanying the economic recovery, such supposedly doomed mass-market magazines as *Better Homes and Gardens* and *Ladies Home Journal* enjoyed a revival.

Videotex

Newspaper companies wish to make sure that they continue to provide information should print be replaced in the future by electronic services transmitted by cable television. Electronic publishing in the United States brought grief to many media companies in the 1980s. The costs are huge, the potential profits enormous, but consumer demand uncertain. In 1983 there were predictions that within a decade the business would have total revenues of $30 billion.[61] For comparison, US daily newspaper industry revenues in 1985 were $20 billion.[62] Banks, telecommunication companies and retailers have all invested heavily in the new industry.

The Knight-Ridder newspaper chain introduced the first complete two-way transaction and information service late in 1983 in the Miami area. Viewtron cost $12 per month to subscribers and about $1 per hour to use. It also required an AT&T terminal, Sceptre, which cost $600. The two-way videotext system provided huge quantities of information: news, local events, encyclopedia access, academic courses, road maps, airline guides and travel information. Viewtron also allowed consumers to link up to 'service providers' who sold services, goods and information. Users could pay bills and bank from their homes. To set up the Miami operation alone cost Knight-Ridder $26 million, but consumers balked at paying $600 for a terminal. In Chicago, Field Enterprises, which had sold off the *Chicago Sun-Times* in 1983 Rupert Murdoch, set up a consortium with Honeywell and the Centel Telephone Company in 1984 to start up Veycom, a similar service to Viewtron. In Los Angeles, the Times Mirror Co., publisher of the *Los Angeles Times*, introduced a similar service.

Potential rivals to newsapers in the infant videotext industry in 1985 included retailers and the banks. High costs encouraged consortiums. For 1986, IBM, CBS and Sears Roebuck planned a $150 million videotext service. Other ventures planned in 1985 combined Citicorp and RCA; GCE, J.D. Penney and a group of French companies; ATT, Bank of America, Chemical Bank and Time Inc.; and Times Mirror Company and Informat.[63]

Despite the huge potential of videotext consumer resistance was high. Customers had found it too expensive and complicated. In 1986 both Times-Mirror and Knight-Ridder abandoned videotext. Nevertheless the success in France of videotext in 1986 augers well for the future of videotext in the USA.[64]

Cable television

In the 1970s cable television, with its potential to be a one-way electronic newspaper, was seen as major threat to the print media. To preserve their role as information providers many US newspaper and magazine publishers diversified into cable. Particularly in big cities there have been delays in awarding franchises and building systems, so that in 1985 Washington, New York, Boston, Chicago, Pittsburgh and Philadelphia still had incomplete systems and only 40 per cent of America's 90 million households were on cable. Nevertheless from 1982 to 1984 basic revenues rose from $30 million to $45 million and Pay-TV revenues from $24 million to $45 million.[65]

Despite the risks, major newspapers have invested in cable. In 1985 they included the *New York Times*, Time Inc., *The Washington Post* and Hearst. The sums involved have been considerable. ABC television's cable operations lost $47 million before ABC abandoned cable in 1984. The two other networks, CBS and RCA, the parent company of the NBC, were still in cable in 1986. In 1984 CBS joined with Hearst and took over the failed RCA Rockefeller Cable Pay Television Entertainment Network. Hearst and ABC were also partners in 1984 in the creation of Lifetime, a 24-hour health and lifestyle channel.[66]

The print media have had some success diversifying to cable television. Of the 32 million cable subscribers to Pay-TV in 1984, over 13 million subscribed to Time Inc.'s Home Box Office (HBO). HBO and its sister Cinemax generated nearly two-thirds of Times' $342 million operating profit in 1983, dwarfing *Time* magazine and her sister publications contribution to the corporation. HBO represented a highly successful print media diversification in the 1980s.[67] The *New York Times* has been another successful investor and innovator in cable television. They modified interactive techniques to create a new form of Pay-TV so that in their New Jersey system consumers had a two-way cable system which allowed them to buy specific programmes, for example a film or sports event, individually.[68] At the same time the VCR (video cassette recorder) boom, begun in the US in 1984, and the dramatic expansion of video rental outlets could challenge movie-based Pay-TV like HBO, as could those basic cable services which carried advertising supported services.

Other diversifications

In 1981 Tribune Company Group, publisher of the *Chicago Tribune* paid $20.5 million for the notoriously unsuccessful Chicago Cubs baseball team. This represented a somewhat bizarre form of vertical integration. Tribune Company Group had diversified into broadcast and television and had rights to cover the Cubs games. Buying the Cubs ensured that Tribune Company Group, which had had its right to televise Yankee games from its New York television station threatened in a challenge from Sports Channel Association cable network, continued to cover the Cubs. Applying its managerial know-how to the Cubs, Tribune nearly doubled players' salaries but still reduced losses from $5 million to $1 million and brought the Cubs the first division title for 39 years.[69]

A similar form of vertical integration to guarantee entertainment supplies involved the backward move by cable companies into film. In the case of Rupert Murdoch's News International the $560 million purchase of Twentieth Century Fox Film Corporation in 1985 guaranteed inputs for his cable interests, following his earlier diversification into cable from newspapers earlier in the 1980s. This ambitious move also provided programme inputs for Murdoch's US and European satellite television system.[70]

In summary, in order to ensure survival in an uncertain world and to reinvest substantial profits earned from newspapers US newspaper firms have been major investors in both the traditional and evolving media. Not all have proven as profitable as newspapers.

PERFORMANCE

Performance in the US newspaper industry in terms of the economic criteria frequently used is highly satisfactory. Newspaper firms are efficient, frequently criticised for that very efficiency in terms such as commercial or cost-conscious. By international standards productivity in 1985 was high and the industry's profit record was considerably above the US industry average. In the US new technology had been introduced quickly in order to stay abreast of rapid change in the other media. The industry was labour-intensive and employed one million people. Each day there were 100 million repeat customers who read the papers and each year advertisers spent over $20 billion, again mostly as repeat buyers.[71]

The economics of product quality were evaluated by *Time* magazine in 1984. Even ten years *Time* tries to identify the ten best US dailies in terms of such dimensions as reporting quality, layout and enterprise. Generally, *Time* concluded that quality had improved over the previous decade with better graphics and photos, better journalistic education, a broader range of syndicated news and features and better coverage of local issues in general despite the growth of chain ownership.[72] No single type of firm organisation nor market structure in the US had a clear-cut propensity to produce a quality paper.

The worldwide dominance of the US press and US news agencies in the 1980s has been sharply criticised and became the source of controversy both within the United States and in the Third World. Whilst much discussion of this controversy and accusation of influence is political there are noteworthy economic implications. These are: Western readers want Western news; Western news is easier and cheaper to collect; Western governments are less obstructive. For sound economic reasons, the world news is dominated by Western news. The US government and press have already responded to the charges, with subsidies to help the Third World press and increase Third World coverage.

The United States press is widely acknowledged to be the freest in the world. Watergate and the eventual resignation of President Richard Nixon, then the most powerful man in the world, attest to the power and freedom of the press. Yet a decade later, in 1983, public confidence in the US press was at an all-time low. Following Watergate nearly 30 per cent of Americans had a greal deal of confidence in the press, by 1983 it had fallen below 15 per cent, even lower than for banks and little better than for lawyers. The National Opinion Research Center which conducted the polls found the press was criticised most frequently for dishonesty and inaccuracy; but also for a lack of compassion, a proneness for the invasion of privacy, an emphasis on bad news, a possible threat to national security and a hypercritical attitude to authority.[73]

These results might suggest the American public is not getting the press product it wants or the quality of press product it wants. It raises the possibility that the reader consumer is not 'king', and in the case of newspapers that the market does not work to meet the consumers' demands. It suggests market failure. Yet all the major consumer, the advertiser, wants is reach. He is otherwise disinterested in content and so delegates that choice to readers. And each day over 110 million people read the US dailies. They vote for them by buying time. The fact that cases of dishonesty and inaccuracy in the United States press are exposed reveals the diversity of information sources and their competitiveness. The fact that fabricated and false stories are exposed by rivals reflects the healthy competitive state of the US press. The fact that major financial scandals involving political leaders in the US, Japan and the Philippines were first disclosed in the US attest to its independence and effectiveness.[74]

The media in the USA is expected to be the major watchdog of government and other large institutions. In the USA by and large it does do its job. It does serve the people, though not equally; the rich and conservative are better served. The public may not like the messages but the press is only the messenger. The public may not like how it carries the messages but it does at least have them offered in a wide variety of forms and is prepared to buy them in enormous quantity. There is always a danger that the government will be allowed to control the press under the guise of restraining so-called press abuses. This threat in itself keeps the press on guard and forces it to be socially responsible.

By comparison with the highly partisan press in the United States up until World War I, the current ideological press of Italy, France and Spain, the more controlled half-free press of Britain or the socially restrained press of Japan, the government regulated press of the United States is remarkably unrestrained and unbiased. There is no comparison with the Third World and Communist countries. For all its weaknesses it compares favourable with the press of the other democracies in terms of freedom, variety and quality.

NOTES

1. On the supply side, the power and influence of the US press unions has been seriously curtailed since 1978 when there were major strikes. The new technology no longer required printers' skills and membership in the

International Typographical Union in 1985 was down to 37,000, or one-third of a decade earlier. Though the *New York Times* still dealt with 14 unions, there were none at the *Los Angeles Times*. Most journalists in 1986 were university-trained and educated and many were reasonably well paid and had high status. Most were members of the Journalists' Guild. There was relatively little government interference in the press and limited regulation. This reflected the Jeffersonian tradition. There was easy access to finance capital, the latest technology, news agencies and newsprint. Supply-side conditions to the USA newspaper industry in 1986 were therefore highly satisfactory by world standards.

2. *Business Week*, 3 February 1986.

3. *Business Week*, 26 August 1986.

4. Most US newspapers keep a fixed ratio between advertisements and editorial, say 60/40.

5. *Journalism Quarterly*, Autumn 1983.

6. *Wall Street Journal*, 14 October 1981.

7. Ibid.

8. *Business Week*, 15 April 1985.

9. *Time*, 21 November 1983.

10. *Newsweek*, 1 February 1982.

11. Ibid.

12. *Business Week*, 27 May 1985.

13. *Washington Post*, 20 April 1985.

14. *Business Week*, 27 May 1985.

15. Ibid.

16. *Business Week*, 8 July 1985.

17. *The Economist*, 26 October 1985.

18. The US spent over $50 billion in 1986 on military research and development for the purpose of national security. Leaks in the newspapers or elsewhere undermine perceived security.

19. *Time*, 15 October 1984.

20. Ibid.

21. *Time*, 2 September 1985.

22. *Business Week*, 29 October 1984.

23. The cases above involved public figures concerned more about their reputations than the size of the settlement. Economic incentives were evolved which encourage the bringing of libel suits and subsequent expensive jury trials which discourage uninhibited reporting. To remove both these economic incentives, upper limits on the amount of libel recovery could be imposed.

24. 'Blenderised' is a derogatory term for smooth, non-controversial editorial content.

25. *US News and World Report*, 11 February 1985.

26. *Time*, 30 April 1984.

27. *US News and World Report*, 11 February 1985.

28. *Business Week*, 12 August 1985.

29. *Business Week*, 16 September 1985.

30. In 1983 Park Newspaper, a small New York-based chain, bought a local paper in Jeffersonville, Indiana called the *Evening News*. In 1979 it had bought the *Daily Herald* in Sapulpa, Oklahoma. In Jeffersonville, Park

was seen as being 'very community oriented', in Sapulpa as having 'lost touch with the community'. Likewise, Copley Newspapers' purchase of the *Evening News* in La Jolla, California was seen as restoring balance in 1983, but its purchase of the *News-Sun* in 1984 in Waukegan, Illinois as creating a gulf between the owners and the community.

31. *Time*, 30 April 1984.
32. Ibid.
33. Ibid.
34. *Time*, 23 November 1985.
35. Ibid.
36. This emphasises once again the soft-edged or blurred limits of the market.
37. *Editor and Publisher Yearbook*, 1985, p. 148.
38. Ibid.
39. *Time*, 8 July 1985.
40. *Business Week*, 13 December 1984.
41. *US News and World Report*, 13 May 1985.
42. *Business Week*, 1 April 1985.
43. *Wall Street Journal*, 13 June 1985.
44. *Wall Street Journal*, 24 June 1985.
45. *The Economist*, 1 February 1986.
46. *Newsweek*, 29 November 1982.
47. *Wall Street Journal*, 17 May 1985.
48. *Journalism Review*, June 1984.

For Murdoch the US market in 1985 had yet to become as successful as the Australian and British markets. Pre-tax profits in the US in 1982 were only $3.3 million. Profits for 1984 were $24 million and were expected to improve further. Losses at the *New York Post* which approached $20 million in 1982 when Tribune launched the *Daily News* there, had been reduced to around $10 million in 1985. Profits were essential to underwrite Murdoch's highly levered non-newspaper operations.

49. *MacLeans*, 31 October 1983.
50. *Canadian Business*, June 1985, p. 237.
51. Peter Dreier, 'The Position of the Press in the US Power Structure', *Social Problems*, February 1982, p. 305.

In 1982 when William Rogers, former Treasury Secretary, worked for Gannett, Gannett's chairman commented: 'Bill Rogers is in a position to make major contributions to Gannett in its dealings with government, on anti-trust matters, with the FCC . . .' When in 1984 the FCC relaxed its rules on cross-ownership of the media Gannett was assured its views would be represented. Likewise the chains' many affiliations to the banks and financial institutions can only help when it is necessary to raise funds.

52. *Time*, 17 January 1983.
53. *Time*, 9 September 1985.
54. *Business Week*, 3 June 1985.
55. *The Economist*, 26 February 1984.
56. *Business Week*, 20 May 1985.
57. *Time*, 28 November 1983.
58. In 1985 *Reader's Digest* (18 million copies) and *TV Guide* (17 million copies) were runners up.

59. *Time*, 5 August 1985.

60. *Business Week*, 24 December 1984.

61. *Fortune*, 14 November 1983.

62. *Business Week*, 14 January 1985.

63. *Business Week*, 14 January 1981.

64. See Chapter 11, page 260.

65. *The Economist*, 12 January 1985.

66. *Business Week*, 3 June 1985.

67. Despite the risks, newspaper companies have continued to enter the cable television market. In 1985 Washington Post Co. paid nearly $400 million for Capital Cities Communications Inc.'s cable television system. There were several bidders for the systems which CCC had to sell to meet federal regulations when it took over ABC network television. In 1985 press baron Rupert Murdoch bought Metromedia for $1.6 billion. Federal regulations required he then sell WCVB-TV in Boston. When the Hearst Corporation paid $450 million for WLVB-TV in 1985 it had to sell the highly acclaimed *Boston Globe* to meet FCC regulations.

68. *Business Week*, 22 July 1983.

69. *Business Week*, 15 October 1984.

70. *Business Week*, 7 October 1985.

71. Perceived product quality has fallen. Public opinion polls showed that confidence in the press had fallen in the period 1976 to 1983. Those with a great deal of confidence fell from 29 per cent to 14 per cent. Perceived product quality had fallen in the following areas: trust, objectivity, justice, image, attitude, protection of privacy, community sensitivity, national loyalty, and responsibility. The press had become more arrogant, remote, pessimistic, biased and hypercritical. Libel suits, the growth of chains, multiple motivations and story fabrications have been discussed and help explain these sentiments. In the reactionary 1980s, aggressive investigative reporting in the Watergate tradition was out of style. When Reagan restricted the press in Grenada in 1983, the White House curb on freedom was supported by 5-1 in letters received. Much of the reader criticisms of the press stems from the perceived over-zealousness of the press.

72. *Time*, 30 April 1984.

73. Ibid.

74. *The Washington Post* disclosed Watergate; *Newsweek* disclosed Prime Minister Tanaka of Japan's acceptance of bribes; the *San Jose Mercury* first revealed the extent of the Marcos corruption.

5

United Kingdom

INTRODUCTION

Britain has some of the world's highest circulation newspapers. In 1986 London's daily newspapers had a combined daily circulation in excess of 14 million. For nearly 90 years London's Fleet Street newspapers have been able to circulate throughout Britain as national papers as a result of Britain's early development and large urbanised population packed into a small geographic area with a good transport system. Few national capitals dominate a country's political economy in the way London does Britain. Consequently, the dominance, tradition, variety and even mystique of London's nationals is unique in the developed world. Britain also has a vital but smaller regional daily press.

The British newspaper industry, both regional and national, in the mid-1980s was in a state of transition as it adjusted belatedly but rapidly to new technology, commercial radio, more television competition, changing tastes, satellites and videotext, all in an environment of still hostile labour relations and considerable government involvement and influence. London's Fleet Street in particular found this transition difficult.

The years 1898 to 1914 saw the rise of the Fleet Street popular press. Between the wars there was rapid circulation growth with national newspaper reading becoming a widespread habit and the *Daily Mirror* achieving a five million circulation. From 1940 to 1957 growth continued in an environment of newsprint shortages and rationing. After 1957 circulation of Fleet Street newspapers levelled off, commercial television began and the era of Fleet Street prosperity ended. Since 1957 newspaper chains have grown in importance in Britain. Until 1986 ownership has changed often, profits all but disappeared and Fleet Street has survived based on cash infusions from North Sea oil, regional newspapers and other outside sources.

Concern over the state of the newspaper industry in Britain has led to many official investigations since 1945, including three Royal Commissions in 1948, 1962 and 1977. These collected considerable information and inspired special newspaper legislation but generally failed to restore a healthy competitive press in the sense of similar profitable newspapers competing head-to-head for the same market. Labour relations legislation in 1980 and 1982 had more effect.

BASIC CONDITIONS

Attitudes and motives

Anthony Sampson, commenting on the press in 1983, noted: 'In the old days press barons were attacked for making large profits out of their newspapers. Today there is more surprise about owners who are prepared to take heavy losses.'[1] Although these heavy losses were often paper losses, it seemed irrational that anybody should wish to own losing, troublesome Fleet Street papers.

In fact, ownership of a national newspaper buys social prominence, political and economic power and influence, sometimes a peerage and occasionally profits. In the regional press newspaper ownership rarely buys a peerage but usually better profits.

Viewing the press as a quasi-public institution all three Royal Commissions examined the motivation of press owners, the implications being that profits were adequate motive to produce paper plates but not newspapers. Newspapers have a special social responsibility and so, it was implied, their owners should be specially motivated.

Mixed motives of gain, power and influence explain why for decades commercially non-viable propositions such as *The Times* and the *Daily Express* have continued in production. They also explain in part why the Fleet Street unions were able to abrogate control of the production process to themselves. In 1979 during the year-long strike at *The Times* Lord Thomson said, 'We have always been conscious in our ownership of these titles that we have duties and responsibilities going beyond purely commercial considerations.'[2] These duties and responsibilities cost him £30 million from 1967 to 1980. The next owner of *The Times*, Murdoch observed, 'third world coverage doesn't sell newspapers'.[3] Still, under his ownership *The Times* continued extensive, if reduced, coverage of foreign affairs.

Most Fleet Street owners by 1986 were conglomerates which could use a newspaper as a vehicle to improve image, extend influence and improve profits in other activities. Such activities are not necessarily clear or widely reported but were brought to public attention with the sale of *The Observer* to Lonrho in 1981 by the Atlantic-Richfield (ARCO) Company, the owner since 1975. Whilst the focus of interest was on the purchaser Lonrho's African interests, ARCO's ownership of *The Observer* had covered the years following the first OPEC crisis when North Sea oil concessions were granted. In the USA in Aspen, Colorado, ARCO ran the Aspen Institute, an influential research institute which made no direct contribution to profits but clearly benefited ARCO in terms of goodwill and other non-pecuniary pay-offs. *The Observer* fell into the same category of image-maker and influence-peddler at ARCO. Likewise, Thomson's financial support of *The Times* helped his other interests in profitable government-regulated industries, notably North Sea oil, commercial television and regional newspapers. In 1984 alone, Thomson International's profits were $93 million with 80 per cent from North Sea oil. From 1959 to 1980 when Thomson owned *The Times* it had lost less than one-third that amount.[4] Indirectly *The Times* had been a good investment.

Fears concerning Rowland of Lonrho's motives for owning *The Observer* proved well-founded. Initially opposed by *The Observer* staff, the sale was referred to the Monopolies Commission which attempted to set up safeguards in the form of five independent directors to protect the public interest and editorial independence.[5] Even at that time the safeguards seemed inadequate and in 1984 Rowland indeed did interfere in the paper's coverage of atrocities in Zimbabwe. It was a brazen flaunting of editorial independence to further Lonrho's economic interests.

The sale of Mirror Newspapers by Reed International in 1984 to publisher Robert Maxwell for $147 million created further concern about press concentration and what motivates newspaper owners. Maxwell's parent company Pergamon Press was registered in Liechtenstein and little was known about it. He had a long but shady history as a successful capitalist, and many observers questioned his motives and suitability as an owner.

Public policy

Until the post-war era public policy regarding the British newspaper industry was essentially passive. Libel laws, tax laws, education acts and similar legislation affected the environment in which a free press operated, but within that context papers were clearly private possessions to be used as their owners wished for their own ends. Somewhat ironically it was only after real alternative media substitutes became available that the Fleet Street press came to be viewed as a quasi-public institution. Threats to close *The Times* from 1978 to 1982 evoked a response that illustrated the common viewpoint that newspapers are special products, and that owners of them merely custodians.[6]

In Britain there is no written constitution and no law dealing specifically with the role of the press. In 1986 there was still no freedom of information act. There are a number of laws which pertain to the operation of the press. There are libel and contempt laws to which the press is subject. In recent years there has been a number of libel cases resulting in newspapers paying heavy damages. The 1926 Judicial Proceedings Act, the 1935 Young Persons' Act and the 1967 Criminal Justice Act all impose restrictions on covering court cases, although some protection for editors is given by the 1952 Defamation Act and the 1960 Administration of Justice Act. The 1911 Official Secrets Act protects the national interests, the 1959 Obscene Publications Act and 1955 Harmful Publications Act deal with morally objectionable and harmful material.[7]

Media competition has been dealt with specifically. The 1965 Monopolies and Mergers Act and the 1973 Fair Trade Act deal with the transfer of ownership of newspapers with an average daily circulation of over 25,000. The 1980 and 1982 Labour Reform Acts affected the terms under which labour was organised banning secondary picketing and closed shops. Whilst not specifically aimed at the media, they were partly inspired by newspapers and newspapers became their testing ground.[8]

Reader demand

Concern over newspaper monopoly in the 1980s in much of the developed world has emphasised structure and the concentration of ownership. The influence of the press in Britain, however, has steadily declined as news and information alternatives have developed, beginning with radio in 1922. In Britain the broadcasting media was slow to develop as a powerful competitor to newspapers. Up until the 1970s both radio and television were tightly controlled by the state, there was no radio advertising and limited television advertising. As entertainment, television was an evening affair with programming beginning late in the afternoon and ending before midnight. Not until 1977 was a fourth television channel started. Even then the state-appointed Independent Broadcasting Authority (IBA) decides who should have the highly profitable commercial franchises which are reviewed every five years. Television content has tended to be directed at the middle-class taste of the IBA since investors want the franchises renewed. Whilst Britain has produced some widely acclaimed television such as 'Brideshead Revisited' and 'Upstairs Downstairs', earning good export earnings in the process, it has failed to mass produce the all day low-brow low-cost mass-appeal game show type fare useful to many shift workers, the old, the sick, and those often just wishing to be passively entertained; and in the process making an audience for advertisers.

Commercial radio was introduced in Britain in the 1970s, and breakfast television was begun in 1983. Until the 1980s government control of the broadcasting media protected newspapers both as an entertainment and an advertising medium, but in the 1980s this protection began to weaken. Since 1983 the British have been the world's greatest users of VCRs, no doubt partly reflecting the limited choice and daytime provision of traditional broadcast. VCRs helped fill the gap and so provided competition to the newspapers; as in other developed countries competition will be provided by more cable television, more satellite television, increased commercial radio and more home computers.

In other words, newspaper demand in Britain in the 1980s faced new challenges from previously muzzled traditional broadcasting media and from the new electronic sources. In 1985 the Peacock Commission even reviewed the heretical possibility of advertising on broadcasts by the BBC.

National newspapers

Demand for national Fleet Street newspapers has fallen slightly since the 1950s but not uniformly across all segments of the market. Between 1957 and 1986 demand for London evening newspapers fell by over two-thirds. This dramatic shift in demand reflects the decline in the use of public transport as more people owned and

Table 5.1: Circulation of UK national newspapers, 1985

Title and foundation date	Owner	Circulation Jan–June 1985
National dailies (mornings)[a]		
'Populars'		
Daily Express (1900)	Fleet Holdings	1,875,291
Daily Mail (1896)	Associated Newspapers Group	1,828,068
Daily Star (1978)	Fleet Holdings	1,434,562
Morning Star (1966)	The People's Press Printing Society	28,251
The Mirror (1903)	Pergamon Press	3,271,861
The Sun (1964)	News International	4,065,647
'Qualities'		
The Daily Telegraph (1855)	Telegraph Newspaper Trust	1,221,092
Financial Times (1888)	Pearson Longman	229,423
The Guardian (1821)	The Guardian and Manchester Evening News	486,984
The Times (1785)	News International	479,640
National Sundays		
'Populars'		
The Mail on Sunday (1982)	Associated Newspapers Group	1,605,228
News of the World (1843)	News International	4,787,233
Sunday Express (1918)	Fleet Holdings	2,405,004
Sunday Mirror (1963)	Pergamon Press	3,210,917
Sunday People (1881)	Pergamon Press	3,089,707
'Qualities'		
The Observer (1791)	George Outram & Co.[b]	745,692
The Sunday Telegraph (1961)	Telegraph Newspaper Trust	689,556
The Sunday Times (1822)	News International	1,257,709

Notes: a. There is one London evening paper, *The Standard* (504,000).
In 1986 a new morning *Today* started. Initial circulation was
under 500,000. Late in 1986 *The Independent* also was
launched.
b. Controlled by Lonrho.
Source: Britain, An Official Handbook (Central Intelligence Office,
London, 1986).

commuted by car, the move of much of the population from central
London to the suburbs, and most noticeably commercial television.
Demand for London morning newspapers also declined with an
overall 15 per cent decline. Traditionally London's dailies are
divided into 'qualities' and 'populars'. There is a wide range of
choice as the national dailies attempt to identify their own market
niches.

The quality newspaper *The Times* has an enviable reputation as one of the world's best newspapers, though it is not without its detractors. Demand for *The Times* comes from 'bishops and professors' in the words of its owner Rupert Murdoch.[9] When in 1980 he tried to increase circulation to include students and intellectuals he found advertisers unresponsive. *The Times* had at one time advertised that 'top people read *The Times* and advertisers were only prepared to pay the paper's high advertising rates so long as readers were top-income people. This reflects the unique character of the newspaper. Since the cover price at *The Times* did not cover the additional newsprint, ink and distribution costs of additional circulation, so, even with no reduction in cover price, increased circulation generated losses.[10] *The Times* re-evaluated its policy.

Also qualifying as a qualty in 1985 was the *Financial Times*, a financial newspaper similar to the *Wall Street Journal* in market focus and with similar ambitions to become an international newspaper. It is said that those who run Britain read the *Financial Times*, those who think they run Britain read *The Times*. The *Financial Times* in 1986 also published in Frankfurt, Germany and Virginia, USA using satellites for international distribution. By far the largest of the so-called qualities in circulation was the pro-Conservative *Daily Telegraph*.

Competing newspapers in the middle of the daily newspaper quality-popular-spectrum were the once dominant *Daily Express* and *Daily Mail*. Finally, much maligned but with far and away the largest circulations were the *Daily Mirror, The Sun* and the upstart *Daily Star*, started in 1982 and published in Manchester. These popular tabloids competed aggressively for a similar market providing lightweight entertainment and titillation with a smattering of current events. As the circulation figures show, demand for these papers was strong. In the first half of the 1980s they were the only profitable daily newspapers from Fleet Street.

The only evening paper published in Fleet Street in 1985 was *The London Standard*. It only circulated in the London area and was formed in 1980 when the *Evening Standard* and *Evening News* finally merged in the face of major decreases in demand for evening papers in the capital and huge losses by both papers.

On Sundays *The Observer* and *The Sunday Times* are published. These are both high quality national weekly newspapers. Their presence largely explains why national weekly news magazines in glossy format, such as America's *Time* or Germany's *Stern*, have had no success in Britain. In 1986 much of the editorial content in

Figure 5.1: Circulation of British daily national newspapers, 1980–85

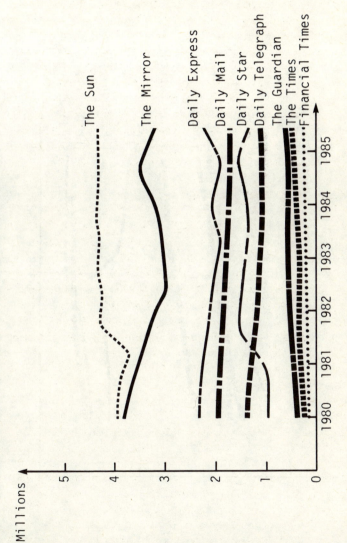

Sources: Audit Bureau of Circulation (ABC); Newspaper Publishers' Assoc. (NPA).

Figure 5.2: Circulation of British Sunday national newspapers, 1980–85

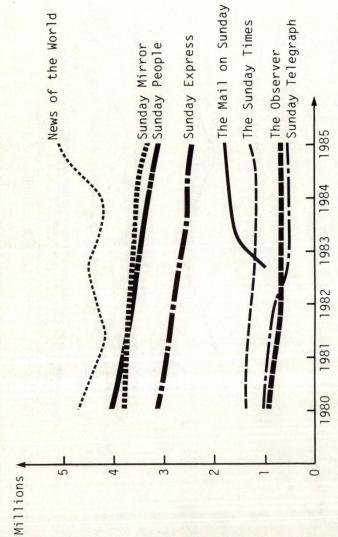

Sources: Audit Bureau of Circulation (ABC); Newspaper Publishers' Assoc. (NPA).

Table 5.2: UK national newspapers total sales, revenues and pre-tax profits

	1980	1981	1982	1983	1984
Total sales (£b)	1.05	0.93	1.05	1.17	1.30
Pre-tax profits (£m)	14	5	(30)[a]	11	24

Note: a. Loss.
Sources: Audit Bureau of Circulation (ABC); Newspaper Publishers' Assoc. (NPA).

both of these Sunday newspapers was less immediate, more analytical and more reflective than in the dailies. *The Sunday Telegraph* was a more downmarket, yet losing version, of *The Sunday Times* and *Observer*. Moving along the spectrum towards 'popularity' were the *Sunday Express* and the *Mail on Sunday* and then the *Sunday Mirror*, the *Sunday People* and the *News of the World*. Sunday newspapers have long been an institution in Britain enjoying large circulations and for years special legislation had allowed newsagents to open on Sundays just to sell newspapers. Comparing Table 5.1, demand on Sunday was very different to weekday demand with *The Sunday Times* and *The Observer* and *Sunday Express* having large circulations whilst the *Sunday Telegraph* did less well than its weekday sister. Popular tabloids sold well seven days a week.

Advertising demand

In 1984 total advertising expenditures in Britain amounted to £6 billion (American). Advertising demand for national newspapers as a proportion of total media advertising had been declining for over 20 years. In 1964 they had accounted for over 20 per cent of total media advertising revenues, in 1975 17 per cent and in 1985 13 per cent.

As Lord Thomson's and Rupert Murdoch's experience showed when they tried to expand circulation at *The Times*, advertisers are interested not in readers' politics but their incomes. High income, high spending, young professionals are the most attractive audience for many advertisers. Students, the unemployed, pensioners, blue-collar workers and welfare recipients are not as desirable to advertisers even though they buy newspapers in considerable numbers.

111

Table 5.3: Distribution of UK advertising revenue, 1964–84

	National newspapers	per cent of all advertising	television	per cent of all advertising
1964	£ 86m	20.8	£ 102m	24.6
1974	£161m	17.8	£ 203m	22.6
1984	£677m	16.7	£1245m	30.7

Source: Advertising Association data.

Their CDE demand for newspapers cannot be converted into high advertising rates.[11] Since they tend to buy left-wing newspapers, there is an economic bias against the survival of left-wing newspapers. The bias stems from the nature of advertising demand.[12]

Consumers usually buy newspapers out of habit. Once ingrained the same paper is bought repetitively unless something occurs to break that habit, for example a newspaper strike, a successful rival newspaper's promotion scheme, a change of format, or a lifestyle change for the individual consumer. This habit aspect of demand helps explain why Fleet Street owners have often been reluctant to engage in strikes, since a strike forces readers to sample competitor's offerings. Habit also explains why new newspapers have a considerable 'loyalty to the familiar' barrier to entry to over-come. Readers of *The Times* have proved exceedingly loyal to the 'Court Circular', the obituary column, *The Times* Crossword, the 'Letters to the Editor', and *The Times* editorials.[13] Even so, after a year-long 1978/9 strike, *The Times* failed to recover fully from the slow erosion of its fringe readers to the *Daily Telegraph*, the *Financial Post* and *The Guardian* until Murdoch moved it downmarket and introduced Portfolio bingo.

Advertising demand for provincial newspapers between 1974 and 1984 increased from £250 million to over £900 million. As a proportion of total advertising demand it fell from 30 per cent to 24 per cent, and even this figure is misleading since it includes local freesheets. Freesheets absorbed nearly £224 million or over 4 per cent of all advertising revenues in 1984. They had been insignificant in 1974. Daily provincial newspapers which attracted 20 per cent of total advertising revenues in 1974 received only 12 per cent in 1984. In 1984 freesheet publishers sent out 24 million copies per week, under nearly 600 titles whilst the number of daily and weekly provincial titles declined.[14] Though some freesheets were put out

Table 5.4: UK newspaper advertising revenues, 1984

		price per page
The Sun	£61.5m	£29,000
Daily Mirror	£71.0m	£25,000
Financial Times	£55.0m	£17,000[a]
The Times	£20.0m	£20,000
Guardian	£17.0m	£17,000

Note: a. To reach one half of one per cent of the population. 99 per
cent of readers are male.
Source: Advertising Association Data.

by local newspaper publishers, and so for them reflected only a transition from run-of-the-press to non-run-of-the-press publishing as they attempted to tailor their organisation to meet advertisers' demand, other freesheets, about half, were put out by upstart non-union firms using the latest technology.

Supply

The new technology's adoption in all countries has meant redundancy for printers whose unions are typically amongst the oldest in any country. As their skills became obsolete the print unions fought a rearguard action to maintain jobs and wages. Nowhere was union success greater than in Fleet Street where until 1986 the unions had prevented the implementation of the new technology, maintained astronomically high wages for members and continued outdated and inefficient manning practices. Their success had had far reaching ramifications for all aspects of the British newspaper industry over the previous two decades.

Labour relations on Fleet Street

Labour theory explains how a successful trade union is able to act as a monopoly, create a labour shortage and drive up the wage. Restrictive trade practices enable unions to increase the number hired at the monopoly wage. Closed shops enable the union to control who is hired. A perishable product strengthens the union since owners cannot stockpile the product in the case of a strike. In Fleet Street until 1986 all these phenomena were observable.

The average annual pay for a linotype operator in 1984 in Fleet Street was about £38,000.[15] This figure was a testimonial to the

113

power of the unions, since linotype skills had been obsolete for 15 years. Most of that pay was economic rent, perhaps £30,000, since without the union, linotype operators would have had to seek jobs as unskilled or semi-skilled workers who in 1984 averaged under £10,000 per year.

In addition Fleet Street linotype operators were deliberately inefficient because of a correction clause in their contract which acted as an incentive to make mistakes. Corrections were rewarded with pay bonuses. Fleet Street productivity was half that of North America or West Germany. So poor was the quality of editorial printing that many advertisers would not use Fleet Street printers. Instead they sent in advertisements already made up by non-Fleet Street printers. The Fleet Street linotype operators were still paid for the advertising work, even though they did not do it.[16]

Previous contracts had created other incentives to inefficiency. One of these was that if a strike was called by another union after a certain proportion of the shift has been worked then full payment was made. Consequently the small electrician's union, EETU, would often strike and lose their pay but would quietly be compensated by all the others who received full payment. Demarcation then prevented anybody except an electrician from switching the machines back on.[17]

Secondary action, at least until successfully challenged in 1984, had been used to strengthen Fleet Street's powerful unions further. In Britain independent distributors of newspapers distributed a wide range of other products. This made them open to intimidation from the print unions. When there was a London strike it was possible for those national papers with Manchester print capacity to print extra copies there. It was unlikely however that the London distributors, whose workers belonged to the Sogat '82 union, would risk handling the Manchester copies out of fear they would be blacked by other unions friendly to the Fleet Street unions.

The National Graphic Association (NGA) in 1985 was one of Britain's most unconventional unions exerting a formidable influence over newspaper industry structure, conduct and performance, particularly on Fleet Street.[18] NGA roots can be traced back to Tudor times. The key units in the NGA are the local branches better known as the chapels. Until 1986 the chapels' power and independence from both their own national body and from newspaper managers rested on a number of factors. Their independence from the national headquarters was largely the result of history. In the 1840s when the first skilled workers' unions were

Table 5.5: Copies of newspapers lost through Fleet Street disruptions in 1985 (in millions)

The News of World	0.3 million copies
The Sunday Times	3.8
Sunday People	7.9
Sunday Mirror	6.3
The Times	0.4
Daily Star	0.7
Financial Times	1.3
The Guardian	5.7
The Daily Telegraph	4.1
Daily Mail	5.4
Daily Express	1.3
The Sun	23.2
Daily Mirror	35.3

Source: The Sunday Times, 19 January 1986.

established, power rested in the local chapels, and the Fleet Street chapels successfully repudiated later attempts by the NGA to extend its control over them. Chapels managed, over the years, to play off one Fleet Street management against another and so erect a body of restrictive practices. These seriously hindered technological advance in Fleet Street.

The NGA's stranglehold was based on the fact that it had a monopoly supply of labour to most composing rooms and many print machine rooms at the 15 Fleet Street national newspapers.[19] To each paper labour was sold for a lump sum. It was the chapel (or union branch) which decided which workers, how many of them, and for whom and for how long there would be work. By playing off one management against another over the years, by exploiting the fact that there were rigid deadlines to be met, the chapels were gradually able to undermine traditional management control of its labour supply and so, 'management's right to manage'.

This development was very costly to the newspapers. Not only was NGA labour expensive but it was also inefficient. Outside Fleet Street in the regional press, cold print had been introduced. But in Fleet Street the domain of the chapels, the old 'hot metal' obsolete technology was still used in 1985. The chapels therefore had retained a vital productive function by successfully resisting the new technology. This made it impossible for the journalists and advertising clerks to put copy straight into the central computer. (See Figure 1.1)

Since chapel power covered all Fleet Street newspapers it was

115

better for the chapel to let a particular newspaper fail rather than allow the paper to use fewer NGA members — even if technology made it possible and economic survival made it necessary. The reason was that members were loyal to the chapel not the newspaper title. If one newspaper failed the chapel could make sure that those members made redundant got the first opportunity at other Fleet Street jobs. Because the NGA controlled entry to the union, and had restricted entry, it was easy to find new jobs for those made redundant if a title should close. Retirement and natural wastage on other titles made this possible. Conversely, should the chapel help a failing newspaper survive by allowing it to use labour more efficiently and also introduce new technology then non-failing newspaper management would press for similar concessions. As a result total chapel employment might be reduced more by helping a failing newspaper survive than by letting it fail.

In the past commentators had observed that if management would unite to form a monopoly in the purchase of chapel labour then the chapels could be weakened. But the temptation for each management to act as a free rider was strong in Fleet Street and offered considerable short-run benefits.[20]

The first advantage as regards the chapels in negotiations was to be found in the nature of production. Unlike steel or toothpaste producers, newspapers cannot keep inventories of newspapers, though some editorial and advertising can be stored. It is a new product each day. It perishes quickly. There are publishing deadlines. If these are not met the whole day's production is lost. The advantage in labour disputes therefore lay with the union for there was always pressure on management to meet its deadline and therefore make concessions. The cumulative effects over the years of these concessions were considerable. Second, the nature of newspaper competition is such that readers and advertisers of a newspaper caught up in a dispute similarly have no inventories to run down. Readers and advertisers quickly switch to competitor newspapers, sometimes for good as *The Times* found after its prolonged 1978/9 strike. Third, having gained a concession at one newspaper the union has little difficulty in gaining similar concessions from the other newspapers. This fact puts enormous pressure on the first newspaper to concede. A long struggle can be expensive. A concession is unlikely to create any comparative cost disadvantage as other newspapers will likely follow suit very quickly. Only through an owners' united front could the newspaper effectively confront the union. For 70 years Fleet Street management were unable to unite successfully.

Many newspaper managements tried individually to retain some labour control and regain the right to manage. When Rupert Murdoch first arrived at Fleet Street in 1969 at *The Sun* he tried but failed. During the 1970s attempts were made at the *Daily Express, The Observer, Financial Times* and most noticeably from 1978 to 1979 at *The Times* by Lord Thomson. But in all cases the other newspapers' managements failed to support these attempts. Short-run advantage from continued production, enhanced by spill-over gains of reader and advertisers from the closed-down rival, seemed to outweigh long-run considerations in every case. The cumulative effect over the years of the failure to meet monopoly were disastrous. First, Fleet Street losses in 1982 were £30 million per year. Total profits from 1980 to 1985 were just £20 million. Second, higher costs were passed on to both advertisers and readers. Advertisers' rates and newspaper prices rose, circulation of the popular newspapers fell from the 1950s, and fewer households took two newspapers. Higher costs drove some advertising to other media. Quality suffered.[21] Economic pressures, exacerbated by the labour situation, led to circulation wars and the rise of such selling gimmickry as bingo, daily nudes, violence and a general decline in editorial standards to levels below those outlined by the Press Council. For example in 1984 the highly regarded *The Guardian* disclosed information known to have been stolen from a public servant.

The quality of newspaper ownership has been affected too, possibly endangering the public trust implicit in the control and management of a newspaper. Rightly or wrongly, *The Times* and *The Sunday Times* are often viewed as public institutions.[22] Lord Thomson's sale in 1980 of these venerable papers was precipitated by the long labour dispute in 1978 and 1979 as much as by the losses incurred.[23]

The losses of *The Times* and *Sunday Times* made these quasi-public institutions unattractive as business propositions to most investors. There were few practical alternatives to accepting Rupert Murdoch's offer to acquire them. The sale raised two issues. First, his News International group already owned a Fleet Street newspaper (*The Sun*), so raising questions of monopoly and market power. Second, unlike the Thomsons, Murdoch had a reputation for becoming involved in editorial policy. Clearly on both competitive and political grounds there were reasonable objections to the sale and some basis for accusations that ownership quality was lowered.

As a result of the Thomson sale to Murdoch, though there were still 15 London-based national daily and Sunday newspapers they were controlled by eight conglomerates of which the three largest, News International, Mirror and Associated News, controlled over 75 per cent of daily circulation and 85 per cent of Sunday circulation.

A year after Thomson sold *The Times* and *The Sunday Times* the editor of *The Times* (and former editor of *The Sunday Times* for 14 years) was forced out. Highly respected journalist Harold Evans claimed interference at Britain's paper of record had begun soon after the sale to Murdoch. If labour troubles had instigated the sale, political interference had enabled Murdoch to buy it. By supporting Mrs Thatcher in the late 1970s in *The Sun* and *News of the World*, the Conservative government allowed the Thomson sale to go through without reference to the Monopoly Commission. Though Murdoch signed agreements guaranteeing editorial freedom, these did not prevent him from giving instructions to his editor as to general editorial content, to the detriment of the papers. There was a clear linkage from poor Fleet Street labour relations to Lord Thomson's decision to sell the newspapers, to the lack of prospective buyers, to the Murdoch purchase and to the decline in product quality that resulted. It was the outcome of political interference and favouritism. It resulted from Murdoch owning *The Sun* and using it aggressively to support Mrs Thatcher in 1979.[24]

Regional labour relations

In the national press an effective monopoly labour supplier faced rival owners which it successfully played off one against the other until 1986. In the regional press a monopoly-monopsony situation usually existed.[25] Regional newspaper owners were more successful in the 1970s and 1980s in gaining acceptance of the new technology, so, lowering their costs to be competitive with the other media for circulation and advertisements. Even so, by contrast to North American and Japanese newspapers, British regional newspapers still used outdated methods and were hampered by restrictive trade practices in the mid-1980s.

In 1984 the Nottingham *Evening Post* was the only newspaper 'where the mighty print unions appeared to have been fully tamed'.[26] There, as in most North American newspapers, journalists used VDTs to write, edit and file stories to the computer to await printing. Despite more pages, 28 composers in Nottingham did the work that 214 had done in 1967. Redundant production workers had been found other jobs at the *Evening Post* and after a long battle both the NGA and the National Union of Journalists (NUJ) had been forced out. The *Evening Post* in 1983 earned £1.35 million in profits. With its 1967 workforce it would have lost over £200,000.

At most other provincial newspapers the battles continued with the NGA into the mid-1980s. To the NGA, direct entry by computer was anathema since it would make at least one-third of its 11,000 members redundant. The provincial press owners, represented by the Newspaper Society, claimed, rightly, that the lowered costs of direct entry were necessary to make the provincial press competitive with other newer methods of advertising in Britain.

A key labour decision for the whole British newspaper industry in the 1980s followed the passing of the Employment Acts of 1980 and 1982. These labour reform acts banned secondary picketing and closed shops. Only those actually involved in a dispute could picket. The new legislation and new balance of power was tested in the historic Messenger affair which began in 1980 at the Stockport Messenger Print Works. There Eddie Shah produced freesheets.

The background to the Messenger affair was that at the Warrington works where the *Stockport Messenger* was printed, Shah had accepted a post-entry closed shop agreement with the NGA.[27] At his other, as yet non-unionist Bury works, he hired some non-union labour. The NGA called out the *Stockport Messenger* printers. Shah fired the NGA workers for breach of contract. The affair simmered. Five months later NGA pickets who were not directly involved in the dispute arrived at the unionist Warrington works. Under the new legislation Shah sought and obtained an injunction. NGA picketing continued. Fines were levied and ignored. The NGA was fined for contempt as well, in all £150,000, and the affair became 'news'.[28]

On Fleet Street there was a supposedly spontaneous sympathetic walk-out. All national newspaper production was lost for two days. Violent picketing took place at Warrington, Shah lost his previous willingness to compromise. The Newspaper Proprietors' Association's opportunity to take on the unions in Fleet Street collapsed when individual owners failed to unite and made agreements to get production going again. Undeterred Shah went to court. A long-time British resident educated at Prince Charles' former school, Gordonstoun, NGA propaganda exploited his Iranian background. Outraged, Shah eventually won a prolonged law suit and the NGA was fined over half a million pounds, a huge amount by British standards.[29]

The importance of the decision for the industry was inestimable.

First, it showed the new labour reform legislation worked. Second, it motivated Shah to launch *Today*, a new national daily, in 1986 free of the restrictive trade practices of Fleet Street. His lower costs pressured the other producers to abandon Fleet Street.

In 1986 the consequences of the Conservative government's laws against secondary action therefore were a transformation of the UK newspaper industry. At the time it was anticipated that the traditional unions would sign agreements similar to that signed by Shah with the electricians' union (EETPU). Instead, at Wapping where Murdoch had built a new print workers and equipped it in great secrecy behind barbed wire fortifications, 500 non-union workers including some EETPU members produced all four News International papers. To avoid blacking by the Sogat '82, the union which traditionally handled distribution, News International contracted out distribution to a courier service (TNT). He also set up separate companies for each stage of production to exploit the new labour restrictions on secondary picketing. Murdoch demonstrated his determination to match Shah's lower costs. He closed his Fleet Street operations, where he had fired 5,000 printers earlier for refusing to sign a legally binding no-strike agreement. By proving that he could produce and distribute his papers without the traditional unions, Murdoch paved the way for *The Guardian, Financial Times* and *The Daily Telegraph* at their new plants. As the traditional unions declared themselves ready to allow large redundancies and new working practices it was clear an era had ended.[30]

Other inputs

Britain produces some newsprint but there are no restrictions on imports. Most journalists receive on-the-job training. There are no journalism schools comparable to those of North America. The major journalists' union is the National Union of Journalists (NUJ). Capital is available from the banks and conglomerate owners and most presses and systems are imported, chiefly from Germany and the United States. Without doubt, the most unusual aspect of the British newspaper supply side has been its labour relations structure.

STRUCTURE

Conglomerate ownership

The British newspaper industry is dominated by conglomerates. To spread risk newspaper firms in Britain have acquired other interests, whilst conglomerates wishing to acquire prestige and influence have purchased Fleet Street newspapers. Amongst recent owners Thomson International and News International are foreign conglomerates which began as newspaper companies. The Canadian conglomerate Argus, which bought *The Daily Telegraph* in 1985, has interests in Canadian newspapers. Amongst the British-based owners, Reed International has its roots in paint, paper and manufacturing. Fleet which was spun off from Trafalgar House had its beginnings in hotels. Lonrho had its origins in resources. Robert Maxwell's empire BPCC was based on printing, packaging and publishing. The *Financial Times* is owned by the Pearson Longman PLC group with many interests including Penguin books, *The Economist*, Lazards Bank, Fairey aerospace and Doulton china. The owners of the *Daily Mail*, Associated News, have expanded from newspapers into other profitable interests including magazines and the regional press. United Newspapers PLC and the Illiffe family holdings until 1985 were the principal regional newspaper chains. In 1985 United bid successfully for Fleet. In London in 1986 only *The Guardian* was owned by a trust which had relied, until 1983 when it finally became profitable, on a subsidy from the Manchester *Evening News*.

Ownership and public policy

In Britain, concentration of the national press has attracted considerable comment, although even more concern has centred on the character of the personalities of the owners involved. This reflects a number of factors but most importantly Britain's attitude towards monopoly. In Britain monopoly *per se*, unlike in the United States, at least until Reagan, has not been regarded necessarily as evil and against the public interest. At the same time, foreigners and *nouveaux riches* are suspect so that Thomson, Maxwell, Murdoch, Anderson, Rowland and even Conrad Black, whose ancestors founded *The Daily Telegraph* which he acquired in 1985, all generated suspicion.[31] Editorials on the sale of *The Times* in 1980, *The Observer* in 1982, *The Mirror* in 1984 and *The Daily Telegraph* in 1985 reflected the attitude that foreigners might not fulfil the public trust.[32] In all these cases, one conglomerate sold to another conglomerate, so that industry concentration was not significantly affected, but there was considerable concern over the motivations and ambitions of the purchasers.

Although there is special newspaper competitions legislation it has had minimal effect on structure. Referrals have been made to the Monopolies Commission, reports have been issued by the Commission, and Royal Commissions have been established, but the overall impact has been limited.[33] One major weakness of the legislation has been its discretionary nature. Following changes made in 1973, the government *may* refer proposed mergers to the Monopolies Commission. The Commission then makes a non-binding report. The sale of the failing Mirror Group to the newsprint, paper and property conglomerate Reed International in 1970 was not referred. The newly-elected Thatcher government declined to use its powers of reference in 1980 when Rupert Murdoch bid for *The Times* and *The Sunday Times*, since News International's paper *The Sun* had been highly supportive of Thatcher in the election of 1979.[34] It is likely the Monopolies Commission, given its mandate, would have had to report against the take-over which gave Murdoch 37 per cent of the national daily newspaper market and 41 per cent of the Sunday market.

The Observer had not supported Mrs Thatcher in 1979. When the oil conglomerate ARCO sold the paper to Lonrho in 1982 the sale was referred to the Monopolies Commission. Lonrho's extensive African interests, the Commission reported, might conflict with 'the accurate presentation of news and free expression of opinion' (1973 Fair Trade Act) and not be in the public interest (1965 Monopolies Act). Despite the reservations of the Monopolies Commission, Lonrho's Tiny Rowland, himself a Thatcher supporter, was permitted to take over the paper. Five independent directors were appointed to oversee editorial independence.

The sale in 1984 of the Mirror newspaper by Reed International to the publisher Robert Maxwell, a staunch Labour Party supporter, was referred and approved. So was the 1985 sale of Fleet's Trafalgar House newspapers to United Newspapers in 1985 and the sale of the Telegraph newspapers in 1986 to Conrad Black.

Barriers to entry and exit

Entering any mature or declining industry necessitates taking market share from somebody else. The easiest way to enter the national newspaper industry in recent years has been to purchase existing newspapers. New newspapers have, however, been launched into the London market. (See Table 5.1).[35]

New newspapers inevitably lose money until they have established a circulation base which can be sold to advertisers. Some, like *The Sunday Telegraph*, never break even requiring constant subsidy. Prolonged subsidies can be crippling for small chains and losses from *The Sunday Telegraph* contributed to the sale of its parent in 1985. In 1986 *Today* required a financial bail-out from Lonrho.

There are also significant barriers to exit from Fleet Street. In 1980 Thomson sold *The Times* and *The Sunday Times* in 1980 for just £12 million, less than the value of the real estate property and other interests, such as a share in Reuters which went with the paper. Reed International sold its printing group Odham, former owners of the *Daily Herald* to Robert Maxwell in 1983 for just £1.5 million. *The Observer* was sold to Lonrho's Mr Rowland for £13 million and in 1985 Rowland was reportedly willing to sell for £7 million. In all cases the redundancy payments which would have had to be made by the owners if operations had been ceased were formidable. A sale, even at less than the market value of the assets involved, was a preferable option. In addition, the quality papers hold a position in Britain of quasi-public institutions. Closing one could raise a public outcry. The qualities have been called 'honorary members of the public sector' enjoying 'commercial immortality'.[36] The likelihood of public opprobrium and loss of goodwill for other conglomerate activities, create an incentive to try to avoid closure, particularly if they are conglomerates with other interests dependent on the state or requiring a good public image.

New entrants

In 1985 Eddie Shah announced plans to launch a new national daily *Today* in 1986. His calculations showed that in Britain a non-union paper produced with the latest electronic technology would have a break-even circulation of just 300,000 and be totally self-supporting from circulation revenues at a sale of 1,500,000. Lower capital costs and labour costs were the basis of the calculations. Shah argued that the new technology and his own defeat of the unions in 1984 had significantly lowered Fleet Street entry barriers.

Shah's *Today* calculations had to be taken seriously as a reasonable estimate of attainable newspaper industry costs in the UK in the mid-1980s. He had no difficulty persuading the City to finance him, a good indicator of realism. The State Bank of Hungary's London branch put up £8 million towards new printing presses and the venture's start-up costs were estimated at £22 million per year.[37] By comparison labour costs alone at the Mirror Group in 1984 were £120 million. In 1986 Shah's staff of 500 produced seven days a week. There were 160 journalists, 140 printers and 40 advertising staff to generate a 40-page tabloid similar to *USA Today* with considerable use of colour and graphics. Editorial staff working in London produced and typeset the paper there, then sent it electronically to five press centres around the country. Situated beside the motorways franchised vans distributed the papers freeing them from the problems of Sogat '82 and using British Rail.

Shah's initial success in financing his brainchild encouraged imitators. In 1986 there were half a dozen plans of different sorts, in different stages, for new national newspapers. Reed International which had owned the *Daily Mirror* until 1984 and owned a share of Britain's first daily freesheet, Birmingham's *Daily News*, had a London daily freesheet under consideration. Robert Maxwell who had bought the *Daily Mirror* from Reed International had a new evening paper or 24-hour daily colour tabloid planned. Murdoch anticipated launching a new evening paper, the *London Post*, downmarket from *The Standard*. The man who tried to save the *Daily Mirror* from Maxwell in 1984, Clive Thornton, in collaboration with the unions intended to launch a new Sunday newspaper. A former city editor for *The Daily Telegraph*, Whittam Smith, made arrangements to produce a new quality daily paper, *The Independent*, which began publication late in 1986. His firm, Newspaper Publishing, had the support of a group of Fleet Street journalists and city merchant bankers.[38]

In all cases planned investments and staffs were small when compared to the over £100 million of modernisation which brought down Lord Hartwell of the Berry family and their *The Daily Telegraph*. Smith planned to spend £5 million on a computerised office but to contract out printing and distribution, and another £5 million on advertising to launch the paper. The new nationals planned to use much smaller staff than the traditional newspapers. Whilst the *Daily Mirror* employed 6,000 staff, Shah planned to use 500 including 120 journalists at *Today*. Thornton planned to use half that number at *News on Sunday*.[39]

During 1985 Murdoch added a further £10 million to the £100 million already invested in the News International print works at Wapping in the old docklands. Begun in 1978 union opposition had prevented a move of his titles from Fleet Street to the new plant earlier. Spurred by the prospect of new low cost entrants the move became imperative. Planned in great secrecy using a dummy company, a Kodak Atex system was installed early in 1985. Similar to the system used at his *Boston Globe*, the system represented virtually the most up-to-date available technology.[40]

Horizontal and vertical integration

There was limited vertical integration in 1986 in the British press, either backward or forward. Reed International, owner of the *Daily Mirror* from 1970 to 1984 is a major print and publishing company supplying paper, ink and printing services. Since these inputs are available from other suppliers, both domestic and overseas, and as there is no protection for these commodities, Reed International had no competitive advantage. Likewise, there was no backward vertical integration into advertising. British newspaper distribution was mostly handled by independent wholesalers and newsagents although United Newspapers PLC owned some 100 retail outlets.

There was horizontal integration. Maxwell's Pergamon Press bought the BPCC (British Printing and Communications Corporation) group in 1981. Within two years he had turned BPCC around, got union co-operation, introduced new technology and made a number of acquisitions and divestitures. Printing accounted for 70 per cent of BPCC's profits, which prints most of Britain's popular women's weeklies. Another major colour producer, Eric Benrose, is owned by Rupert Murdoch. As tabloids moved to colour and magazines so the complementary of Maxwell's and Murdoch's printing and newspaper activities increased.

Newspaper Publishers' Association

The Newspaper Publishers' Association (NPA) was, until 1985, the eleven-member employers' association in Fleet Street. It was an ineffective body, not surprisingly given the rivalry of its members. It had failed miserably over the years in co-ordinating efforts to combat union excesses and to create a strategy to make Fleet Street profitable. In 1985 Maxwell and Murdoch resigned whilst new-comers United Newspapers and Shah did not join.[41]

Structure and the stock market

The influence of the stock market, the treadmill effect, on newspaper structure and conduct was illustrated in Britain by the sale of the Mirror Group of papers in 1984.[42] The parent, Reed International, which had bought the paper in 1981 as part of its paper and packaging conglomerate, sold the paper to Robert Maxwell.

The opportunity to sell the papers resulted in part from the 1983 Reuter News Agency's decision to go public. By keeping their Reuters shares in the company, Reed planned to spin off the Mirror Group as a separate offering on the stock exchange. Prior to this the losses, the redundancy liabilities and trade unions' influence had made a public offering impossible. During 1983 and 1984 efforts were made to make the paper attractive for flotation. Plans for a new printing plant in Manchester and the use of web-offset were made. A no-disruptions agreement with the unions was negotiated, and details of the new company's articles of association were drawn up. These would have restricted any shareholder from holding over 15 per cent of the company and encouraged worker participation. Reed anticipated receiving about £50 million from the sale of the new company.[43]

Then, Robert Maxwell who had a long history of seeking a Fleet Street proprietorship entered negotiations. At different times he had been a contender for the *News of the World* (1969), *The Observer* (1983) and *The Times* (1980). Robert Maxwell clearly and rationally valued the company higher than would a large number of small anonymous investors. The influence, prestige, challenge, tax write-offs and possible benefits for his other printing interests were benefits unavailable to a fragmented ownership. Maxwell's offer of £113.4 million for the Mirror Group therefore created a dilemma for Reed between profits and public trust. Obligations to Reed shareholders required that they sell to the highest bidder, in other words to Maxwell whose bid was possibly worth £50 million more than a stock market offering would generate.

New investment

In 1985 most of the Fleet Street newspapers had plans to invest in new facilities and in huge redundancy payments. In effect redundancy payments were the purchase of work-rents from the unions. Newspapers planned on buying back the capitalised value of concessions made by the owners and the government to the unions over the previous decades. If successful, British newspapers would move from technical obsolescence and losses to modernisation and profits. Redundancy payments at *The Daily Telegraph* were £38 million to eliminate 800 jobs or £45,000 per job. Fleet Holdings PLC needed to eliminate four times as many jobs. The total Fleet Street redundancy bill was estimated to approach £400 million. That was as much as the newspaper owners planned to spend on new printing facilities in London's former docklands and Manchester.

Since from 1980 to 1984 Fleet Street profits averaged only £5 million annually, raising the capital for the new investments had to come from elsewhere than retained profits. Robert Maxwell's plans for the Mirror Group were announced in 1985.[44] Maxwell arranged for a group of banks to lease 20 new presses to print newspapers from the MAN Roland Group in West Germany at a cost of over £60 million. These would go to his printing works in the former London docklands. An additional £25 million was set aside for redundancy payments. Asset stripping was familiar work to Maxwell and in 1985 a 49 per cent share of the Mirror Group's Scottish newspapers, the *Daily Record* and *Sunday Mail* were offered to the public raising over £20 million.[45]

Whilst the conglomerates could use either profits from their other operations or borrow using their other operations as collateral, *The Guardian*, and *The Daily Telegraph*, had no such option. In 1985 the Daily Telegraph Group offered redundancy payments of £38 million in order to reduce staff by 800 to 1,200. A similar amount was required to finance two new printing plants in London and Manchester. Both the *Telegraph* and *The Sunday Telegraph* had been losing market share and money and survival depended on modernisation. To raise £30 million the Berry family which had controlled the paper since 1927, placed 40 per cent of the family-owned company with private investors. The major investor was Conrad Black, a Canadian millionaire who contributed £10 million. In fact a great-great-great-grandson of one of *The Daily Telegraph*'s founders, Black had received an agreement of first option of control should the Berry family decide to give up the paper.[46] Late in

127

1985, as the Berry's financial difficulties increased Black exercised his option claiming he was not another 'chump in the Commonwealth willing to pay for the privilege of losing money on a London paper'.[47] Simple arithmetic showed that saving 800 jobs at £25,000 per year at the Telegraph Group would convert a 1984 £900,000 loss into a £19 million profit, less the additional debt charges of about £4 million to finance the modernisation. With Eddie Shah, Robert Maxwell, Rupert Murdoch and the EEPTU poised to break the old unions, Black appeared to have bought a bargain.

CONDUCT

The 1976 British Royal Commission commented 'freedom and variety in the expression of opinion and presentation of views is an element which does not enter into the conduct of the competitor industries and that is of paramount public interest'.[48] Whilst there is limited newspaper competition for readers in the regional press, competition, rivalry, even hatred and contempt, as well as variety, are hallmarks of Fleet Street. Firms' conduct in Fleet Street reflects this competition to include product differentiation, price competition, product quality, service, promotional games, advertising, services to advertisers, research subsidies and format. In 1986 no other developed country enjoyed the variety of Britain's dailies.

Product differentiation on Fleet Street

Sensationalism

In terms of circulation, sensational tabloids dominate the British press and have done so since the 1930s. Once dominant, the *Daily Mirror* with a circulation of five million in the 1950s was undercut in the 1970s by Rupert Murdoch and his *Sun*. The *Daily Mirror* quickly retaliated by offering similar sex and sensational content. In 1978 Trafalgar House which had bought out the Beaverbrook Express chain in 1977 launched a new newspaper from Manchester called the *Daily Star*. Applying the same sort of formula, circulation of the newcomer grew in six years to over 1.5 million largely at the expense of the other two.[49] Above them the British reader had the choice of two middle-brow and four quality dailies in 1986, and the prospect of yet more choice to come.

Format

Another tactic is a change of format. In the 1970s the *Daily Mail* converted to tabloid format and the *Daily Express* soon followed, so making the papers more convenient for commuters and possibly less formidable to readers familiar with the *Mirror* and *Sun*. Adding colour and graphics increases costs but again is unlikely to lead to destructive retaliation from rivals. They may increase advertising revenues but in 1986 advertisers had not responded strongly to colour advertisements in newspapers preferring the better quality of colour in magazines.

Magazines

In 1980 only three papers enclosed a colour magazine. They were the 'qualities', the *The Sunday Times*, *The Sunday Telegraph* and *The Observer*. By 1982, the *Sunday Express*, *News of the World* and the *Mail on Sunday*, launched in 1982, carried magazines.

In 1980, the three colour supplements received £50 million worth of advertising. The new down-market entries quickly caused an eleven per cent decline in their market terms of advertising lines carried despite the qualities offering discounts. In 1984 the total revenues of all the supplements exceeded £100 million.[50] The new magazines had also attracted additional advertising.

Sunday magazines in Britain have been expensive to launch. The cost for the first year of the *Mail on Sunday*'s magazine was reported to be £8.5 million, that of the *News of the World*, £7 million. However, they helped stop circulation declines temporarily at both the *Sunday Express* and *News of the World*. Circulation at the non-supplement Sunday populars fell. A six per cent fall at the *Sunday Mirror* cost approximately £9 million in lost revenues and an eleven per cent fall at the *Sunday People* cost £17 million over the first six months of 1982.[51]

In 1983 those popular Sundays with magazine supplements, except the *Mail on Sunday*, lost market share whilst the *Sunday Mirror* and *People* recouped some of their losses. Magazine supplements had had only a temporary effect on market share. They were expensive to both those who did and did not start supplements.

The *Mail on Sunday* with its lavish colour supplement, comics and heavy advertising promotions certainly drew readers from all the Sunday papers. It was also successful in attracting new readers to Sunday reading. In 1983 its circulation grew from under 1 million to over 1.5 million. The *Mail on Sunday*'s great success was in large part attributed to the lush quality of the colour supplement. Of its

1.5 million circulation approximately half came from the other Sundays.

Changing focus: The Times revival

The Times of London is a remarkable product. In 1986 its circulation was about four per cent of that of *Yomiuri Shimbun*, Japan's leading newspaper. Despite this, its international status and influence was formidable. In 1985 at a dinner in Washington to honour the 200th anniversary of US-British diplomatic relations, Prime Minister Thatcher addressed President Reagan: '. . . 1985 marks the 200th anniversary of a favourite British institution, *The Times* newspaper.'[52] Few other commercial products would be so honoured.

Meanwhile *The Times'* current owner, to whom Mrs Thatcher was indebted for election support in 1979, was planning to become an American citizen. This section examines his product strategy to nearly double circulation from 1980 to 1985 and to cut losses.

Former editor Harold Evans said Murdoch regarded 'news and entertainment as the same thing'.[53] At *The Times* he modified the formula used at the *Sun* and *New York Post* but it was a similar strategy. He moved down-market, swung to the political right and added more pictures. He held down prices when its rival *The Guardian* raised them. He introduced 'portfolio', a form of bingo. He followed his own adage that Third World news does not sell newspapers and reduced international coverage. The proportion of soft news increased. The first editor under Murdoch, Harold Evans, resigned after 13 months, reputedly for £450,000, over the issue of editorial independence, and Murdoch's support for the Conservative prime minister. Murdoch replaced him and continued the popularising trend under an editor, Charles Douglas-Hume, an establishment man and nephew of former Prime Minister Sir Alex Douglas-Hume. When he died another like-thinking editor Michael Wilson was appointed.

The move down-market by *The Times* alarmed some people who felt the paper had abrogated its leadership role and now pandered to popular taste. Yet as a leader for 'Top People' *The Times* did not have a flawless history. One pre-war editor said: 'I try to see that nothing appears which might give offence to Herr Hitler';[54] another deputy editor demanded that Stalin was treated with 'proper reverant discretion'.[55] *The Times* employed the spy and art critic Anthony Blunt. Much of its content before Murdoch was more appropriate to a magazine. Popularising the paper did not necessarily mean a loss of quality particularly if it made it commercially viable and prevented failure or government subsidy. Murdoch may have saved *The Times* from the afflictions of *Le Monde* in 1985 by making it less pompous and more colourful.

Content and rivalry

There is intense rivalry in Fleet Street. When Thomson opposed the unions for eleven months from 1978 to 1979 other newspapers exercised little restraint in going for his market. *The Observer* began publishing part of the paper on Wednesdays so that it could carry more editorials and advertising.[56]

Sensational stories sell newspapers. In Britain the *Daily Mail* earned an unenviable reputation with revealing, but unchecked, stories about bribes by British Leyland which later proved groundless. In 1983 *The Sunday Times* published the false Hitler diaries which it had bought from *Stern* in Germany. Censoring and excluding content, however, is arguably of greater public concern than poor quality content. Whilst success in suppressing news requires that the suppression is not discovered, ownership intervention to suppress news has occurred for economic motives and been uncovered.

A case of suppression at *The Observer* in 1984 reflected this less admirable aspect of newspaper conduct. Lonrho in 1984 was a London-based conglomerate with extensive multi-million dollar interests in Zimbabwe, formerly the British colony of Rhodesia. Lonrho's Zimbabwe interests included such illiquid investments as coffee and timber plantations, ranches, mines and textile plants. Clearly Lonrho had to make great efforts not to upset any current government. When Zimbabwe moved to independence and black majority rule in 1980 Lonrho had supported the winning faction of Joshua NKomo. When NKomo's hated rival Robert Mugabe replaced NKomo, Lonrho quickly cultivated Mugabe, whilst quietly paying NKomo's hotel bills in London. Like the support of NKomo in exile, Lonrho's 1981 purchase of *The Observer*, a paper renowned for its Africa coverage, made sense at the time as a form of insurance.[57]

Tribal warfare took the form of a government campaign. Reports of atrocities in 1983 in NKomo's tribal stronghold of Matabeleland included torture, rape, systematic starvation and mass murder. These were as well covered as possible by *The Observer*.[58] Though

UNESCO has frequently complained of poor Third World coverage by the Western press, Mugabe ordered his Information Ministry 'not to continue to overstretch itself in wanting coverage in overseas papers', but did not deny the charges of rape, torture and mass murder.[59] *The Observer*'s editor, Donald Trelford, who himself had visited Zimbabwe, had clearly acted responsibly as a Western journalist in his comprehensive coverage. At the same time he had compromised Lonrho's considerable economic interests.

Rowland, Lonrho's chairman, wrote a letter to Mugabe. It was not unreasonable for him to 'unreservedly dissociate' himself and Lonrho from the article. He had however promised there would be editorial independence. His other comments on Trelford's conduct being 'discourteous, disingenuous, and wrong in the editor of a serious paper, widely read in Africa', and on the article 'containing unsubstantiated material' and being 'sensational' were therefore not reasonable. These were critical issues of human rights not to be dismissed, as Mugabe tried to do, as 'mischief making'.[60]

In London, the five independent directors vindicated Trelford and condemned Rowland for interfering with editorial freedom. Rowland had complained to them that Trelford and his journalists had failed to 'do their utmost to protect the commercial viability of the paper'.[61] Rowland's frustrations with *The Observer* were understandable. For most conglomerate owners, losses at the newspapers could be offset by benefits, such as television licences and North Sea oil concessions. Even if owning a paper did not help, it rarely harmed. They were good insurance in most instances. However, *The Observer* had jeopardised Lonrho's African interests as well as losing some £2 million per year. His editorial influence had been intended for economic gain.

The events would not have occurred if (i) labour legislation and owner concessions over the years had not made Fleet Street newspapers unattractive investments for most investors; (ii) government had applied its own mergers legislation and had not allowed unsuitable owners with potential conflicts of interest to take over newspapers. Therefore, having created an unprofitable environment in which only conglomerate owners who wanted to use the newspaper for influence and profit elsewhere would own them, the consequent conduct was predictable.

Pricing competition and subsidies

In Australia, Britain and America Murdoch had adopted aggressive price policies. In Britain he has held the price of *The Times* below that of *The Guardian* and forced *The Daily Telegraph* to hold its price. He has held the price of the *Sun* below that of the *Mirror*.

At *The Times*, where his main rivals, *The Guardian* and *The Daily Telegraph* in 1985 were owned by a trust and a small family company, the longer-term consequences were serious. *The Guardian* was barely profitable. *The Daily Telegraph* in 1985 lost about £15 million, required new outside financing, and was forced to sell. At the *Daily Mirror* Maxwell met the *Sun*'s price competition when he took over the *Daily Mirror* and appeared quite prepared to compete on any terms with rival Murdoch. As new national newspapers like *Today* and *The Independent* appeared in 1986, including the possibility of daily freesheets, price competition for both readers and advertisers entered a new age.

By 1985 there were 724 weekly and bi-weekly freesheets being produced and distributed in Britain. Weekly freesheets had taken over or replaced some 250 traditional paid-for weeklies. Lower costs to produce small volumes had made freesheets commercially viable, such as the Birmingham *Daily News*, part-owned by Reed International. Daily free newspapers require a larger advertising base than weekly freesheets but Glasgow, Manchester, Bristol, Leeds, Newcastle, Liverpool and Bradford could all probably support daily freesheets and are expected to have them by 1990.

Cross-subsidies for 20 years have been necessary to keep nearly all Fleet Street newspapers alive. Some cross-subsidies have been seen as unethical and as unfair trade practices. When Thomson advertised *The Scotsman* at low rates on his new Scottish television in unused spots in the late 1950s this was seen as unfair. In 1984 in the Lonrho interference affair at *The Observer* over Zimbabwe, Rowland threatened to withdraw extensive Volkswagen car advertising from the paper.[62] Rowland controlled the major firm importing Volkswagens to Britain. Again this was seen to be wrong. For a conglomerate to absorb losses was acceptable but to cross-subsidise advertising was not, although in no case has a court case resulted.

Regional conduct

The concentration of ownership of the regional press since 1945 had

Table 5.6: British regional newspapers with circulations (over 100,000)

Birmingham	Evening Mail[a] (1870)	282,000
	Daily News (1984) — FREE	301,000
Hull	The Daily Mail (1885)	110,000
Leeds	Evening Post[a] (1890)	153,000
	Yorkshire Post (1754)	87,000
Liverpool	Echo[a] (1879)	213,000
Manchester	Evening News[a] (1868)	320,000
Newcastle	Evening Chronicle[a] (1885)	149,000
Nottingham	Evening Post[a] (1878)	137,000
Portsmouth	The News[a] (1877)	99,000
Sheffield	The Star[a] (1887)	152,000
Wolverhampton	Express and Star[a] (1874)	336,000
Edinburgh	Evening News[a] (1873)	125,000
	The Scotsman (1817)	96,000
Glasgow	Daily Record[b] (1895)	759,000
	Evening Times[a] (1876)	182,000
	Herald (1782)	119,000
	Sunday Mail[a] (1982)	822,000
	Sunday Post (1920)	1,500,000

Notes: a. Evening.
     b. The *Daily Record* is a Scottish version of the *Mirror*.
Source: Editor and Publisher Year Book, 1986.

Table 5.7: British regional newspapers, number of titles and share of advertising revenues, 1974 and 1984

	1974		1984	
	Number of titles	Share of UK ad revenues %	Number of titles	Share of UK ad revenues %
Daily and Sunday	130	19	117	13
Weeklies	1154	11	949	5
Freesheets	—	—	580	6
	1284	30	1646	24

Notes: a. 1984 newspaper advertising revenues were £697m.
     b. From 1974 to 1984 freesheet advertising revenues rose from under £10m to nearly £200m.
Sources: Newspaper Society; Advertising Association.

been much criticised for the loss of local content, local reporting and local loyalties.

British regional newspapers show once again how a familiar vehicle abandons old and develops new functions. Display advertising has been eroded by television since 1960 but classifieds expanded as people had more consumer durables and services to sell and exchange. Local television and radio cover local stories and have made readers less reliant since 1970 for community news coverage on the regional press. At the same time, a more affluent, educated population wants to be informed about issues that affect them, particularly coming events, local sports, local government and local entertainment. In a global village where all are exposed to world events, local scandals and local news breakthroughs are apt to appear less than world shattering, and if they are, they are picked up by the national media. In other words, the regional newspaper has become a bulletin board and a transmitter of routine issues and events. The market for local news scoops in local newspapers had been much reduced by 1986. Monopoly regional newspapers in Britain provided a competent routine service which was profitable if mundane. Monopoly ownership had enabled the regional owners to move faster than Fleet Street towards improved technology, lower costs and greater efficiency.

In Britain Thomson's small newspaper formula has been less successful than in North America in the 1980s. First, as shown in Chapter 2, there is competition from the London dailies in geographically compact Britain for all of Thomson's 60 regional papers. Second, UK newspaper advertising demand plummeted as unemployment in Britain rose ten-fold to over three million over the decade from 1973. Newspaper advertising lines for employment at Thomson regional newspapers fell from 37 million to seven million. £20 million of annual revenues were lost. Finally, and critically, the 1980s saw the rise of freesheets. By 1985 there were over 700 freesheets. With lower editorial content and so editorial costs, and with the ability to use contract printing to avoid union restrictive practices and so reduce production costs, freesheets' advertising revenues share increased rapidly surpassing that of paid-for local newspapers in 1984. To prevent new entrants to its markets, Thomson established freesheets in all areas where it had paid for regionals in the 1980s.

Britain's geographic compactness could lead to regional consolidation with zoned editions of nationals or larger nationals in the future. The prospect of more free provincial dailies existed for the late 1980s, following the example of the free Birmingham *Daily News* launched in 1985.

Promotional bingo games

Newspapers are usually reluctant to engage in price competition since to suppliers it is an unprofitable negative sum game.[63] Consequently, they tend to compete in other safer dimensions involving product differentiation. Many promotional schemes have also proved to be negative sum games and unprofitable for newspapers.[64] In 1982 bingo games were begun by the tabloids and did little more than confuse the readers and advertising markets and increase costs.

Promotions add to costs at all newspapers and, unlike content improvements, add to neither circulation nor advertising revenues for the industry. From 1982 to 1984 circulation at each of the populars remained virtually unchanged. There was a stalemate. In 1984 the *Daily Mirror* spent £6 million to guarantee to make a *Mirror* millionaire.[65] It mailed a card with a number on it to every household in Britain, to the consternation of the postal system. If the number matched that in the *Mirror* the household won £1 million. The newspaper's front page became just a lottery advertisement. The costs of this circulation war certainly exceeded total industry profits from 1982 to 1984 and cost £50 million.[66]

One real problem was how to end bingo. For example, should the *Sun*, which started the war, decide to end bingo unilaterally and so lose just ten per cent of its four million sales for just three months, it would lose £5 million in circulation revenues alone. Bingo for newspapers is not only a negative sum but also a non-symmetric game, easy to start but difficult to end.[67]

At *The Times* the 'Portfolio', bingo games with other product changes had a dramatic effect on circulation. Part of *The Times'* success resulted from the fact that *The Guardian* and *The Daily Telegraph* refused to follow suit and play games.[68] As an exercise in game theory, the other qualities response created a winning strategy for Murdoch.

Press councils

Following the 1948 Royal Commission, a Press Council was established in 1953. The 1961 Royal Commission was highly critical of the Press Council for not reporting on the economic problems of the press. It was still much criticised in the 1980s.

In practice the Press Council has not met expectations. It was intended to be a non-governmental ombudsman and watchdog of the press. It would give 'prompt and impartial consideration to any complaints made by individuals, chapels and unions' about the press. For the press it would discourage the introduction of laws which might curb their activities. It would provide an expeditious, inexpensive and fair adjudication of complaints. Financed by the proprietors but independent of them, the Press Council would also be free of government intervention. As a watchdog the Press Council should have improved industry performance.

Its very presence may have done so, but its own performance has been criticised. In 1980 the National Union of Journalists (NUJ) withdrew from the Press Council. The NUJ claimed it was a creative agent of the proprietors and failed to meet its stated objectives to 'preserve the established freedom of the press and to keep under review developments likely to restrict the supply of information of public interest and importance'.[69]

Its procedures suffered from long delays, unnecessary obstacles, a lack of financial resources to investigate complaints and lack of authority over how the press reported its adjudications. It was too large with 36 members, in comparison the Swedish Press Council had five experts and could act much more quickly. As structured it was a less than satisfactory alternative to libel litigation. For the proprietors the small sums put up to fund the Press Council could be viewed as insurance money against greater government interventions. Underfunding, however, rendered it impotent.

PERFORMANCE

Fleet Street until 1986 still dominated the British press both economically and in terms of influence. Journalistically the best of Fleet Street was as good as any in the world. Economically it was a disaster. In terms of the allocation and efficient use of scarce resources, Fleet Street in 1985 was a disgrace. Monopoly labour and restrictive practices increased costs to levels which made most of the national dailies unprofitable. They survived on subsidies. Whilst subsidies to newspapers may well be desirable because of associated externalities (the cultural and social benefits), Fleet Street subsidies from large conglomerates had a number of drawbacks: (i) the conglomerates tended to tire of the losses from owning the papers and pass them along as Cadbury, Carr, Beaverbrook, Astor, Thomson, Reed, Berry, ARCO, and others have done; (ii) frequently changed ownership leads to instability and uncertainty for workers, readers and advertisers; (iii) owners underwriting huge losses may justifiably feel they have a right to interfere in editorial policy; (iv) the supply of acceptable tycoons could run out leading to low quality or to closure.

With a rationalised labour force in the national press losses will be reduced and eliminated in most cases. Viable newspapers should then attract a wide range of new potential owners and a more stable ownership. Failure by both owners and government to reform labour relations in Fleet Street posed a real threat to the structure and performance of the British national press. Events in early 1986 were to be welcomed.[70]

The employment benefits of using obsolete technology on Fleet Street were small. Restrictive trade practices appear to keep jobs for those who would otherwise become technologically unemployed. As with all cases of protection, those whose jobs are protected can be clearly identified and are highly vocal. Those who might benefit from job opportunities created should protection be eliminated cannot be identified, are usually unaware of their deprivation and therefore have no voice. The Newspaper Society represents the provincial press owners. It reported in 1984 that in the USA over the period 1968 to 1977, when most American newspapers switched to direct entry, industry employment actually increased from 345,000 to 393,000, though total production workers declined by 10,000 and membership in the ITU fell from 110,000 to 38,000. The Newspaper Society felt that, as in the USA, net job losses from modernisation and elimination of restrictive practices might even be negative. In other words, increased newspaper competitiveness, the improvement and expansion of auxiliary servicces, more marketing jobs and other new opportunities would tend to create more jobs.

NOTES

1. A. Sampson, *The Changing Anatomy of Britain* (Random House, New York, 1982), p. 299.

2. Susan Goldenberg, *The Thomson Empire* (Bantam Books, NY, 1984), p. 53.

3. M. Leapman, *Barefaced Cheek* (Hodder and Stoughton, London, 1983), p. 84.

4. *The Financial Post*, 31 August 1985.

5. *The Economist*, 23 June 1984.

6. *Encounter*, vol. LVIII (2) 1982, p. 56.

7. *Europa Year Book* (Europa Publications, London, 1985), p. 987.

8. *The Economist*, 22 February 1986.

9. *Encounter*, vol. LVIII (2) 1982, p. 56.

10. M. Leapman, *Barefaced Cheek*, p. 93.

11. A and B class readers represent professionals and upper management; CDE include semi-skilled and unskilled workers.

12. In the market advertisers want to reach readers with high incomes. The voting system for content therefore approximates one vote per dollar of income.

As a result, in Britain, since World War II, left-wing newspapers even with large circulations, have succumbed to the pressures of the advertising marketplace and a lack of wealthy left-wing sponsors willing and able to support them. In 1960 the *News Chronicle*, despite a large number of readers, closed. It had been owned by the Cadbury Trust and had echoed the left-wing liberal Quaker principles of the Cadburys. Purchased by the Associated News group it was merged into the right-of-centre *Daily Mail*. In 1961 a similar fate befell the left-wing *Daily Herald* when its owners, Odham, sold out to the Daily Mirror group. The Daily Mirror group at that time was left-of-centre and in direct competition to the *Herald*. They closed the paper, retitled it the *Sun*, attempted to move up-market to attract a non-partisan audience and more advertising, failed and in 1969 sold the paper to Rupert Murdoch. Murdoch had entered the British market in 1968 purchasing a major interest in the Sunday best seller, *News of the World*, so beating the take-over plan of the left-wing Labour-supporting entrepreneur Robert Maxwell.

In 1984 Maxwell finally entered the national newspaper market when he bought the Mirror Group for £100 million cash from Reed International. Reed International in turn had bought the Mirror Group in 1970. Reed International, a large diversified conglomerate had had little interest in left-wing politics, so that Maxwell's purchase revived an old connection between the *Mirror* and Labour and an old rivalry between Maxwell and Murdoch.

13. Readers, unlike with other products, often have a deep loyalty to one part of a paper, for example the Bridge Column or the Court Circular.

14. *The Sunday Times*, 21 July 1985.

15. *The Economist*, 25 January 1986.

16. *London Illustrated News*, 12 October 1984.

17. Ibid.

18. *The Economist*, 8 February 1986.

19. *Encounter*, vol. LVIII (2) 1982, p. 56.

20. In economic terms a free rider is a consumer who enjoys a benefit without contributing to the cost.

21. For example, the paper had to be put to bed earlier, meaning deadlines were earlier.

22. *Encounter*, vol. LVIII (2) 1982, p. 56.

23. Susan Goldenburg, *The Thomson Empire*, p. 61.

24. *World Press Report*, July 1984.

25. A monopoly-monopsony situation refers to a one buyer–one seller situation.

26. *The Economist*, 7 April 1984.

27. *Financial Times*, 3 December 1984.

28. Ibid.

29. Ibid.

30. *New Statesman*, 3 May 1985.

31. *Financial Post*, 1 July 1985.

32. *Encounter*, vol. LVIII (2) 1982, p. 56 and *The Economist*, 15 May 1985.

33. To circumvent the Monopolies Commission, *The Times* and *The Sunday Times* were treated as a single unit, and therefore a failing newspaper, so exempting the sale from the law's restrictions on concentration.

34. On 3 May 1979 Mrs Thatcher even replaced the page three daily nude in the *Sun*.

35. These included *The Sunday Telegraph* (1961), the *Sun* (1962), the *Daily Star* (1978), the *Mail on Sunday* (1982) and *Today* (1986). These still existed in 1986 although *The Sunday Telegraph* continued to require a cross-subsidy from its sister, *The Daily Telegraph*. Not all new entrants succeeded. In 1979 James Goldsmith attempted to launch a weekly newspaper, *Now!*, along the lines of *Time* magazine which would have competed with the Sunday papers. It closed in 1980. In 1982 the *Sunday Standard* in Scotland lasted one year.

36. *Illustrated London News*, 12 October 1984.

37. *The Economist*, 25 May 1985.

38. *The Economist*, 25 January 1986.

39. Ibid.

40. *Business Week*, 3 September 1984.

41. *New Statesman*, 2 December 1983.

42. See Chapter 2, pp. 33–4.

43. *News Statesman*, 2 December 1983.

44. Maxwell's Pergamon Holdings Foundation was registered in Liechtenstein and the ultimate ownership of the privately-owned group was unknown. Its 1980 performance, however, had been spectacular. From 1980 to 1984 Pergamon's pre-tax profits rose twelve-fold to £45 million and British Printing and Communications (BPCC) turned £11 million losses in 1980 to £38 million profits in 1984. Pre-tax profits for 1986 were expected to be over £65 million.

45. *The Sunday Times*, 2 July 1985.

46. *Financial Post*, 1 July 1985.

In the early 1980s Black owned Capital Radio in London as well as 20 newspapers in Canada.

47. *The Economist*, 15 May 1985.

48. Great Britain, Royal Commission on the Press, 1974–7, *Final Report* (HMSO, London, 1977), p. 304.

49. *The Economist*, 30 October 1982.

50. *The Spectator*, 5 May 1984.

51. Ibid.

52. *Time*, 11 March 1985.

53. *World Press Report*, July 1984.

54. *Encounter*, vol. LVIII (2) 1982, p. 56.

55. Ibid.

56. Incidentally, this revealed that much of the content of the Sunday

newspapers is not news in the sense of being quickly dated and that the Sunday newspapers in terms of function more closely approximate weekly magazines like *The Economist, Time* and *Der Speigel*.

57. *The Economist*, 25 June 1984.

58. *The Economist*, 21 April 1984.

59. Associated Press, 26 April 1984.

60. *The Economist*, 23 June 1984.

61. Ibid.

62. *The Economist*, 28 April 1984.

63. A negative sum game is one in which total losses exceed total gains although one player may end up ahead.

The reader demand for newspapers is inelastic so that lowering prices for *all* newspapers causes total revenues to fall.

64. In 1929 Julias Elias, later Lord Southcliffe, bought the *Daily Herald* and ushered in a circulation war. His ambition was to reach a circulation of two million. At a reported cost of £12 million, equivalent to £200 million in 1985 values, he achieved this goal in 1933. By then 40 per cent of Fleet Street staff were canvassers. New subscribers to the *Daily Herald* were given the complete works of Charles Dickens, the *Daily Mail* serialised Dickens' 'Life of Christ', and readers could get free insurance, dictionaries and coupons.

65. *Daily Mirror*, 23 August 1984.

66. *The Spectator*, 4 February 1984.

67. Ibid.

68. Nevertheless *The Guardian*'s circulation still grew from 1980 to 1985 by over 200 per cent to over 400,000.

69. *New Statesman*, 1 July 1983.

70. In 1986 the Mirror group earned over £20 million, a nearly four-fold increase under Maxwell. *The Times* newspapers experienced cost savings of over £40 million after leaving Fleet Street.

6

Europe

The newspaper industry of Europe offers several contrasts in basic conditions and structure. Northern countries of Europe such as the Scandinavian countries and Germany have high per capita newspaper consumption similar to Britain's (see Table 1.4). This chapter examines Germany as an example of northern Europe's newspaper industries. France represents a newspaper industry in decline and tending more to the southern European pattern. Southern Europe's industry is typified by low circulation and limited growth. The specific cases of France, Italy, Spain and Greece are examined.

GERMANY

Despite two world wars Germany has close cultural ties to Britain and the United States. Like them, Germany acquired the newspaper habit in the days before broadcasting.

Historically there is a two-way link to the United States. Many Germans emigrated to the USA, the first foreign-language newspaper in the United States was German, and Germans had a formative influence on the early US newspaper industry. Then, after 1945, the Allies, some of whom were of German extraction, helped restructure the German newspaper industry.

Basic conditions

With this background the German newspaper industry is mostly an unsurprising hybrid of its US and British counterparts. Germany's large geographic size compared to Britain has made it difficult and

Table 6.1: Major German newspapers with circulations, 1985

Hamburg	
Bild Zeitung (1952)	5,900,000
Bild Am Sonntag (1956)	3,000,000
Die Welt (1946)	244,000
Die Zeit (1946)	481,000
Deutsches Allgemeines Sonntagsblatt (1948)	132,000
Hamburger Abendblatt (1948)	276,000
Hamburger Morgenpost (1949)	145,000
Wikako Hamburg Group[a]	607,000
Bonn	
Bonner Rundschau (1945)	64,000
General Anzeiger (1725)	80,000
Frankfurt	
Abendpost Nachtausgabe (1948)	167,500
Frankfurter Allgemeine (1949)	378,000
Frankfurter Neue Presse	141,000
Frankfurter Rundschau	217,800
Dusseldorf	
Anzeiger — Cooperation Nordrhein[a]	1,700,000
Dusseldorf Express	161,000
Handelsblatt	95,000
Rheinische Post	142,000
Westdeutsche Zeitung	211,000
Zeitungsgneppe RWR[a]	350,000
Munich	
Abendzeitung/8-Uhr-Blatt	270,000
Müncher Merkur	167,000
Süddeutsche Zeitung	350,000

Note: a. a group of local editions.
Source: Editor and Publisher Year Book, 1985.

expensive to establish national newspapers. Furthermore, its history as a collection of states — it is still made up of eleven — meant no capital comparable to London or Paris developed during the nineteenth century in terms of population, so encouraging regional papers. The press system set up by the Allies after World War II established a free press similar to their own. In terms of circulation per capita, productivity, owner motivation, industry concentration and advertising demand the West German press has many similarities with those of the USA and Britain.

Hamburg and Frankfurt are the largest cities in Germany. As in Britain, morning newspapers dominate the market. Unlike Britain, most morning papers in Germany in 1986 were regional. The only national newspapers were four quality papers, *Die Welt*, the *Frankfurter Allgemine Zeitung* (FAL), the *Frankfurter Rundschau* and the *Süddeutsche Zeitung*. There was one popular national daily, *Bild-Zeitung* (BZ), sold as a tabloid in multiple centres. In 1985 *BZ* dominated the German market. It had a circulation of 5.9 million, over a quarter of total German 21 million circulation. No other paper sold more than 750,000. The Sunday newspaper habit had not developed in Germany by 1986 and most newspapers did not print on Sundays when total circulation fell to under three million.[1]

Structure

In 1985, in Germany Axel Springer controlled 29 per cent of the market through his company Springer. Both Springer's *BZ* and quality *Die Welt* faced limited competition. *BZ* was highly profitable and appealed to popular taste. *Die Welt* was a money-loser and was cross-subsidised by its sister publication, the popular *BZ*. *Die Welt*'s closest competition in the quality market was *FAL*.

Die Welt was set up by the British government in 1946 to be a German equivalent of *The Times* of London. Produced with subsidies from the City of Hamburg, owned by the British government and protected by licence controls which gave it a monopoly, circulation in 1945 exceeded one million. With the end of controls, four hundred new papers started in Germany and *Die Welt*'s circulation dropped to under 300,000. In 1952 the British sold *Die Welt* to the politically acceptable Axel Springer.[2] In 1952 he started *BZ* basing it on the *Daily Mirror* of London. Within twelve years Springer controlled 30 per cent of the German daily market and 80 per cent of the small Sunday market.

Die Welt lost over $100 million between 1970 and 1985.[3] Despite a circulation of less than 250,000 there were special Hamburg and Berlin editions. Whilst *Die Welt* claimed to be a national paper it sold mostly in the Ruhr. Clearly an extra-parliamentary right-wing political organ in the 1970s, cost-cutting measures were made in the early 1980s. These included introduction of the latest cold-type technology, a new printing centre, a leftwards move editorially, a movement of headquarters to Bonn, a reduction in the labour force including that of the editorial staff from 300 to 120, a reduction in the number of pages to 16, of which only four were advertisements, a reduction in the number of foreign correspondents from 15 to eight with greater reliance on Springer's

Figure 6.1: The Springer empire, 1985

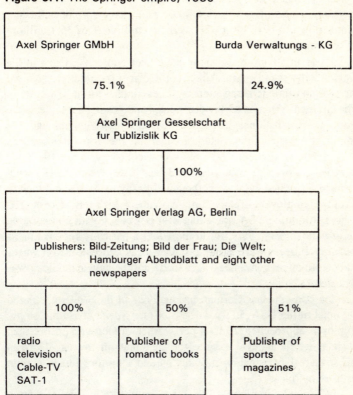

Source: The Economist, 1 June 1985.

own foreign news service SAD and the elimination of some money-losing rural distributions.[4]

Many of these cost-cutting measures at *Die Welt* paralleled those attempted by Murdoch at *The Times* in the 1980s where losses since 1970 had been of a similar financial magnitude. Also like Murdoch's News International, Springer had diversified. Like Murdoch, Springer had created a magazine empire and invested in the electronic media. Like Murdoch, in 1985 Springer diversified into the electronic media when he obtained a 35 per cent share in the news service for West Germany's SAT-1 cable television service.[5] In Germany 450,000 households had cable in 1985, a figure expected to grow five-fold by 1990. As with Murdoch in Britain, further newspaper expansion had become impossible for Springer in

145

Germany. The industry was mature with little growth potential, and the German National Cartel Office would have forbidden further acquisitions. In 1983 his profits were $13 million (DM 36.1 million) on a turnover of $930 million.[6]

Labour relations in Germany have been more like those in the United States than Britain. After World War II the allies reorganised the German unions along industry lines similar to the US system. The German system is highly centralised and general agreements are made at the national level between the trade unions and the employers' associations. Details are then a matter for works councils to negotiate. As in the USA cold-type technology in the 1970s led to strikes. For both countries 1978 was a key year. In Germany plans to introduce the new methods led firstly to strikes and then to a united employers' retaliation involving a lock-out at over 100 papers. As in the USA, the balance of power lay with co-operating non-fractious employers. As in the USA, a basically regional press meant employers were not rivals. Generous concessions on wages and employment guarantees were made but the new technology was accepted.[7]

As a consequence German productivity in the 1980s compared with that of the USA. In the early 1980s newsprint consumption per employee approached 20 tons per worker in Germany, more than twice the British level despite the fact that on average German newspapers have smaller circulations and therefore fail to exploit scale economies.[8]

In Germany circulations in 1985 were generally smaller than in Britain and the USA and many cities still had two newspapers. The general forces operating to create local monopolies elsewhere also existed in Germany but a 1978 report of the Bundestag stated that two-thirds of the population still had a morning choice.[9] One explanation for the restrained Jackal effect has been the lack of television advertising.[10] In Germany in 1986 it was limited to just 20 minutes per day.[11] It is good insurance against monopoly therefore, as well as to obtain reach, for advertisers to support second newspapers.[12]

Media concentration has concerned the German government. In 1965 changes in competitions policy were made in order to maintain a diversity of views and opinions. The Press Kommission took 20 per cent of the national market as a critical cut-off figure as did the Italian, Canadian and Swedish governments later. If a firm had more than 20 per cent then it was felt there was cause for concern. The viewpoint espoused in this book is that such approaches had become simplistic by the 1980s and (i) ignored competition from other media and (ii) misidentified the appropriate market which was local and regional. In fact recognising this the German National Cartel Office has over-ridden its own recommendations. In Germany, Springer's *BZ* alone took 25 per cent of the market. His other publications took under ten per cent of the market. Springer had 80 per cent of the Sunday market which would be cause for concern in Britain or the USA but not in Germany because the Sunday market is so small. No other newspaper publisher has even ten per cent of the daily market.

If Germany in 1986 had no significant Sunday market it did have a vital weekly news magazine tradition. An examination of the contents of British quality Sunday papers reveals much material reviewing, analysing and discussing the week's events as well as other more timeless material such as book excerpts and biographies. But Germany's lack of Sunday newspapers and Britain's lack of weekly middle-brow photo-news magazines reflect the soft-edged nature of the newspaper industry. The vehicle is different, but their function is similar. When, therefore, *Stern* magazine announced in 1983 'the journalistic scoop of the post World War era' its negotiations for the sale of the syndicated rights were to the *Sunday Times* newspaper in Britain but to *Panorama* magazine in Italy and *Paris Match* magazine in France.[13]

In conclusion, the German newspaper industry in 1986 was well established, mature, profitable and efficient. It was largely a regional press. *Bild-Zeitung*'s dominance of the tabloid market had no counterpart in other countries, and Germany's strict limitation on television advertising was exceptional.

FRANCE

Supply and demand

France, unlike the United States, Britain, Canada and Australia, has a long history of state involvement in industry generally. With this background it is not surprising to find state influence on the press in France in 1986 to be all pervasive.[14] The French government has means to 'suborn, seduce and, if necessary, silence the press' which are not available in Canada, Australia, Japan, the USA, West Germany or Britain.[15] In 1985 President Mitterand declared 'Freedom needs to be regulated.'[16]

After World War II and the liberation the French press made a

Table 6.2: The newspapers of Paris with circulations, 1985

L'Aurore (1944)	220,000
La Croix (1883)	118,000
Les Echos[a] (1908)	65,000
L'Equippe (1946)	326,000
Le Figaro (1828)	332,000
France-Soir (1944)	550,000
L'Humanité[b] (1904)	150,000
International Herald Tribune[c] (1887)	140,000
Libération (1973)	150,000
Le Journal de Dimanche (1946)	360,000
Le Matin de Paris (1977)	137,000
Le Monde (1944)	450,000
Paris-Turf	150,000
Le Parisien Libéré	342,000
Le Quotodien de Paris	72,000

Notes: a. Business national paper.
      b. Communist.
      c. English-language international.
Source: Editor and Publisher Year Book, 1985.

virtual new start. In 1939, 31 Parisian dailies accounted for 63 per cent of French production. In 1975 just three of these dailies remained and all Parisian dailies accounted for just 35 per cent of French production. In 1978 there were 13 dailies published in Paris. Their total daily circulation in 1980 was 3.8 million, down from five million and 28 dailies in 1946. By 1986 total circulation had declined to under 2.5 million.[17] Meanwhile the provincial dailies had a circulation of 7.5 million in 1980, down from nine million in 1946. These were very prosperous, unlike their Parisian counterparts. The dominant Hersant group (France's largest chain) used profits from its successful provincials, 22 in 1986, as well as its 14 magazines to help finance its three money-losing nationals, *Le Figaro, France-Soir* and *l'Aurore*.

The basic legislation governing the French press was passed in 1881 and was generally very liberal. It established a free press. Offences were limited to libel, defamation, official secrets, offensive material and disturbing the peace.[18] This legislation was modified after the liberation but the government's influence is expressed through other means such as control of the banking system, ownership and control of much of the broadcasting media, tax breaks and subsidies to the media, appointments to the media, ownership and control of much printing and placement of advertising, a monopoly of the dissemination of news via France's only press agency the Agence France Presse (AFP) and the licensing of journalists. In addition there are many informal links between the press and politics. In 1977, for example, the heads of the Hersant chain, of *France-Soir* (France's largest newspaper circulation), of the Provençal group, and of l'Express group were all Deputies to the National Assembly. The head of *Jours de France* and the editor of *L'Aurore* were both Senators.[19] The French state blatantly 'rewards its friends and punishes its enemies'. In 1981 under Giscard d'Estang the nationalised banks helped Hersant in a take-over by providing finance. In 1984 the socialist Mitterand government clearly intended to punish the same Hersant when a press bill was introduced to the National Assembly 'to free journalists and newspapers from undue pressure from government by press groups and advertisers'.[20] Whilst the intent may have been laudable, editors and journalists of all political persuasions condemned the bill for its vindictiveness and hypocrisy. Only Hersant would be affected whilst the state monopolies of AFP, the advertising agencies, television and radio would be unaffected. However, since the legislation was not retroactive Hersant did not have to dismantle his empire. Furthermore as a member of the European Senate he was immune from prosecution.

Mitterand's phoney competition legislation failed to daunt Hersant. Anticipating the socialist election loss of March 1986, he flaunted the law late in 1985. He acquired five more papers. He purchased Delaroche, publisher of *Le Progrès*, the leading daily paper in Lyons and four others. Meanwhile his son purchased *L'Union* in Reims. This meant he had 40 per cent of the largest market (Paris), nearly 100 per cent of the second largest market (Lyons) and nearly 25 per cent of the total regional market.[21] In Lyons the other major daily was Hersant's own *Le Dauphiné Libéré* and the Delaroche purchase ended years of close rivalry in a typical Jackal effect situation.[22] Since it gave Hersant a monopoly, the Delaroche market share was worth more to Hersant than anybody else.

Since the French government is the major owner of both the major sources of content, advertising and news, and of the major substitutes for newspapers, radio and TV, its influence is formidable. Up until 1982 the French state had a monopoly of all radio within France although commercial radio to France was transmitted from outside the country and attracted large French audiences.[23] The two largest were RTL from Luxembourg and Europe No. 1 from Saarbrucken. Even then, in order to have some control over content the French government became a major shareholder of these stations. Since 1982 private radio stations have been permitted in France and have provided competition for the limited advertising, which previously went to newspapers. Limited television advertising was first introduced within France on the three state news channels in 1982, although French viewers in some areas had received signals with commercials from Luxembourg, Belgium, Germany and Monaco before then.[24]

Much of the French government's regulation favours the press. In 1982 deregulation of radio led to chaos as over 1,000 new stations were set up. Consequently the decision to allow private television in 1985 was taken with caution. The Bredin Report on commercial television expressed concern over the effect of commercial television on press advertising.[25] Anticipating slow total advertising growth until 1990 of $330 million per year, Mitterand's government decided that only two new national channels should be established.[26] In 1985 television advertising took only 17 per cent of all advertising in France versus over 30 per cent in Britain and North America and 50 per cent in Spain.[27] The new channels were limited to 24 minutes of advertising a day and advertisements by publishing companies, chain retailers and of liquor and alcohol were all banned. These regulations all helped protect newspapers. Clearly in the late 1980s newspapers in France will be especially vulnerable as their share of the limited advertising dollar declines (see Table 2.1) and as other broadcasting and electronic media expand and develop.

The advertising industry in France in 1985 had a unique structure. It was dominated by two firms, Havas and Publicis, both French-owned and both advertising agencies as well as advertising booking agencies. Together they sold 90 per cent of all provincial newspaper space.[28] Since the state was the majority shareholder of the largest booking agency, Havas, the state had a formidable potential to influence private sector newspaper advertising content, either by withdrawing advertising or threatening to do so. In addition, in France, the state is the major buyer of advertising. Air France, Renault, SNCF and other nationalised industries have huge advertising budgets. Also public utilities, the post office and many government departments advertise. Withdrawal of state advertising would be critical for any newspaper.

State influence in 1986 extended beyond advertising to other newspaper inputs. First, Agence France Presse was under state control even though it was theoretically autonomous. The state provided 60 per cent of its revenue and appointed three members to the ruling council. Most provincial newspapers subscribe only to AFP. Much of the information transmitted to AFP subscribers inevitably came from various government department press releases and other government sources. Second, small newspapers were guaranteed newsprint at the same price as large newspapers through the state-regulated newsprint purchasing co-operative.[29] Third, and most importantly, the NMPP (Nouvelles Méssageries de la Presse Parisienne) co-operative newspaper distribution system must carry all publications without bias. This had enabled the widespread distribution of limited-interest papers like the communist *L'Humanité*.

The pace at which the new production methods are introduced depends critically on labour legislation. In France the printers' union, the Syndicat du Lure, representing mostly craft skills dated back to the nineteenth century. They had a very powerful monopoly, but were less successful in fighting progress than the British. One reason for this was the Moisant Law of 1956. This made closed shops illegal, whereas it was not until 1982 that Mrs Thatcher banned closed shops. The printers union in Paris, like its Fleet Street equivalent, had negotiated extremely favourable working conditions and salaries in the 1960s and 1970s. A series of strikes in the late 1970s resulted in negotiations permitting the new technology.[30] The newspapers' owners had been organised since 1925 in the National Federation of French Newspapers but had, like the Fleet Street owners, failed to support each other in a united front against the unions.

Journalists in France have been organised since 1918. In 1935 the National Assembly introduced a work code for journalists which had two especially important provisions:

(i) the 'clause de conscience' which provides for generous compensation should a journalist leave a newspaper because the newspapers has changed its ideology, for example if there is a change of editor or owner;
(ii) special taxation for journalists under which 30 per cent of their gross income is not taxed.[31]

Structure and conduct

Increased concentration of the press has occurred in France as elsewhere. Whilst circulation since 1914 was little changed in 1985,

Table 6.3: French provincial newspapers with circulations, 1985

City	Newspaper	Circulation
Angers	Le Courier de L'Ouest (1944)	112,000
Bordeaux	Sud Ouest (1944)	365,000
Clermont-Ferrand	La Montague (Centre France) (19)	256,000
Grenoble	Le Dauphiné Libéré (1944)	427,000
Lille	Liberté (1944)	103,000
Lyons	Le Progrès (1859)	354,000
Marseilles	La Marseillaise (1944)	165,000
Marseilles	Le Provençal (1944)	345,000
Metz	Le Republican Lorrain (1919)	202,000
Montpellier	Midi Libre (1944)	191,000
Morlain	Le Telegramme de Brest (1944)	203,000
Mulhouse	L'Alsace (1944)	134,000
Nancy	L'Est Republicain (1889)	259,000
Nantes	L'Eclair (1945)	707,000
Nice	Nice Matin (1944)	261,700
Poitiers	Centre Presse (1958)	123,700
Reims	L'Union (1944)	127,000
Strasbourg	Les Dernières Nouvelles d'Alsace (1877)	233,000
Toulouse	Le Dépêche du Midi (1870)	253,000
Tours	La Nouvelle Republique (1944)	281,000

Source: Editor and Publisher Year Book, 1986.

the number of daily papers in Paris had fallen from 60 to ten, whilst provincial newspaper titles had fallen from 242 to 75.[32] The process of rising concentration in France has been characterised by the Jackal effect and the 'natural monopoly' characteristic of the industry, but also by one additional force unique in France. This is the advertising-booking agencies system. Large provincial newspapers after World War II formed groups who pooled their advertising and sold space through advertising agencies for the group as a whole. Economies of scale in set-up and administration enabled the groups to sell space at a lower price per consumer reached, so under-cutting non-group competitors. By 1969, Publicis and Havas placed over three-quarters of their advertisements with the nine largest groups.

In 1975 two dominant information groups emerged in France when the Provost newspaper and magazine holdings were sold. Robert Hersant bought *Le Figaro* and Hachette purchased many of the magazines.[33] In 1981 the arms manufacturer Matra, better known in Europe perhaps for its Matra Formula 1 racing cars, took over Hachette.

Hachette, before being sold to Matra, was a huge publishing multinational whose origins dated back to 1848. For supporting

Louis Napoleon, Louis Hachette obtained a monopoly of railway station kiosk bookstalls for the new developing transport system. By 1970 Hachette controlled over 90 per cent of the distribution of the national press.[34]

By 1985, Hachette was both vertically integrated forward into distribution and backwards into printing. Horizontally Hachette had interests in periodicals, books, video, radio, television (Radio-Télé Luxembourg), advertising and real estate. Hachette had ranked as France's 68th largest corporation in 1977 before the sale to Matra with only about 20 per cent of earnings derived from its press holdings. Hachette's major shareholders were the Hachette family and the Banque Paribas.[35]

The Hersant empire in 1986 was a contrast to Hachette. Based mainly on the press it was a relatively new company headed by high-profile leader Robert Hersant whose own personal history dated back to his collaboration with the Nazis in 1940.[36] By 1986 Robert Hersant's empire had grown to include three Parisian dailies and 21 provincial dailies.

Hersant built his empire from a magazine *L'Auto-Journal* which he acquired after World War II. By 1970 Hersant had expanded this into a small newspaper chain. Initiating the concept of advertising groups discussed above, he acquired local newspaper monopolies in Lille in the 1960s and Le Havre in the early 1970s. He then expanded to his native Rouen and in 1975 bought *Le Figaro* in Paris. He had influenced all his earlier acquisitions editorially so that they had a right-wing pro-Gaullist editorial slant. In 1975 there were other potential purchasers for *Le Figaro*. Although Hersant had created his provincial empire by borrowing and was already highly levered, finance was made available to his holding company, SOCPRESS. Banque Verdas, in which the armaments manufacturer Marcel Dassault, who had close ties to Prime Minister Chirac, had a major interest, and the state-owned Banque Nationale de Paris arranged funds. Over the next two years SOCPRESS's debt more than doubled as Hersant paid out over F20 million as indemnities to journalists as a result of the 'right of conscience' law. Hersant continued to make further purchases including *France-Soir* in 1977. By 1980 the Hersant group owned 12 dailies, 9 provincial weeklies and 11 magazines.[37] In 1982 Hersant took a major holding in *Le Dauphiné Libéré* so adding 410,000 in daily sales in the Lyons area, $24 million in losses, and a 40th publication to his press empire.[38]

Just as Gaullist support had helped Hersant build up his empire, so the Socialists after their 1982 election sought to bring him down.

Press concentration has been an issue over the last two decades in most of the Western democracies. The French press bill introduced into the National Assembly late in 1983 to deal with press concentration may therefore have been doing the right things. In the case of France it did them for the wrong motive — revenge. Hersant's newspapers had continuously attacked the Mitterand government since 1982. The 1984 bill prevented any group from controlling more than three national newspapers, or a national newspaper and a provincial newspaper if their combined circulation exceeded 15 per cent of French national circulation or 15 per cent of a region's circulation. In 1983 Hersant controlled 40 per cent of national daily sales and 15 per cent of provincial daily sales.[39]

Significant barriers to entry exist in the shrinking French newspaper industry although government support and subsidies have led to attempts to establish new newspapers.[40] The advertising booking agencies, the facts that readers are creatures of habit, that advertisers are loathe to risk advertising dollars on new papers and finally, that for decades France has been a shrinking market for readers with growing alternatives for advertisers, have all inhibited entry.

The heterogeneous nature of market demand in France aided by the distribution system was reflected in the variety of newspaps found in 1985 in the small Paris market (see Table 6.2). The left-wing *Le Monde* which carried no pictures or cartoons until 1984 was still, in 1985, one of the world's most influential newspapers.

Founded in 1944 *Le Monde*'s origin can be traced back to *Le Temps*, a nineteenth-century newspaper confiscated in late 1942 from the steel trust, Comité des Ferges. Thirty journalists from *Le Temps* who had not collaborated with the Nazis were given partial ownership of the new newspaper.[41] In 1973 the journalists' association held 40 per cent, management 20 per cent, moral guarantors 25 per cent and various individuals the rest of the shares. *Le Monde* had been a success in terms of circulation up until the early 1980s, increasing circulation from 170,000 in 1961 to 350,000 in 1968 and 550,000 in 1982. *Le Monde* was always financially and politically vulnerable. All the other Parisian dailies lost money and were cross-subsidised from the provincial newspapers and the other activities of the groups that owned them. *Le Monde* had no other sources to draw upon.

Until 1983 *Le Monde* had successfully increased circulation in Paris, the provinces and internationally. In the 1980s foreign sales approached 100,000 daily. Its audience was attractive to advertisers since they were young and professional. However, *Le Monde*'s 40th anniversary in 1985 found the paper virtually bankrupt and in crisis. Financial losses, a loss of direction, falling circulation and internal strife in 1985 plagued France's most famous paper. Its economic difficulties stemmed from (i) government subsidised competition, (ii) its democratic employee-owned organisation, (iii) high costs,[42] (iv) changing commercial tastes[43] and (v) falling quality and loss of identity.[44]

By 1985 *Le Matin* and *Libération* had siphoned off a significant proportion of *Le Monde*'s readers. Both were relative newcomers. *Libération* began in 1973, *Le Matin* in 1977. In 1969 *Le Monde* had actually had an 800,000 circulation following the 1968 crisis, in 1982 it was 550,000 but in 1984 it had fallen to 370,000.

Libération's origins were hardly promising. Founded by existentialist Jean Paul Sartre and run by a group of Maoists and Trotskyists to be a voice of the people, it had limited capital, would accept no advertising, paid everybody the same salary, and in the name of equality had no bylines for journalists and no need for unions. The then powerful monopoly print unions had so little faith in *Libération*'s future they did not even oppose the introduction of the latest photo-composition equipment or its lack of unions.[45] Yet by 1985 the serious, non-elitist tabloid *Libération* had a growing circulation of 130,000 in the shrinking Parisian market. Though it still made a loss its survival could be credited to the following. Most importantly, the French government provides loans and subsidies to low-circulation newspapers to make up for the lack of advertising. Second, its latest technology and lack of unions meant costs in 1983 per page were, reportedly, one-tenth of *Le Monde*'s.[46] Third, its dynamic editor since 1974, Serge July, was given permission by the staff in 1981 to reorganise the paper. He closed the paper for five months, hired new editorial staff, moved the paper to a more libertarian anti-Marxist slant, allowed suitably inclined businessmen to invest in the paper, increased the reportage budget, and established *Libération* as a less sombre intellectual rival to *Le Monde*, particularly among the young.[47] July was successful, achieving circulation growth in a declining market. Fourth, under French law all papers are guaranteed distribution.

Le Monde's unique form of organisation also proved a problem once it had developed economic problems following losses of $2 million and $3 million in 1982 and 1983. Photographs, cartoons and weekend supplements belatedly added in 1984 failed to stem the losses. Organised as a trust, with no outside finances available, *Le*

Monde's only hope was to cut costs. A new editor introduced drastic measures for 1985, including pay cuts, voluntary redundancies, selling a 25 per cent share to outside shareholders, a sale and lease-back of the headquarters and investment in new production methods. Still journalists maintained control by retaining 35 per cent of the stock, despite the sale of 12 per cent to readers. The shock of the crisis seemed to revive the spirit of the paper.[48] In 1985 it scooped *Libération* when it exposed the French government's involvement in the sinking of the Greenpeace peace boat in New Zealand. Circulation rose above 500,000.

Reflecting the 'reverse onus' basis of the Roman law system of France, any reports using information of a judicial, military or government nature must be cleared before publication. This inhibits investigative reporting within France, as do laws which severely limit investigations of the private lives of public figures and libel laws which allow prosecutions of newspapers for false reports even if newspapers believed them to be true. When in 1985 *Le Monde* halted its circulation decline with its revelations about the French government's sabotage of the peace ship in New Zealand waters, it was only possible because the events occurred outside France.

Performance

In terms of performance, the experience of the French press is not dissimilar to that of other Western countries. The Jackal effect has operated leading to the establishment outside Paris of profitable local monopolies. High profits for monopoly survivors encouraged the development of newspaper chains. A virtual state monopoly of television and radio until 1982 prevented significant cross-media ownership. Many newspapers are owned by conglomerates, whose major interests are outside newspapers.

From 1973 to 1986, Paris newspaper circulation declined from 3.5 million to under 2.3 million. All papers suffered. The Socialist *Le Matin* founded in 1977 lost F10 million ($850,000) in 1982. Its circulation declined from 738,000 in 1982 to 137,000 in 1985. The right-wing papers belonging to press baron Robert Hersant fared no better. Even his popular best selling *France-Soir* lost money, as did *Le Figaro* and *L'Aurore*. Hersant claimed with justification that without his cost-cutting measures and subsidies all three would have folded by 1982. The growth of *Libération*, which in 1981 required additional financing from supportive businessmen to cover losses, therefore added competition to the Parisian market. Yet the overall outcome in 1985 was not satisfactory. On its own, Hersant's rescue of failing newspapers was desirable. So were *Libération*'s and *Le Matin*'s new voices. But together they jeopardised *Le Monde*'s viability so that all made losses. For how long and on what terms subsidies for Parisian newspapers will be forthcoming was unclear in 1986.

The real problem for French newspapers was inadequate demand. Per capita consumption has been declining for decades. By 1986 it was below 200 per thousand, much lower than in the rest of northern Europe and North America. Demand is decreasing to southern European levels.

ITALY

Demand and supply

In 1875, when mass circulation newspapers were being founded across Britain and the United States, more than two out of three Italians were still illiterate. Italian newspapers with the exception of *Il Corriere della Sera* have never had an international reputation for quality. In 1985 Italy had one of the lowest per capita consumption levels of newspapers amongst developed countries. Only one person in ten bought a newspaper. Total circulation was little more than half that of one of Japan's big dailies or about the same as Britain's *Daily Mirror*. Italy's failure to acquire the newspaper habit results partly from its late development. Radio, television, scooters, cars and other consumer goods have pre-empted the demands of newspapers for readers' time and income. Italy also has a café tradition of open air discussion. Since 1960 Spain has had a similar experience. Rapid economic development in both countries has not encouraged newspaper readership. In Italy as in Spain, the lack of a democratic tradition has also worked against the development of widespread newspaper readership. Political involvement in newspapers and government regulations have further discouraged growth in newspaper demand. Price controls on newspapers have forced greater dependence on advertisers and encouraged lower editorial budgets. Since the government enjoyed a monopoly of television until 1983 a weakened press was to their political advantage.

There are many explanations for low Italian newspaper consumption. (i) Italians have an oral rather than a written tradition.[49]

Table 6.4: Major Italian newspapers with circulations, 1985

		Orientation
Milan (population 1.6 million)		
Il Corriere della Sera (1876)	534,000	
Il Giorale (1974)	179,000	
Il Giorno (1965)	180,000	
Il Sole — 24 ore (1965)	138,000	Financial
La Gazzeta dello Sport (1896)	215,000	
La Notte (1952)	154,000	
L'Occhio (1974)	80,000	
L'Unità (1924)	296,000	Communist
Rome (population 2.9 million)		
Avanti (1896)	130,000	Socialist
Corriere dello Sport Stadio (1924)	170,000	
Daily American (1945)	80,000	English
Il Giornio (1969)	50,000	Business
Il Globo (1945)	57,000	Financial
Il Manifesto (1971)	70,000	Communist
Il Messagero (1897)	300,000	
Il Popolo (1944)		
Il Tempo (1944)	148,000	Conservative
La Republica (1976)	400,000	
L'Unità (1924)	300,000	Communist
Paesa Sera (1949)	200,000	Socialist
Turin		
La Stampa (1896)	500,000	

Source: Editor and Publisher Year Book, 1985.

(ii) Language diversity in Italy as well as many dialects makes reading a newspaper, even in 1985 by many so-called literate people, a formidable task.[50] A survey in 1976 found that 78 per cent of the population could not easily read a newspaper and that 33 per cent could not read a newspaper.[51] For many Italian citizens, newspapers are hard to read and not worth the effort. Potential readers instead rely on television and a vast selection of glossy popular magazines which outsell newspapers by a three to one ratio. (iii) The Italian newspaper distribution system does not favour the widespread readership of newspapers. All newspapers are sold at news-stands and there is no home delivery such as occurs in Britain, Japan and the United States. To operate a news-stand a permit is granted by a joint committee of publishers and news-stand operators. The latter have a vested interest in preventing new entrants to the distribution of papers so that in Italy there are only half the number of news-stands on a per capita basis as in France, or one stand for every 2,500 persons. The operators then collect a 35 per cent commission on each copy sold, compared to 20 per cent to 25 per cent in most developed countries.[52] In 1986 a law to allow a wider distribution of newspapers went before Parliament.

In 1976 the Italian courts decided that the state broadcasting system RAI only had a monopoly of national broadcasting and in the following years hundreds of local commercial FM stations were started.[53] These merely reinforced the tendency of those who had never started to read papers not to do so. There is little reason to think that those who read newspapers stopped, since there was no change in circulation trends discernible. It did mean one more competitor for the advertising dollar and for potential new readers.

The potential bias of Italian newspapers further limits their market. Surveys have shown that the majority of people do not believe that Italian newspapers tell the truth, nor that they are politically neutral.[54] In fact Italian newspapers are preoccupied with politics and many issues that elsewhere would be hard news are reported as political issues in Italy. The Christian Democrats in 1985 controlled one state television news broadcast, TG1, the Socialists the other, TG2. Politics infuse Italian institutions which in other countries are apolitical, for example, movies, the arts and broadcasting, the banks and the many nationalised industries. Newspapers are politicised and hire politicised journalists.

Political links are more influential in all Latin countries and taken to extremes in Italy and Greece. As in France, in Italy there is a 'clause de conscience', whereby, should a newspaper change its ideological stance, journalists can be awarded considerable indemnities. In Italy these have been laid down as one month's salary for every year of service. They act as a powerful lever for employees to influence management and also act as a deterrent to labour mobility.[55]

Political party newspapers still exist in Italy. They attract little advertising, advertisers generally avoid political associations and distribution costs are higher because they wish to reach readers who the commercial press would be willing to forego on the basis of marginal cost-benefit analysis. They may also get subsidies from those wishing to buy favour. In 1975 the US Securities and Exchange Commission divulged that Gulf Oil had contributed over half a million dollars to the papers of both the Christian Democrats and the Socialists, though they had not bought advertising space.[56]

The state recognises twelve professions in Italy. The last to be recognised was that of the journalists in 1963. The state decides what

159

constitutes journalism, who becomes a journalist and who benefits from being a journalist.[57] Entry is restricted but those who obtain entry receive many favours and protections. They get travel discounts on airlines and the autostradas as well as on the already heavily subsidised railway system.[58] They get high salaries because, like doctors in the USA, entry is restricted. In fact, in 1985 Italian journalists were better paid than doctors. Writers who have not been admitted to the Order of Journalists can be fined and are fined by the courts if they work as journalists. To join the Order a journalist must have served an apprenticeship on a newspaper and passed an exam. The hitch is that to serve an apprenticeship an aspiring journalist must first be employed at a newspaper, and to get a job on a newspaper requires influence. By law it is illegal to publish a newspaper or a magazine unless all staff members are apprentices or members of the Order. In other words journalism is a state-sanctioned closed shop which brings financial rewards to the journalists, but political control to the state. The system is defended on the grounds that it protects journalists from pressure from employers to write contrary to their conscience and protects the public from journalism that sells sensationalism and appeals to base taste.[59]

The Order of Journalists is not a union but a professional order or form of state registration. In Italy journalists have high social status and high incomes. Most journalists are male, university educated and enjoy considerable job-security. Whereas in the United States the journalist takes the professional view that political commitment should not appear in his reporting and that editorial positions are the prerogative of the owner, in Italy journalists do include political views and do not tolerate editing of their stories.

There is limited evidence about bribes and hush money in this politicised environment. In Italy Giovanni Spadolini, historian and journalist, editor of *Il Corriere* in the early 1970s, Prime Minister in 1981 and author, wrote a book detailing bribery in political journalism since the turn of the century.[60] He revealed that bribery was widespread and that the price for Catholic journalists was less than for Socialists. Whether bribery makes any difference to what journalists write cannot be known. In countries such as Italy, Spain and much of the developing world where bribery and corruption is endemic in society in general, it is to be expected in the press too. This lower credibility of the press decreases demand for newspapers in general and reinforces the oral tradition.

Structure and conduct

Most newspapers lose money in Italy despite the assistance of the government with a number of subsidies. There are discounts on newsprint financed by a special tax on all other forms of paper. There are extraordinary tax exemptions on many aspects of the newspaper business including on new plants and offices. There is no sales tax on the actual papers. There are special rates for the transport of newsprint and of newspapers on the railways and cheap rates on the telephones and telegraphs. None of these is sufficient to make the press viable so that they must rely on either state or conglomerate support.

There have been new entrants to the newspaper market. In 1976, a year when Italy's daily newspapers lost $90 million, a new tabloid newspaper *La Republica* was launched. By 1985 only *Il Corriere della Sera* sold more copies, but *La Republica* sold more copies outside Rome and Milan. *La Republica* had therefore established itself as a national daily by identifying a market niche for hard news and non-partisan editorial and in 1985 earned a small profit. From 1983 to 1986 circulation doubled to 485,000. Though independent, the paper's financial supporters included the weekly *L'Expresso* and the publishing group Mondadori, in turn part of the de Benedetti conglomerate. *La Republica*'s success served as stimulus to the other major Italian newspapers to acquire new technology and popularise content causing an increase in overall newspaper consumption.

Since the Italian reader market is limited it is not surprising that newspapers lose money. Nevertheless, there has been keen competition to own them. As on Fleet Street the explanation lies in the ability to propagate a viewpoint, to defend the owner, to help make friends of influence and to curry favour.

The four national papers in Italy all had conglomerate owners in 1985 and a history of support from wealthy outsiders. An important reshuffling of ownership occurred in 1974.[61] In 1973 three out of four heirs to the original Crespi family founders of *Il Corriere* decided to sell out. Also in 1973 the feuding Perrone family who had take each other to court over 35 times in the previous 20 years finally broke up and one family segment sold out their shares in *Il Messaggero* to another magazine company, Rusconi. In 1974 the chemical giant Montedison took over the ownership of *Il Messaggero* from Rusconi. Montedison had also started *Il Giorno* in 1956, had directed advertisements to *Il Tempo*, and provided financial help to the financial paper *Il Globo* as well as other papers in Turin which competed with *La Stampa*. ENI, the huge state-owned conglomerate, has financial interests in Montedison so that the newspapers owned by Montedison are ultimately linked to the state.

Despite the overall failure of the mass circulation press certain events in the 1980s involving the elite *Il Corriere* were significant. These events reflected the political and economic influence of ownership of the newspaper of record.

In 1982, Roberto Calvi, a major backer of Rizzoli Editore, the publisher of the country's leading paper, *Il Corriere della Sera* of Milan, was discovered hanging from London's Blackfriars Bridge. Days later an international scandal broke when Calvi's Banco Ambrosiano nearly collapsed revealing dubious financial connections to the Vatican. Calvi was also connected to Italy's infamous P2 Masonic Lodge. So was Angelo Rizzoli, Chairman of Rizzoli Editore and owner of *Il Corriere* since 1974. By 1983 Rizzoli's own finances had become desperate. He owed $325 million.[62] Court-appointed overseers of the company were instructed to sell the paper.

The 1983 sale of *Il Corriere* had parallels to the 1980 sale of London's *The Times*. Both papers were regarded as national institutions. Though circulation in 1984 hovered below the half million mark the paper's influence within Italy was still considerable.

The financial troubles at *Il Corriere* could be traced back to 1972 when the paper's editorial moved to the left, supporting abortion and divorce.[63] This increased demand. In 1974 the original owners, the Crespi famliy, decided to sell. Though some journalists hoped to set up *Il Corriere* as a trust, the publishing company Rizzoli with more financial and political clout gained control.

Rizzoli poured money into *Il Corriere* for new cold-type technology, computerisation and a Rome edition. To overcome distribution problems Rizzoli integrated downwards and bought out the distribution system. Rizzoli also diversified and introduced new magazines using *Il Corriere* staff. But do to all this Rizzoli had to borrow heaviliy. There were rumours of political involvement with the Christian Democrats, of loans from Fiat through Swiss banks, of intervention by the Prime Minister in 1977 in the appointment of the editor. By 1981 Rizzoli's losses and debts were unmanageable. He therefore sold a 40 per cent interest in *Il Corriere* to the banker Roberto Calvi for L6.3 million. Rizzoli continued to hold 50.2 per cent and the Rothschild Bank of Zurich 9.8 per cent. Bruno Viscenti, the President of Olivetti Corporation and also of the Republican

Party, was appointed by the government as guarantor of *Il Corriere*'s editorial independence.[64]

After the suspicious death of Calvi and collapse of Calvi's Banco Ambrosiano, *Il Corriere* was placed in receivership. Rizzoli group's major creditor was the Nuovo Banco Ambrosiano. Banks under Italian law cannot own interests in the press. The paper had to be sold and was put up for sale in 1984.[65]

There was no shortage of would-be buyers for the loss-making but influential *Il Corriere*. Both the Socialists and Christian Democrats reportedly asked businessmen close to their parties to make offers.[66] In the end neither political party was successful with *Il Corriere*. Hours before the court-appointed deadline for the sale of the paper a group of free enterprise independent-minded businessmen outbid the offers of all the party-affiliated groups.

The successful group had interesting motives. Led by Giovanni Agnelli of Fiat and Leopoldo Pirelli of Pirelli tyres, the group represented the business establishment of Northern Italy. Newspapers are not a natural diversification for the likes of Fiat and Pirelli and there is little synergy between cars and the press. But for $33 million they bought a 60 per cent share in Rizzoli which guaranteed independence for *Il Corriere* from the politicians in Rome as well as a voice for the business interests centred around Milan. Announcing plans to spend $33 million on capital expenditures for 1985 in the loss-making enterprise, a spokesman for the news owners still claimed it made 'good business sense'. Nevertheless its chances of making a profit as a newspaper were slight.[67]

Like much of the press in southern Europe, the Italian press was bankrupt by the 1980s. In 1981, total losses at the press had amounted to £180 million. Legislation was passed in 1981 whereby groups with less than 20 per cent of the market could receive subsidies. These amounted in 1981 to £90 million. Subsidies to smaller papers in effect meant subsidies to political party newspapers.

In 1986 Italy, even more than France, illustrated that an affluent, educated population did not assure a viable press. Similar difficulties handicapped the press throughout southern Europe and Latin America.

GREECE

The Greek newspaper industry faced many problems similar to other

Table 6.5: Major Greek newspapers with circulations, 1985

Apogevmatini (founded 1956)	114,000
Ethnos (founded 1981)[a]	203,000
Ta Nea (founded 1944)	189,000

Note: a. In 1981, 89,000
Source: Editor and Publisher Year Book, 1986.

countries in southern Europe and Latin America in 1985. Greece in 1985 reflected the problems of a partisan press. It revealed how a plethora of papers, contrary to conventional wisdom, is not necessarily to the advantage of the public. Circulation was under one million in a population of nearly 9.4 million. This circulation on a per capita basis was similar to Italy and Spain. Like Italy and Spain, literacy was almost universal (92 per cent) in Greece. Like them, Greece has experienced political instability and a right-wing dictatorship in living history. From 1967 to 1974 a military junta imposed censorship, surveillance and import duties on newsprint. Circulation then fell from 1.2 million in 1967 to 365,000 in 1971. With the return of democracy, circulation had increased to 910,000 by 1983.

Over half of all dailies are sold in Athens (population 3.5 million) and the choice is formidable. In 1984, 29 newspapers were sold there. In 1983 there were 118 Greek dailies in all and 14 claimed to be national dailies. Only three had circulations exceeding 100,000. All were partisan. All received funding of some sort either from the government or other parties. Limited reader demand, small circulations and low advertising revenues made loans and political funding an essential fact of life. In 1980 out of $80 million total advertising expenditures in Greece, government-owned television absorbed 47 per cent, newspapers attracted just 28 per cent.

In 1983 the conditions under which the industry operated were modified following the closure of Greece's most respected paper of record, *To Vinia* in 1982 and rumours that a successful new entrant *Ethnos*, Greece's first tabloid, was Soviet-financed.[68] Devaluation of the drachma in 1982 exacerbated problems as newsprint costs rose but intense competition meant few newspapers felt able to raise prices. Most that did later rolled them back when their circulations slumped.

The Greek government feared such intense 'unhealthy' competition would eventually lead to more closures and monopoly.[69] In 1983 the government therefore introduced special economic legislation to regulate the press and reduce competition. It (i) banned newspaper advertising on radio and television; (ii) set a maximum of 90 pages per paper per week; (iii) set a basic selling price and (iv) implemented laws to control the time that morning and afternoon papers could be published. The incentive to conform was the threat to withdraw duty-free newsprint and distribution licences. The government also ended its practice of giving loans to newspapers.[70]

In terms of conduct in 1985 there was price competition. Generally papers were alarmist, sensational and partisan. Most were opinionated and enjoyed low credibility. Greece's ideological pluralism was reflected in its newspapers. They provided an outlet to the people for political parties, but the results were bewildering to the politically uncommitted reader.

SPAIN

Spain's rapid transition from an illiterate rural population to a prosperous literate urban one exemplifies the economic difficulties that will face newspaper industries in Third World countries that successfully develop economically in the future. As in Italy and Greece in the 1980s, only one person in every ten bought a paper in Spain. Consequently total daily circulation in Spain in 1985 was under four million, less than the *Sun* alone in Britain. The Spanish market in 1986 was small and lacked promise.

Table 6.6: Major daily newspapers of Spain with circulations, 1985

Madrid	
ABC (1905)	127,000
El Alcázar (1936)	95,000
Diario (1976)	125,000
El Pais	348,000
Pueblo[a] (1940)	45,000
La Región Internacional[b] (1935)	110,000
Barcelona	
El Peródico (1978)	170,000
La Vanguardia Esperato (1881)	192,000

Notes: a. State-owned.
      b. Catholic.
Source: Editor and Publisher Year Book, 1985.

In 1976 media censorship ended and the post-Franco era began. After 40 years the press was declared free. New publications were started, but the basic conditions for a flourishing commercially viable press to develop were not there. Government-owned television had already captured the bulk of the potential newspaper-reader market as viewers. Television advertising had also claimed a share of the advertising market during the 1970s. As in Italy, weekly gossip and news magazines in combination with daily radio and television met the press needs of many Spaniards.

There was also government competition to discourage new entrants to the industry. The government had inherited a large number of newspapers from the Franco regime which it continued to produce and subsidise in competition with the private sector. For example, before the government closed the Madrid daily *Arriba* in 1979 it lost the equivalent of four dollars on every copy sold.[71] The Spanish government also set television advertising rates which were amongst the lowest in Europe, whilst newsprint prices were amongst the highest because of a protective tariff and taxes.

Consequently in 1985 no Spanish newspaper had a really significant circulation. Circulation figures for Spain's two major cities are given in Table 6.6.

CONCLUSION

The experiences of the southern European countries show that the timing of economic take-off is an important determinant of the size of the newspaper market. Italy, Spain and Greece were all late developers in the European Economic Community. For their standard of living all have low newspaper circulations when compared to their northern partners and North America at a similar stage of development. Broadcasting and weekly magazines have largely pre-empted the mass reader market for daily newspapers. These comments also apply to South America where political instability further reduces the incentive to supply newspapers.

NOTES

1. *Editor and Publisher Year Book*, 1985, p. 201.
2. M. Walker, *Power of the Press*, p. 93.
3. *The Economist*, 1 June 1985.

4. *World Press Report*, July 1982.

5. *The Economist*, 1 June 1985.

6. Ibid.

7. *National Institute for Economic Research*, February 1981, p. 81.

8. Ibid.

9. Ibid.

10. See pp. 28–9 for full Jackal argument.

11. Satellite television enables advertisements to be beamed in from outside Germany.

12. Limited broadcast advertising can have two effects. It can (i) reduce total advertising demand and (ii) increase newspaper advertising demand. If it even partly increases newspaper demand then the prospects for second newspapers are improved.

13. The scoop was a hoax involving the faked secret diaries of Adolf Hitler. The case revealed the dangers of commercial journalism. At *Stern* the unofficial motto was 'Everything that money can buy'. *Newsweek* did not publish, but the reputations of *Stern* and London's *Sunday Times* were tarnished.

14. One reason for extensive state intervention in the French press and its general acceptance is that after World War II many confiscated newspapers were held by a state holding company for nearly a decade. This established the idea of state involvement in both industry structure and conduct. The range of involvement still covers a broad spectrum. State financial assistance to the press was estimated in 1976 to be worth about eight times the gross income of the largest Parisian newspaper. Most of this aid was from lost revenues to the state as a result of tax concessions and subsidies. Special postal rates accounted for over half the total. Other significant items included value added taxes not collected and tax breaks for journalists. As well there were railway subsidies, telephone and telegram subsidies, special tax concessions on profits reinvested, and assistance to the international distribution of newspapers. In 1969 the Linden Report examined the role of the journalists' association. In 1972 the Drancourt Commission reported to the National Assembly on the economic situation of the newspaper industry. In 1984 the Bredin Report examined the impact of television. Permanent agencies monitor circulation (Official Circulation Board), advertising (Truth in Advertising Board) and consumers (Centre for the Study of Consumers of the Press). Censorship powers in times of crisis are considerable. The state determines what is a crisis, as it did during the Algeria crisis in the late 1950s when *L'Humanité* was suppressed and various issues of *Le Monde, La Croix* (Catholic), *L'Aurore* and *L'Express* were banned.

Newspaper conduct in the area of content is seriously constrained in France by extensive state involvement. Direct political interference is widespread, whilst on the economic side the state has many weapons with which to cajole newspapers to implement self-censorship, including financial assistance, placement of advertisements, licensing of journalists, investment loans from the state banks, tax harassment, expensive libel suits and anti-trust laws. Despite this and the virtual state monopoly of the television and radio media there is considerable diversity of opinion expressed in French newspapers.

15. *The Economist*, 24 December 1984.

16. *Editor and Publisher Year Book*, 1985, p. 201.

17. Ibid.

18. *Europa Year Book* (Europa Publications, London, 1985), p. 486.

19. Antoine De Tarlé, 'The Press and the State' in A. Smith, *Newspapers and Democracy* (MIT Press, Cambridge, 1980), p. 128.

20. *The Economist*, 24 December 1983.

21. *Business Week*, 20 January 1986.

22. See Jackal effect argument, p. 29.

23. *Europa Year Book*, 1985, p. 421.

24. *New Statesman*, 23 December 1983.

25. *Business Week*, 24 February 1986.

26. In 1986, before the elections, the opposition said it was inclined to privatise the state-owned television channel Antenne 2 if they came to power. Reflecting pervasive French politics, the Socialists had denied a television channel to Hersant. Hersant however was favoured by the new government for ownership of Antenne 2.

27. *Business Week*, 24 February 1986.

28. Ibid.

29. Since 1944 the price of newsprint has been controlled and since the formation of the EEC, newsprint production has declined and imports increased.

30. In 1979 the Paris-based *International Herald Tribune* was given permission for journalists to direct access the typesetting process after threatening to leave France. One hundred out of 130 printers were dismissed. These developments enabled Hersant to build and use a modern printing plant in the Paris suburb of St Dennis. There he prints *Le Figaro, France-Soir, l'Aurore* and *Paris Turf*, after they have been set by photo-composition at their own Paris separate headquarters. As a result the four papers required only 1200 production workers, half the previous number needed for the same work. By exploiting economies of scale productivity improved although inefficiencies at the newsprint and distribution levels remained. He obtained further cost reductions by co-ordinating advertisements.

31. *Europa Year Book*, (Europa Publications, London, 1985), p. 422.

32. *Editor and Publisher Year Book*, 1985, p. 206.

33. J.W. Frieburg, *The French Press: Class, State and Ideology*, (Praeger, New York, N.Y., 1981), p. 168.

34. Hachette held 49 per cent of the NMPP co-operative as well as its own distribution company.

35. Paribas, through a subsidiary owned 20 per cent of Power Corporation of Canada. Power Corporation held a virtual monopoly of French-language papers in parts of Quebec.

36. *The Economist*, 10 March 1986.

37. *The Economist*, 23 June 1979.

38. Hersant's financial secrecy is not unique. As private corporations, both Maxwell in Britain and Newhouse in the USA have kept their financial transactions from the public eye.

39. In defence of Hersant from the Socialists' attacks certain economic issues arise. First, many of his provincial acquisitions had been failing newspapers whose demise would have lowered competition. Group take-

overs do not necessarily lower competition in a region if the alternative is closure. Second, in 1983 only Hersant in France owned three national newspapers. Influence depends on market share not numbers of newspapers and *Le Monde* alone enjoyed more than 15 per cent of the national market in 1983. Third, newspaper markets are highly segmented and within the Paris newspaper market, dailies such as *L'Equippe* (sports), *L'Humanité* (Communists) and *L'Aurore* (right-wing) were at best distant substitutes. Fourth, by the 1980s many media commentators felt that the real threat to press freedom came when there was cross-media control. In France this was not the same problem as in Britain, the United States and Canada where most city newspapers had a local monopoly, since in France television, in 1985, was still a virtual monopoly controlled by the state. The legislation appeared politically contrived and hypocritical.

40. In 1965 Marcel Dassault, the arms manufacturer who later financed Hersant, set up *Vingt-Quatre Heures* to compete with *Le Monde*. In 1977 a group including the Michelin family set up *J'Informe*, again to compete with *Le Monde*. Both ventures were short-lived, failing to attract sufficient readers or identify a market niche despite rich parents. The left-wing *Le Matin* started in 1977 was more successful though never profitable.

41. *L'Express*, 7 December 1984.

42. During the 1970s, *Le Monde*'s success had brought profits. Staff grew, salaries rose above average levels, but investment in new plants and union concessions did not take place. In 1985 *Libération*'s production costs were one-tenth of *Le Monde*'s. In 1980 advertising in *Le Monde* brought 70 per cent of revenues and was 45 per cent of content, but in the 1980s as circulation fell, so did advertising revenues. By 1985 the cash flow to finance the $10 million of required capital improvements was no longer available. As circulation declined and television advertising expanded, *Le Monde*'s finances became increasingly bleak. Government price controls made it impossible to raise circulation revenues.

43. Until Mitterand's 1981 victory for the Socialists, *Le Monde*'s left-wing opposition to D'Estang was rigorous and obligatory reading for bureaucrats, opinion-makers and students. Its franchise was clear. After 1981 *Le Monde*, until the Greenpeace affair in 1985, seemed slower to criticise and less independent. *Libération* and the major newsweekly magazines *L'Express* and *Le Nouvel Observateur* filled the gap, and did so in a more entertaining format.

44. Newspaper quality is hard to define, let alone identify and analyse. Still, in the 1980s *Le Monde*'s democratic but cumbersome time-consuming and laborious method of choosing a new editor, tending eventually to elect a play-safe compromise, led to dissatisfaction, political infighting and a misdirection of effort. Threats of salary cuts and declining circulation further compounded problems of declining morale and loss of flair. Not surprisingly, many observers felt *Le Monde*'s standard had declined.

45. *New Society*, 11 August 1983.

46. *L'Express*, 7 December 1984.

47. In terms of product strategy *Libération* identified an unfilled market niche. It mixed excellent reporting and serious analysis with photos, crude cartoons, verbal jokes and a letters page. This contrasted with the grey, ponderous, opinionated newspaper *Le Monde* had become, lacking photos

and entertainment. The progressive *Le Matin*, though less weighty in terms of editorial, had also attracted *Le Monde* readers.

48. *The Economist*, 21 December 1985.

49. Italians are not generally great readers. They enjoy the outside, face-to-face communications and personal contact, unlike the British, the Scandinavians and the Germans who, in general, are more reserved. Northern Europeans also have to bear a harsher climate which has prevented a lifestyle of public discussions. Television, however, has appeared able to pull people off the streets of Italy in a way newspapers had not.

50. W. Porter, *The Italian Journalist*, (University of Michigan Press, Ann Arbour, 1983), p. 78. Until the late nineteenth century Italian was only spoken in Tuscany and Rome and even in 1986 Romano was the patois of the capital. The oral and non-verbal traditions live on in the non-verbal gestures and the variety of dialects and regional languages, whilst newspapers continue to be written in the style and language of the elite.

51. Ibid.

52. Ibid.

53. *Europa Year Book*, 1985, p. 642.

54. W. Porter, *The Italian Journalist*, p. 83.

55. In 1974 under a new owner, *Il Corriere* moved editorially to the left. A group of angered journalists founded a new newspaper and took *Il Corriere* to court under the *clause de conscience*. They lost the case, but had they been successful then Italy's leading paper *Il Corriere* would have been bankrupted.

56. Most party newspapers, however, are a drain on party funds and the largest of all, *L'Unitá* of the Communist Party, with a 1984 circulation of 296,000, required heavy party support.

57. W. Porter, *The Italian Journalist*, p. 89.

58. Ibid.

59. Whatever the merits of these arguments the system has its roots in the methods used by the Fascists to control the press. The Order of Journalists takes an interest in, and has a concern for, such matters as political stance, editorial coverage and balance and professional status. Journalists also have a union, the National Federation of the Press which most journalists, but not all, join. It negotiates at the national level setting the terms and conditions for all journalists and was inspirational in the establishment of the Order of Journalists.

60. W. Porter, *The Italian Journalist*, p. 86.

61. After 1945, unlike the situation in France and Germany, Italian newspapers were not confiscated for failing to oppose the Fascists. The old pattern of ownership continued.

62. *The Economist*, 26 February 1983.

63. W. Porter, *The Italian Journalist*, p. 87. It also brought new competition. Disgruntled *Il Corriere* journalists, backed by advertisements from the Montedison combine worth 12,000,000 lires, formed a new daily *Giornale Nuovo*, 'to combat the demagogic attitude of the new *Corriere*'.

64. *The Economist*, 26 February 1983.

65. *Business Week*, 22 October 1984.

66. For example, Socialist Prime Minister Bettino Craxi who had successfully sued *Il Corriere*'s editor early in 1984 for asserting the

Socialists 'sided with the thieves rather than the cops' in Italy's political scandals, favoured a sale to one Attilio Monti. Monti owned papers in Bologna, Florence and Trieste. To circumvent Italy's anti-trust law which limits newspaper ownership to 20 per cent of the market, Monti transferred formal ownership of some of his papers to his daughter. In August 1984 Craxi demonstrated his willingness to intervene in the media for political ends. His Socialist friend and supporter, Milan developer Silvio Berluscari, was permitted to buy out his only remaining rival in Italian commercial television, so creating a television monopoly. *The Economist*, 15 September 1984.

67. *The Economist*, 15 September 1984. As insurance, as a means of reducing further government involvement in the economy, as political and economic influence, as a public relations exercise, and a tax loss it probably did make sense to buy *Il Corriere*.

68. In an interview on PBS television, 'Journalism Report', 17 February 1985.

69. Ibid.

70. Ibid.

71. *The Economist*, 23 June 1979.

7

Japan

INTRODUCTION AND BACKGROUND

Any industry structure, its conduct and performance is dependent on its basic conditions. Japan's cultural history influences all aspects of the economy and Japan's huge newspaper industry is no exception. It can only be understood in the light of Japanese economic history and its feudal heritage.

Common values, the subordination of the individual to the group, the importance of the nation and the acceptance of authority, are reflected in the newspaper market. A homogeneous unquestioning disciplined population gets very similar newspapers. Likewise, newspaper owners, journalists and editors closely tied to the establishment carp and criticise, but are ultimately loyal to Japan before either abstract principles like a free press or even before profits. The feudal heritage affects demand, supply, conduct and ultimately industry performance in the huge Japanese newspaper industry.

Japan is a traditional society but a relative newcomer to the world of newspapers. Most Western countries predated Japan by a good century. Within Japan the first newspapers were English-language papers for despised foreigners, English, Americans and Portuguese. The first Japanese daily newspaper *Yokohama Mainichi Shimbun* appeared only in 1871. In 1872 the *Tokyo Nichi-Nichi* appeared explicitly to serve the Meiji government. Its introduction followed passage of the 1871 Newspaper Ordinance. This stated that newspapers 'should enlighten the people in the interest of governing the nation'.[1] Opposition newspapers were given short shrift and oppressed. Political influence and patronage have therefore characterised the Japanese press since its beginnings. More independent

172

newspapers were begun in the 1880s including *Osaka Asahi Shimbun* and *Osaka Mainichi Shimbun*, two of the three largest newspapers in the world in 1986. By 1911 both had circulations over 300,000. The largest paper in the world in 1986, *Yomiuri Shimbun* was founded as a literary newspaper in 1874 but changed its format in 1924.

The Japanese press had never been free before 1947 and had been seriously curtailed during the 1930s. In 1945 the Japanese press was reorganised under General Douglas MacArthur. It was a reorganisation in that most of the old papers and their personnel carried on, unlike in Germay were the Nazi newspapers were closed down. Censorship ended in 1948. Japan received her independence in 1952. Much of the current industry structure therefore is less than 40 years old. It is basically a free press considerably influenced by the United States model in which three huge national dailies the *Asahi, Mainichi* and *Yomiuri* dominate.[2]

Many of the laws and much of the economic infrastructure of the Japanese newspaper industry date back to the post-war era. Superficially Japan's press has much in common with the US press. Clearly a 'fourth estate' function was intended by the occupation forces and exists in theory. Yet, like so many other aspects of Japanese society and their economy, conventions, loyalties, customs and traditions exert a powerful all pervading influence. These affect behaviour in ways hard to comprehend for the individualistic, legalistic Western observer.

BASIC CONDITIONS

The press and particularly *Asahi Shimbun* are regarded more as a part of the establishment and bureaucracy than watchdogs of it. Through connections at the big universities, where all journalists are recruited, the press had close connections to government, the *zaibatsu* (the small number of old families who own and control much of Japan's industry and finance), political factions and academia. Journalism, in fact, is the first-choice career among graduates. Journalists are better paid than their government counterparts. They are certainly very close to those they cover, even writing for them, advising them and socialising with them. Two decades ago following the resignation of Japan's Premier Vishi *The Economist* wrote, 'Violence is not only that of pistols and fists, that of the pen is more dangerous.'[3] Self-restraint and self-censorship by the press

Table 7.1: Major Japanese newspapers with circulations, 1985

Osaka (district population, 15.4 million)	
Asahi Shimbun[a]	2,160,000
Mainichi Daily News[b]	n/a
Mainichi Shimbun[a]	1,460,000
Nihon Keija Shimbun[d] (1950)	541,000
Ojaka Sports	332,000
Sankei Shimbun (1933)	1,150,000
Yomiuri Shimbun[e]	2,100,000
Tokyo (district population, 26.4 million)	
Asahi Evening News[b]	38,000
Asahi Shimbun (1888)	3,830,000
Japan Times[b] (1897)	50,000
Mainichi Daily News (1922)	n/a
Mainichi Shimbun	1,810,000
Nihon Keizai Shimbun	1,190,000
Sankei Shimbun	1,920,000
Sports Nippon (1949)	775,000
The Daily Yomiuri[b] (1955)	n/a
Chunichi Shimbun (1942)	804,000
Tokyo Sports (1959)	203,000
Yomiuri Shimbun (1874)	5,490,000

Notes: a. total *Asahi* circulation 7,800,000.
     b. English-language.
     c. total *Mainichi* circulation 4,300,000.
     d. total *Nihon* circulation 3,000,000
     e. total *Yomiuri* circulation 8,700,000.
Source: Editor and Publisher Year Book, 1985.

tend to mask the very real power of the press in Japan.

Politically Japan is a one-party state and a corporate state. The dominant Liberal Democratic Party (LDP) is made up of five factions largely supported by business. The largest faction in the LDP in 1985 was still led by ex-Prime Minister Tanaka. Since his own forced resignation over bribes from Lockheed a decade earlier he had acted as kingmaker or 'old shogun in the shadows', naming Japan's three subsequent prime ministers. He maintained his power base with money. Tanaka, it was reported in 1985, personally provided all but 35 of his 120-member faction with Y4 million ($16,000) per year each just to keep them loyal to him. This was over and above what the faction gave them. For the other 35 he obtained lucrative official positions including cabinet seats. The press, it was reported, was lavishly entertained by Tanaka's faction and much encouraged to play the gambling game Mah Jong, at which they were suspiciously lucky. Tanaka's own finances came largely from companies who regarded Tanaka as a good investment, even after the 1974 Lockheed bribes scandal which unseated him.

Yomiuri, Asahi and *Mainichi* in 1985 were the three biggest newspapers in the world, though their growth ceased in 1983. *Yomiuri*'s total circulation alone was greater than that of all the United States' 17 largest dailies put together, or three times total Australian circulation or two times total Canadian circulation. It was greater than total Franch circulation, and comparable to total Fleet Street circulation. By newspaper scales the big three are behemoths. They are highly competitive, technically advanced, similar in organisation and make only the most modest profits. All operate under press laws copied from the United States but applied in a distinctly Japanese manner.

Japanese journalists in 1986 should have been the envy of journalists around the world. They had high prestige, job tenure, good salaries and modest work-loads. All journalists at the major newspapers were university graduates with broad training in history, political science, economics and languages. Each year 5,000 graduates apply to take examinations which qualify them for a newspaper job. In 1983 Yomiuri accepted just 38 after the gruelling written and oral exams were completed.[4] Once appointed the rewards were considerable. The average salary for 10,000 Japanese journalists in 1986 was over $30,000 and life tenure virtually guaranteed.

The quality of journalistic input is very high. In addition the papers have huge staffs, as many as 10,000 at each of the 'big three'.[5] Yet in the Japanese wonderland of productivity and quality it can be argued that these resources are wasted. In line with the Japanese ethos of group responsibility, all stories are filed anonymously. There is very little investigative journalism, journalists from different papers co-operate together at the press clubs [called krishna clubs] where they work. They rarely ask public officials surprise questions. Life tenure at the newspaper and anonymity as reporters curbs initiative. Adding to the narrowness of outlook of Japanese journalists is the method of recruiting journalists. Nearly all come from two universities, Waseda and Tokyo and immediately upon graduation join a newspaper. They then stay with that newspaper for life, job mobility being the exception. As a result little content competition emerges. Caution and co-operation with each other, government officials and advertisers, is the custom. Japanese newspapers are all much the same.

All this if viewed as inefficiency and waste reflects a Western concept of the role of a press. A free press is a contradiction in terms for Japan, where mutual obligation and obedience, loyalty and dependency, underscore the common purpose. Journalists see their role as informing and educating but the watchdog role of the Western press is muted. Even where matters arise which have to be exposed, the Japanese approach is not for a 'scoop' or 'exclusive' but for co-operation between newspapers. They decide jointly what should be done and what is in the common interest.

The press therefore is more of a partner with the government and industry in the national purpose. It participates in the informal linkages between government, finance and industry which make society work. It expects to be consulted before politics are instituted and accepts a duty to mould public opinion. It is legally free under the post-war constitution but morally constrained by an older tradition. That tradition serves to remove some of the spice and zest of Western newspapers and eliminates much content competition. However, there can be intense competition on matters which do not affect the *status quo* and the common good and journalists can be zealous. It was reported that in the 1968 student riots gung-ho reporters were more trouble than the students.[6]

Japanese news coverage is exceedingly comprehensive. Content comes from four main formal sources: (i) Japanese news agencies, (ii) international news agencies, (iii) press clubs and (v) newspapers' own bureaus.

There are two Japanese news agencies. Kyodo News Service which is a non-profit, non-government agency made up of the leading newspapers. Jiji Press, a co-operative, is the second news agency concentrating on business and economic news. NHK Radio also runs a news service.

Foreign news makes up a greater proportion of Japanese content than is typical of Western newspapers. Given Japan's dependence on the international economy this is understandable, and to satisfy the demand for international news all the major newspapers subscribe to the major international news agencies. *Asahi*, for example, subscribes to 27. In addition they run their own bureaus overseas. In 1983 *Yomiuri* had 28 overseas bureaus which it used for exclusives and to supplement the wire services.[7]

Within Japan *Yomiuri* had a further 436 bureaus. Its major rivals employed similar numbers of bureaus. With editorial staffs of approximately 3,000 at each of the 'big three', they each outnumbered the *New York Times* by four to one, or London's *The Times*, *Le Monde*, the *Globe and Mail* and *The Australian* added together.

One of the major obstacles to any Japanese newspaper achieving an international reputation as a great newspaper is the krishna club, the press clubs system. It is in the press clubs that, by Western standards, high quality journalistic inputs are diverted to producing mediocre output. It is here that the attitude of co-operation, common purpose and consultation, which helps make for the production of high quality consumer goods, suffocates a free press.

Press clubs are uniquely Japanese. They were set up in 1949 to provide friendship and goodwill between reporters and the various government agencies and major social, political and economic organisations with which the press regularly had to deal. In 1983 there was a press club, for example, at each of the 47 police prefectures, at the Bank of Japan and at the Japanese Socialist Party. There are as many as 200 reporters at each club. By 1984 the clubs had evolved beyond their original modest goals to become a means by which correspondents controlled the flow of news.[8]

From a Western viewpoint, the press club system has many drawbacks. (i) The press clubs have become the main source through which agencies distributed news. Most non-journalists, magazine journalists and foreigners are either excluded from the press clubs or else tolerated on restricted terms. The newspaper journalists have created a *de facto* monopoly of news gathering. (ii) Expulsion from the press club for a journalist is a career disaster. He is no longer able to collect news. Given the lifetime job appointment system he will find it virtually impossible to get on another paper. Consequently the press club system encourages timidity. It encourages journalists to co-operate, to follow. (iii) The press club modifies perspective. Each day journalists commute to the club at the agency they cover. Inevitably a tendency to identify with the agency develops so that, for example, what is good for Toyota becomes good for Japan. Journalists become quasi-public servants at the larger clubs such as Foreign Affairs and the Ministry of International Trade and Industry (MITI) and public relations officers at the big corporations. (iv) The press clubs encourage and facilitate patronage. Politicians may take a Gomperistic approach, 'punishing friends and rewarding enemies'. With a monopoly of news sources, politicians and other influential public figures host favoured journalists in their homes. The outcome, as illustrated by the Tanaka affair cover-up in 1974, is predictable.

For the newspapers the advantages of press clubs are considerable. They facilitate the news-gathering process, dignify the process and give the newspaper a competitive advantage over the other media who are excluded.

Reporters excluded from the krishna clubs work at a disadvantage since they cannot cover the news. Similarly sources without krishna clubs are deprived of equal access to the press and are at a disadvantage in promoting their views. The distortions created by the krishna clubs were illustrated by events at the Ministry of International Trade and Industry in 1984. When MITI was proposing new software legislation which would have been harmful to the United States, MITI was initially able to enjoy favourable press coverage through its krishna club. The US Embassy with no krishna club took the unusual step of inviting Japanese reporters to a hearing of the US point of view and the favourable press coverage ended. Both MITI and US viewpoints were then fairly presented, and the bill was not passed.[9]

The point remains. For the 12,000 reporters at some 400 official krishna clubs the easy access of officials to reporters and *vice versa* is highly efficient and convenient. It is also unfair. Non-member reporters and organisations are excluded, including most magazine reporters, foreign correspondents and foreign corporations. The bias results more from the krishna structure than from sycophancy amongst reporters.

The forces of co-operation and social unity that dull the editorial side of the Japanese newspaper facilitate the production side. Culture, rapid economic growth and lifetime employment have made trade unions co-operative partners as the newspapers have introduced new technology to meet the competition of newer media. The Japanese newspaper industry was the first in the world to introduce facsimile printing (1959) or home printing (Expo 1970). It was the leader in 1984 in the use of computers. The Japanese language creates problems for the press. In 1982 *Asahi* claimed to have the most modern press system in the world, yet all stories had to be written longhand because Japanese uses 2,000 ideographs. Ideographs meant that facsimile transmission, first developed in the 1950s by Britain's *Manchester Guardian*, was of great benefit to Japan and first introduced in 1959 at *Asahi*. There is virtually no opposition from the unions which are organised along company lines and, as in other Japanese industries, encourage company loyalty and mutual goals. Newspapers' poor financial state after 1983, as circulation stagnated, further encouraged co-operation.

Japan's neo-feudalism extends to its attitude to women in the labour market. Though changing, few women enter the workforce with the idea of building a career. Nowhere is their secondary position more apparent than in the newspaper industry. There are virtually no women on the editorial staff, 20 out of 3,000 at *Asahi* in 1980 for instance, but over 200,000 females were employed industry-wide delivering papers door to door in part-time dead-end jobs.[10]

Demand

Japan's highly literate and densely populated island population has many similarities with that of Britain. In 1984 the Japanese population was 119 million. The high density of the population, virtually all literate, enabled Japanese newspapers to enjoy the third-largest market in the world, exceeded by only the USSR and USA.

Crowded living conditions have pressured the Japanese to use the media extensively for entertainment. The average Japanese in 1982 watched 3.5 hours of television per day compared to about two hours for most citizens of Western countries. Still, the Japanese had the highest per capita consumption of daily newspapers in the world at 560 per thousand. In addition there has been a spectacular rise in the circulation of weekly magazines. The Japanese would appear to be 'information junkies', but in fact the bulk of demand is for soft news. The magazines, newspapers and television emphasise sports, entertainment and gossip. In general there is political apathy, a reflection of the remaining feudal aspects of society. There is, however, little scope for further daily newspaper growth. Since 1950 the birth rate has been steadily falling, from 28 per thousand in 1950 to 13 per cent in 1984, abortion is freely available, and it is unlikely that more daily newspapers per household can be sold.

Japanese daily newspapers lack the variety of Western newspapers. All major Japanese newspapers consider themselves politically independent and are politically cautious. There is a limited market for newspapers that cater to the intellectual as do the *New York Times, Le Monde* and the *Guardian*. The Confucian heritage makes sex and gore for the general audience unacceptable in most circumstances so excluding popular tabloids like the *Sun* in Britain or the *New York Post* in New York. Political apathy limits demand for partisan newspapers like the *Daily Mirror* or *Daily Express* in Britain, *Die Welt* in Germany, or the *Washington Post* in the United States. One specialist market niche, however, does exist. Demand for the business newspaper the *Nihon Keizai* known as the 'Nikkei' is three million per day, surpassing worldwide circulation of the *Wall Street Journal* (2.1 million) or the *Financial Times* of London (300,000).

The homogeneous nature of demand, the use of facsimile printing, the density of population and the natural Jackal effect tendency of large newspapers to squeeze out the smaller explain why the Japanese newspaper industry in 1986 was dominated by just five nationals and three regionals. In 1983 38 per cent of Japan's 34 million households bought *Yomiuri*, but *Asahi* and *Mainichi* also had huge circulations.

The big five, also including *Nihon* and *Sankei*, enjoyed 59 per cent of total circulation for Japan's 127 daily newspapers in 1985 but this share was lower than it was in 1974 at 64 per cent, when there were 110 dailies. This fall in market share reflected the increased share of the market of the regional newspapers, which are regional only in terms of the region served. In format and scope they are similar to the big three. Their growth reflects the rapid growth of the medium-sized cities in Japan.

Japanese daily newspapers can be divided into three categories — general, sports, specialised (e.g. business). General newspapers can be further subdivided into national, bloc or regional, and local. These categories of general paper refer only to area of circulation not content and format; locals circulate in just one prefecture, bloc in several, nationals in all prefectures. Japan has 47 prefectures. The five nationals circulate throughout the archipelago. Bloc papers circulation in one region consisting of several prefectures. Several of these are very large by Western standards as shown in Table 7.1 and dominate their regions in some cases. Only in Tokyo, Osaka and Kukuoka do the big three dominate. All nationals maintain editorial offices and plants in Tokyo and Osaka and in up to three other centres.

In 1984, 92 per cent of Japanese newspapers were home-delivered, 7.5 per cent were sold from news-stands and 0.5 per cent sent by mail. Home delivery required some 23,000 news agencies which in turn employed 428,000 workers, mostly juveniles and women. Most dailies were sold as sets. A set consisted of a 20-page morning edition and a smaller ten-page evening edition.

Advertising demand

With relatively slow population growth and a virtually saturated market, the Japanese newspaper circulation market is clearly mature. However, rapid economic growth in the past 30 years has been accompanied by increased total advertising expenditures so that

Table 7.2: Media share of Japanese advertising (%)

Year	Newspapers	Magazines	Radio	TV	Other
1955	55.3	5.7	16.1	1.5	21.4
1965	35.8	5.6	4.7	32.2	21.7
1975	33.1	5.4	4.8	34.0	22.7
1980	31.1	5.6	5.2	34.6	23.5

Source: Fukutake, *Japanese Society Today* (University of Tokyo Press, Tokyo, 1981), p. 102.

not only have total advertising expenditures on newspapers risen, they have also risen as a proportion of total newspaper revenues. By 1980 they accounted for 60 per cent of total revenues.

1980 was a watershed year. Total expenditures on newspaper advertisements started to decline and continued to decline through the first half of the 1980s. In 1983 circulation also began a decline at the big five. Newspapers' share of advertising expenditures had been falling since 1955 but so long as total revenues rose this was not a crucial issue. The fall in advertisement revenues hit *Mainichi* and *Asahi* hard enough to jeopardise their financial independence and make them increasingly dependent on the banks for survival. As in other countries with an established newspaper habit, readers' and advertisers' demand for newspapers had so far proved resistant in the face of new media alternatives. However, it was reported in 1984 that the Japanese were going through a phenomenon known as 'the rejection of the printed word', and observers noted, for example, that fewer and fewer commuters were to be seen reading magazines.[11]

STRUCTURE AND CONDUCT

The Japanese newspaper industry, dominated by the five big national newspapers and three large regionals, is highly concentrated. In Japan's case the national market is probably the correct market in which to estimate concentration ratios. *Yomiuri* and *Asahi* are competitive products in a sense that, for example, the *Los Angeles Times* and *Washington Post* are not, nor even the *New York Times* and *New York Post*.

The big three newspapers are all published by conglomerate giants with diverse outside interests. In common with most of the world's large newspaper companies, the dominant firms in Japan are also horizontally integrated within the media.

Asahi's other interests include smaller dailies, weeklies, weekly magazines, monthly magazines, books and the sponsorship of cultural activities including welfare societies, ballet, judo, art and orchestras. English- and French-language copies of *Asahi* are produced. *Yomiuri*'s interests include radio and television. It set up the first commercial television network, NTV. *Yomiuri* also owns the famous *Yomiuri Giants* baseball team, operates *Yomiuri* Amusement Park, supports an orchestra, owns real estate, operates a junior college of science and engineering, owns golf courses and operates travel bureaus.[12]

Mainichi's main business is daily newspapers. *Mainichi Shimbun*, based in Osaka, is the oldest and the third-largest Japanese daily, well behind the *Yomiuri* and *Asahi*. Mainichi produces three other dailies of note. The first is for elementary schoolchildren, the second for junior high school children, and the last, the weekly *Mainichi Daily News*, a separate English-language paper.[13] *Mainichi* also produces weeklies, magazines and books including a braille weekly and a Chinese-language business quarterly. *Mainichi*, like the other big two, sponsors several thousand cultural and sports events each year. It is impossible to disentangle the economic benefits from the Japanese social responsibility that motivates the sponsorship of activities ranging from high school championships to international art exhibitions.

Mainichi Shimbun in 1983 employed 6,000 employees excluding delivery workers, the same number as the *Daily Mirror* to produce twice as many newspapers. Editorial and news gathering employed 2,000. The paper had 83 branch offices and produced over 100 regional editions each day. Regional editions were like North American zoned editions with a page or two of local and regional news inserted in the national edition. As well as subscribing to all major news services, *Mainichi Shimbun* invested heavily in labour and capital. It kept 15 highly paid and highly qualified foreign correspondents in 15 countries. In Japan *Mainichi* had had specially made vehicles built to facilitate the transmission of news and photos. There were also eight Cessna aeroplanes and helicopters available to give reporters support.

High concentration can be traced back to the occupation era after World War II. When breaking up the old *zaibatsu*, the cartels which had been established in much secondary industry before the war, the occupation forces excluded the press in the belief that such interference conflicted with the principles of non-government intervention in the media. Instead they removed many of those who had run the press as a wartime propaganda machine.

One of the laws passed in 1951 sought to prevent powerful groups gaining control of the press. By it Japanese newspaper companies cannot sell shares to the public. Most shares are held by staff and by management and in trust for emloyees. Ironically, this has opened the back door to government influence. Social responsibility has already been given as a sufficient explanation for Japan's timid establishment line style of reporting. At *Asahi* and *Mainichi* it was reinforced by 1985 by their poor financial state as circulation stagnated and profits fell. At both, the financial linkages from the papers to the banks to the government meant they continued at the pleasure of the establishment. The banks could bring down either or both if they wished. To raise capital the newspapers borrow from the banks which are government-controlled. Though the newspapers claimed in 1983 to be free from influence, the record of establishment pressure exemplified by the Tanaka affair was less than satisfactory.

The editors and publishers of the different Japanese newspapers co-operate on new technology, ethics, editorial policy and even circulation and sales through their association, *Nihon Shimbun Kyokai* — the Japanese Newspaper Publishers' and Editors' Association (JNPEA). But JNPEA is no cartel. There has been intense rivalry between the major newspapers, particularly in terms of non-price competition. As in other countries, Japanese newspapers have tended to avoid price competition, though discounts on subscriptions are offered. In 1984 all the big three charged Y2600 (nearly $12 per month) for home delivery or Y70 for morning editions at news-stands and Y40 for evening editions (about 35¢ and 20¢). The early 1980s saw impressive circulation wars in Japan. In the late 1970s *Yomiuri* challenged the number one *Asahi* for circulation supremacy. The circulation war began with door-to-door salesmen offering gifts such as pots, kettles and mattresses. Then came digital watches for new subscribers. Finally Kodak Instamatics and even colour televisions were given away. Price discounts and free subscriptions to sports magazines also helped, but tickets to watch the record-breaking fanatically-followed first-place *Yomiuri Giants* baseball team may have been the most valued incentive. By 1978 *Yomiuri* had taken the lead circulation in highly heirarchical-conscious Japan. The circulation war continued until 1982 when the Japanese Fair Trade Commission intervened.

When competition got out of hand, as it had by 1982, the JNPEA and the Fair Trade Commission resolved the matter with the minimal use of legal sanctions in a spirit of mutual co-operation and recognition of the industry's common interest. This demonstrated the Japanese industrial genius for compromise. It also showed how JNPEA is a self-regulating body rather than a cartel.[14] The intensity of rivalry between the big three has been such that, since 1977, *Mainichi* in third place has teetered on the brink of bankruptcy.

There is limited vertical integration in the Japanese newspaper industry. As in Britain and Australia, the bulk of distribution is done by independent retailers. Unlike Australia, there is no backward integration into newsprint, virtually all of which is produced in Japan with imported logs. Nor, unlike France, are the newspaper firms involved in advertising. The newspapers do co-operate in the news agencies Kyodo and Jiji. To the extent that they rely more heavily on their own news sources than Western newspapers, they might be considered to be vertically integrated into news gathering. Likewise their relationship with the unions and production workers, in which an obligation to ensure lifetime jobs is undertaken, might be viewed as an investment in human capital, in the ownership and control of a co-operative labour input. The same applies to journalists who with lifetime job guarantees are a fixed cost to a Japanese newspaper in contrast to the 'hire and fire' of American newspaper industry which makes them a variable cost.[15]

Over 70 per cent of the Japanese 23,000 stores are exclusive sales stores with contracts to sell just one paper.[16] The distribution stores make additional income by using the newspaper as a vehicle to carry flyers and other advertising material which they insert into newspapers before delivery to homes. As products, Japanese newspapers are small in size in comparison to North American newspapers running to about 30 pages per set in 1985, up from about 14 in 1955.[17] Morning editions with up to 20 pages tend to be slightly larger than evening editions. In addition there are supplements several times weekly. Stores compete vigorously each month to renew subscriptions and persuade households to switch from competitors. They canvass, give discounts, offer gifts, make introductory offers and use all the market techniques more familiar to purchasers of North American weekly news magazines like *Newsweek*. The stores also sell the weeklies, monthlies, books and other products of their contracting newspaper company. Even so, they require subsidies from the newspaper companies.

There are barriers to entry. First, new papers may have difficulty raising capital since they cannot form public companies and the banks are under government influence. Second, access to the press clubs, an essential prerequisite for entry, although relaxed by Nihon Shimbun Kyokai in the late 1970s, is still a barrier. Third, since 1983 both circulation and advertising growth have ceased. That means any new entrant must take sales away from an existing paper.

To maintain high market penetration the papers cater the paper to the locality. In 1969 *Asahi* already offered 42 different daily editions and 124 local sub-editions from its five plants. Morning and evening editions were constantly updated as new sources arrived. Huge staffs, modern technology, high density of population, huge volumes and co-operative workforces all made this possible.[18]

Among the few injunctions the Japanese Fair Trades Commission has granted has been one stopping the practice of selling additional newspaper subscriptions at below marginal cost. When newspapers like *Yomiuri* and *Asahi* each reach over one-third of all households they become formidable weapons of propaganda for the newspaper firms' other activities. A good press has never harmed Japan's most popular baseball team, the Yomiuri Giants. They enjoy top coverage on Yomiuri NTV television and in *Yomiuri Shimbun*. The value of this publicity machine is obviously beyond estimate, but the big three in Japan have traditionally, like most competitive newspapers around the world, made inadequate profits and received subsidies from their other business.

PERFORMANCE

There is in the Japan newspaper industry a curious mix for a Western observer of intense marketing rivalry and unreasonable content restraint. The competition for subscriptions, to meet regional needs, to introduce colour, to be up to date is all very real. The restraint on content, co-operating on stories and editorial policy, respecting advertisers interest, avoiding sex and scandal is also very real and can lead to outcomes which to Westerners are unsatisfactory in a democracy. The Tanaka affair could have been to a Japanese newspaper what Watergate was to the *Washington Post*, an exclusive of historical significance. Instead 'mutual responsibility' by the big three squashed the story. It was reporting by free-lance reporters, excluded from the press clubs, for *Burgeo Shuzu*, a monthly magazine, following up on a story in the American weekly magazine *Newsweek*, which eventually persuaded the large newspapers to air the scandal. The criticism can be made with justification that Japan's big newspapers are involved in 'results journalism'. They are followers not leaders.

Nevertheless, on its own terms the Japanese press is free. Over 1,000 magazines employ free-lance reporters and are free to publish the results of their investigations. Between 1974 and 1985 the number of dailies increased from 110 to 127. In 1975 *Nikkai Gendai*, for example, was started, a tabloid sold on the streets of Tokyo, aimed at radicals and covering the unorthodox and more controversial. There are new entrants. There are new products. There is intense competition. There are no monopoly profits. There is less fragmentation of the market than in most Western countries either regionally, as in the USA, or politically, as in France, or in terms of popularity, as in Britain. This means there is less market power for newspapers. Economically, Japanese newspapers are highly efficient, using the latest equipment and highly skilled labour. Product quality suffers for cultural, not economic, reasons.

In summary, there is a unique cultural dimension to the structure of the Japanese newspaper industry. Supposedly free, there are powerful informal links between the newspapers, the government, big industry — both as a news source and an advertiser — and the banks. Legally free, the newspaper industry is culturally bound and this affects conduct and performance.

NOTES

1. John Lent, *The Asian Newspapers' Reluctant Revolution* (Iowa State Press, Iowa, 1981), p. 43.
2. After their defeat in World War II, the Japanese for a time were forced to yield control of their country to American occupation forces. The new Japanese constitution promulgated under American auspices in 1947 was thoroughly democratic — United States style. Yet it remains doubtful whether Japanese conceptions of self, society and status relationships, together with all the recognised proprieties of social conduct between social unequals really permit more than lip service to the egalitarian, individualistic and fundamentally alien political ideals so carefully enshrined in the constitution.
3. *Columbia Journalism Review*, 17 March 1984.
4. *Time*, 1 August 1983.
5. In 1975 48 per cent of the big three's staff were graduates compared to a workforce average of 13 per cent.
6. A. Smith, *Newspaper and Democracy* (MIT Press, Cambridge, Mass., 1980), p. 164.

186

7. M. Walker, *The Power and the Influence* (Quartet Books, New York, 1982), p. 205.

8. *Far Eastern Review*, 7 January 1984.

9. Ibid.

10. *Nieman Reports*, Winter 1980, pp. 17–23.

11. *Far Eastern Review*, 1 June 1984.

12. *Time*, 1 August 1983.

13. *Nieman Reports*, Winter 1980, pp. 17–23.

14. *Time*, 1 August 1983.

15. Ibid.

16. Ibid.

17. M. Walker, *The Power and the Influence*, p. 207.

18. *Time*, 1 August 1983. In terms of content *Time* in 1958 described Japanese newspapers as 'impartiality gone haywire', but a generation later in 1983 reported it has 'become less of a monolith'. *Yomiuri* is more conservative, sensational and supportive of the government. *Mainichi* is more philosophical and intellectual. *Asahi* has been described as 'authoritarian' in its views. Content and format is similar in all three.

8

Canada and Australia

One theme of this book is that the non-Communist press is biased to serve the affluent. It serves affluent countries. The reason is that the poor are not a market for advertisers. The very fact that this book devotes a whole chapter to Canada and Australia reflects this. Together, their population equals one quarter that of all Arab countries combined, and five per cent of the population of India, yet their newspaper industries are significantly larger, as Table 1.3 illustrates. The two countries have much in common, not the least of which has been their recent nurture and export of two outstanding press barons, Canada's Roy Thomson and Australia's Rupert Murdoch.

CANADA

Over three-quarters of the Canadian population live within 100 miles of the United States, a country ten times Canada's size in terms of population.

To avoid a cultural take-over Canadian governments have placed restraints both on ownership and content of the media.[1] In 1986, Canadians on average watched 24 hours of television a week, most of it from the United States, but spent less than five hours reading a Canadian newspaper. Threats of cultural imperialism have led to content laws for radio and television programmes. The commitment to freedom of expression, outlined in the 1982 constitution, requires that, except for libel and national security content, newspapers must be free as to editorial content.[2] Control of the press is limited to Canadian proprietors. Consequently a paradoxical situation exists in Canada whereby all newspapers are controlled by Canadian

Table 8.1: Major Canadian newspapers with circulations, 1985

Calgary	Calgary Herald	131,000
	Calgary Sun	71,000
Edmonton	Edmonton Journal	163,000
	Edmonton Sun	79,000
Vancouver	The Province	167,000
	The Sun	279,000
Victoria	Times-Colonist	77,000
Winnipeg	Winnipeg Free Press	174,000
Halifax	Chronicle Herald	80,000
Waterloo	Kitchener-Waterloo Record	75,000
London	The Canada Free Press	127,000
Ottawa	The Citizen	188,000
Timmins	The Daily Press	13,000
Toronto	The Globe and Mail	314,000
	The Toronto Star	517,000
	Toronto Sun	268,000
Windsor	The Windsor Star	85,000
Montreal	The Gazette	196,000
	Le Journal de Montreal	308,000
	La Presse	188,000
Quebec	Le Journal de Quebec	103,000
	Le Soleil	111,000

Source: Editor and Publisher Year Book, 1986.

newspaper proprietors, some of whom even have sizeable press holdings overseas, but they rely for much of the content for their Canadian papers on the international news agencies and American syndicates.[3] Canada understands Third World concerns of media imperialism.

Canadian newspapers, in 1986, operated in the unique environment of a relatively small, affluent, dispersed bilingual population of 24 million dominated by a huge powerful neighbour, the United States. Nevertheless, until the 1980s, geography meant Canada was a dispersed collection of largely non-competing markets for newspapers.[4] Since World War II, the operation of the Jackal effect has destroyed daily newspaper competition in Canada and local newspaper monopolies have evolved. The resulting local newspaper monopolies in Canada are generally very profitable. Consequently, in Canada in the 1980s, there is no real daily newspaper competition and a few national or regional chains dominate the industry. At the national level, Canada has the most highly concentrated press in the Western world.

The relatively small size of the Canadian markets has caused the largest Canadian newspaper firms to expand outside of the Canadian

189

market. In 1986, Canada's Thomson International had become the second largest chain, in terms of papers owned, in the USA. Though Thomson had more US newspapers than Canadian newspapers in 1986, he commanded less than five per cent of US daily circulation versus over 20 per cent of the Canadian market.

Basic conditions

Demand

Despite its proximity to the United States, the Canadian newspaper market is not a reflection of that market. Whilst US circulation peaked in 1973, Canadian circulation continued to grow into the 1980s rising from 5.2 million to 5.3 million from 1984 to 1985. The Canadian market has greater potential for growth than the US with a daily circulation per thousand in 1985 of only 230 per 1,000 versus 300 per 1,000 in the United States. Dailies dominated the Canadian newspaper industry attracting the bulk of circulation and advertising revenues.

Canadian newspaper circulations individually are small by international standards. Only five daily newspapers in 1986 had circulations exceeding 250,000 and 17 over 100,000. In 1981 local and classified advertisements generated $775 million in revenues versus $192 million from national advertising whilst circulation sales generated $400 million. The total 1985 circulation of 5.3 million was spread over 117 daily newspapers. Eighty newspapers with 4.3 million circulation were in the English language, the remaining one million circulation French.

The pattern of Canadian newspaper demand has shifted drastically away from afternoon newspapers. In 1971, 75 per cent (3.5 million) of Canadian dailies were afternoon papers. By 1981, only 50 per cent (2.7 million) were afternoon papers. Meanwhile mornings had more than doubled circulation to over 2.6 million. Sunday circulation increased from just 45,000 in 1970 to over 1.5 million in 1981. As elsewhere, increased evening television news, a decline in the use of public transport, a higher female participation ratio, and more single-headed families largely explain this change.

A more intense weekday lifestyle has also created new market demands. Easy, quick to read, sensational tabloids accounted for 20 per cent of the total market in 1984 and nearly half of all the French-language press. Yet the first English-language tabloid in Canada, the *Toronto Sun*, was introduced only in 1971. By 1984, the *Toronto*

Table 8.2: Canadian advertising expenditures, by media, 1985

Media	%	$m
Daily Newspapers	24.7	1,500
Catalogues and Direct Mail	22.5	1,400
Television	17.1	1,000
Radio	9.4	572
Weekly Newspapers	5.7	347
Magazines	4.1	248
Outdoor, Business Papers, Directories, etc.	16.5	1,433
	100.0	6,500

Source: Maclean-Hunter advertising agency.

Sun was Canada's fourth-largest newspaper. Tabloids were subsequently introduced in the 1970s in Halifax, Winnipeg, Montreal, Edmonton and Vancouver. Canada was also a late developing market in the field of large broad-appeal Sunday newspapers. Filled with comics, magazines, features and supplements they infringed upon the traditional market for weekly news and feature magazines. They were helped by legislation passed in 1974 which made Canadian advertisements placed in US weeklies like *Time*, which sold widely in Canada, non tax-deductible. By 1984 ten Canadian dailies published such Sunday editions, usually selling for 50¢, twice the price of the weekday edition.

Between 1973 and 1985 both the importance and composition of advertising demand for newspapers changed. Circulation revenues fell. Advertising revenues rose to 80 per cent. Revenues from non-run-of-the-press advertising such as inserts, shoppers and special supplements grew from under 2 per cent to 6 per cent between 1973 and 1980 and then doubled again to 1985. These non-run-of-the-press revenues meant a new function for the Canadian newspaper. Since, in many cases, the paper did not even print the insert, it meant the newspaper had evolved into a simple distribution vehicle.

Supply

Newsprint is one of Canada's major export products. Whilst many other countries subsidise newsprint for their newspapers Canadian newspapers pay the world price. Unlike in Australia and the United States, there is no vertical integration into newsprint products.

The Canadian labour supply situation is similar to that of the United States. Journalists are generally university educated and well paid. A Thomson journalist with six years' experience earned an annual salary of $34,000 in 1985. Production labour for the most part has accepted the new technology with less resistance than its European counterparts. Large chains, local monopolies and the Gomperist philosophy of accommodation explain this.

The 1980 *Royal Commission on the Press*, the Kent Report, observed that between 1973 and 1980 Canadian newspapers relied increasingly on purchased news.[5] Internally- or locally-generated news costs as a proportion of total expenditure declined.[6] Sceptics, such as Kent, saw the decline of local editorial content as a weak aspect of conglomerate ownership and high concentration in Canada.[7] This is debatable. It also reflected the changing relative costs and changing tastes of a more mobile society. Furthermore, the real economic choice for a failing newspaper, which was often the case in Canada, was usually closure or conglomerate ownership. The community was better served by the latter choice if the choice was between either a conglomerate paper or else no local paper or a government-subsidised 'independent' paper.[8]

The 1980 Royal Commission also took the view that the conglomerates Thomson and Southam, especially the former, were principally profit-motivated seeing their papers as a 'licence to print money' or as cash cows to finance other ventures. Certainly small newspapers in Canada with circulations below 250,000 per week had been immensely profitable earning 45 per cent on net assets employed in 1980. Large newspapers were less profitable. However, Thomson's determined efforts to make *The Globe and Mail*, which they acquired in 1981, Canada's quality daily have led to losses. Further, Thomson-trained journalists are sought in advertisements for journailsts, suggesting Thomson creates journalism quality. Southam, meanwhile, has a reputation for giving editors total independence, both from Southam's owners and, because of Southam's size, from local pressures. In other words, Canada's two dominant chains, when assessed against realistic economic alternatives, have much to commend them.

Structure

In 1980, the Canadian Royal Commission reported gloomily on the state of Canadian newspapers concluding that matters had deteriorated since a Senate Study on the Mass Media had reported in 1970.[9] The Kent Report was particularly concerned by high concentration in the newspaper industry as well as high profits and an apparent lack of newspaper competition.[10]

In 1984 Southam Newspapers Inc. with 14 daily newspapers controlled 27 per cent of total circulation. Thomson newspapers with 40 daily newspapers controlled 22 per cent. Together they held 59 per cent of English-language circulation. At the national level no developed country has so concentrated a newspaper industry.[11] Yet national concentration is not the appropriate market definition for inferring monopoly power particularly in a country as vast as Canada. Regional and local markets are more appropriate. In Canada, Southam and Thomson have avoided all-out head-to-head competition with each other, unlike Australian chains, so enjoying local monopolies and high profits for their papers.

Regional monopolies: Irving and Péladeau

The Irving family shows how, in a geographically large country like Canada organised as a loose federation, one not very large corporation of no great national significance can dominate one region.

By international standards, the Irving Industrial Group with sales of $1.9 billion in 1983 is not a large conglomerate. But in the small province of New Brunswick in Maritime Canada, Irving ranked as the biggest company in all the Atlantic Provinces and the biggest employer, even bigger than the government. The personal power of the Irving family in the province is overwhelming. Like Thomson, the basis of their empire is oil refining, but they also have major interests in pulp and paper, forestry and shipbuilding as well as interests in cement, convenience stores, food processing, truck and bus lines, steel mills, tugboats, car dealerships and motor parts manufacturing. Most controversially they also own the only four daily newspapers in the province, the largest television station and a radio station.[12]

In 1977 the Irving Group was involved in a newspaper trial which was significant for several reasons. It became a landmark case not just in the field of newspapers but for Canadian combines' policy generally.[13] The trial came about because over the period 1948 to 1971 Irving obtained a controlling interest over all five dailies in New Brunswick. Irving was charged under the monopolies and mergers section of the combines legislation. In the original case Irving was acquitted on the first monopoly charge on the novel grounds that all five dailies had had a local monopoly before the Irving take-overs, so that clearly there could not have been an elimination of competition. There had been no competition to begin with. However, they were found guilty on the second charge that the

193

monopoly was likely to be detrimental to the public interest, in that a diversity of opinion was less likely with one owner. On appeal the Supreme Court felt otherwise. First, the Supreme Court held that the legislation treated the newspaper as a product, or physical object like a paper plate, rather than as a vehicle to carry ideas. The court could not comment on the quality of the content. Second, the court observed that the chain had increased the circulation of all five dailies, that capital investment had been made in them, that loss-making papers had been subsidised so as to continue in production, and that there was no proof of detriment to the public despite all the theoretical evidence produced to suggest otherwise. The onus of proof was on the Crown and the Crown was unable to prove, as the law requires, that a single owner of the five dailies in New Brunswick would be detrimental to the public.[14] Elegant theory and extrapolations from other cases were not enough.

In 1985, the *Moncton Journal* was finally closed after years of losses, in part because the Irving group suffered financial difficulties as its oil and forestry interests experienced industry-wide downturns. In all likelihood the *Moncton Journal* had only survived as long as it did because it was owned by a conglomerate with deep pockets. The prestige, the value of a popular voice, and the possibility that economic growth and technological improvement in the long run might make the paper viable made subsidy of the endeavour worthwhile.

The Province of Québec, isolated by both language and culture from the rest of Canada, also has a dominant newspaper publisher in the form of Pierre Péladeau. He founded Quebecor, Canada's eighth-largest media company in 1985 with sales of just over a quarter billion dollars. Péladeau owns dailies in Quebec's two major cities, Montreal and Quebec City, and weeklies throughout the province. His flagship is the *Journal de Montreal*, Montreal's biggest circulation paper and Canada's second largest, with a circulation of over 300,000. It is a tabloid with a rich mixture of sex, crime and sport. Like Thomson, Péladeau is prepared to support the quality press and in 1984 took over publication and distribution of the small circulation, trust-owned, financially troubled and highly respected *Le Devoir*. Also like Thomson, Péladeau has found no room to expand in his original French-Canadian market, but unlike him he has been unsuccessful in both English-speaking Canada and the USA.[15]

All the major media companies in Canada have interests in the USA. Southam has diversified out of newspapers and in Atlanta owns a large printing operation and is a major investor in Infomat, a database services operation. Maclean-Hunter, who bought a 49.7 per cent shareholding in the Toronto Sun Publishing Company in 1982, owns cable television in New Jersey and Michigan as well as owning the *Houston Post*.

Concentration

The newspaper situation in the Province of New Brunswick points to the irrelevance of national concentration ratios in Canada. Given Canada's loose federal structure and the geographical isolation of many of Canada's communities, a newspaper publisher with but a small fraction of the total Canadian newspaper market can have a powerful and influential local newspaper monopoly. In New Brunswick Irving Newspapers Inc. enjoyed just 2.4 per cent of Canadian total circulation in 1984. This, however, represented the total circulation of the province. More alarming in New Brunswick is the fact that the Irving family also controls the broadcasting media across the province. In parts of the provinces of British Columbia, Saskatchewan and Alberta even smaller chains enjoy a total monopoly of the newspaper market.[16]

Table 8.3: Canadian media corporations' incomes, 1984

Company	Net income (C$m)
Thomson Newspapers[a]	153.8
Anglo-Canadian Telephone	58.3
Maclean-Hunter	49.2
Southam	44.4
Torstar	20.3
Bator Broadcasting	15.2
Toronto Sun Publishing	14.3
Selkirk Communications	13.9
Quebecor	11.4

Note: a. Thomson International is a separate company which in 1985 earned over $3 billion.
Source: Canadian Reviews.

For practical purposes, even in the large cities, there is no newspaper competition in Canada. In Toronto there are three daily newspapers but they serve different market niches and only compete marginally. The Toronto-based *Globe and Mail* is a quality paper currently establishing itself as Canada's first national newspaper using satellite transmission. The *Toronto Telegram* fits the

Figure 8.1: The Thomson empire, 1985

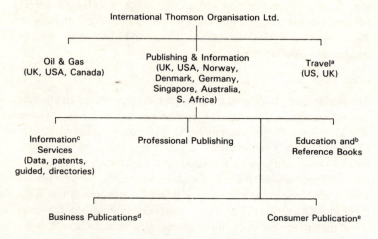

Notes: a. Includes Britannia Airways, Lunn Poly, Unitours.
       b. Includes Jane's Publishing.
       c. Includes Ward's Automotive (US) and Glass's Guide (UK).
       d. Includes 80 US business publications.
       e. Includes 83 daily and weekly newspapers in Britain.

traditional broadsheet metropolitan daily format. *The Toronto Sun* is a tabloid aimed at the young and the commuter, who would probably not otherwise buy a newspaper. Likewise, new tabloids in Edmonton, Calgary, Halifax, Winnipeg and Vancouver claim to seek a new audience and only marginally compete with the traditional broadsheet daily. In Montreal there are four dailies each appealing to different market segments. *The Gazette* of Montreal achieved an English-language monopoly in 1979 by virtue of the Jackal effect and the closure of the *Morning Star*. *Le Devoir* is a small circulation quality paper of great repute and appeals to the intelligentsia. *Le Journal de Montreal* is a hugely successful tabloid and *La Presse* is a traditional metro daily. Quebec City has a tabloid and a traditional daily.

The real danger to press freedom occurs not with newspaper monopolies *per se*, but when media conglomerates develop control of all the media in a given region. Like most successful newspaper chains, Canadian chains have expanded into related fields, driven by the small relative size of the market, fear of tougher anti-trust legislation, and the desire to spread risks. The pattern outlined in

Chapter 2, whereby a successful newspaper chain diversifies and grows using its newspapers as a cash cow, so that eventually newspapers are but a minor part of its total activities, is observable in the case of both Canadian giants, Southam and Thomson.[17]

Southam and Thomson dwarf all other Canadian newspaper interests, although large conglomerates have newspaper interests and are potential competitors. The *Toronto Star* is owned by Torstar which owns no other daily newspapers though it has wide interests in broadcasting and magazines. The *Toronto Star* is Canada's largest newspaper with a circulation exceeding half a million making Torstar Canada's third-largest newspaper company. Canada's fourth-largest daily newspaper publisher's main business is not newspapers. Maclean-Hunter which publishes tabloids in Toronto, Calgary, Edmonton, Winnipeg and Halifax is a book and magazine publishing company which diversified into newspapers in the 1980s when it purchased a major interest in Sun Publishing. Small, yet potentially powerful English-speaking regional monopolies are held by Irving, Sterling Publications and Armadale even though each has less than three per cent of total Canadian circulation. In Quebec three chains share 95 per cent of the market.[18]

Such a market structure would suggest formidable barriers to entry. Large conglomerates have the resources to endure short-term losses in a given market to drive out any would-be intruder. In any case, the history of the newspaper industry in all countries shows that most markets can sustain one profitable newspaper or two or more unprofitable ones. In fact, there have been successful entrants to the still growing newspaper markets of Canada. They fall into three categories. First, as in other developed countries, there is the ongoing process of birth, marriage and death amongst weekly community newspapers, often freesheets with very small, very local circulations. Second, Thomson's *Globe and Mail* using advanced satellite technology became available in most Canadian urban centres for early morning street sale and home delivery by 1984. In 1983, as a possible harbinger of future developments, a Province of British Columbia (BC) zoned edition of the *Globe and Mail* appeared with a full BC affairs daily supplement when a prolonged strike at the Southam-owned Vancouver *Sun* occurred. Third, weeklies are sometimes converted to dailies, a process often adopted by Thomson following take-overs of small community weeklies.

The newspaper industry, as noted, is not capital intensive so capital is not a major entry barrier. The *Elmira Independent* was launched in 1978 for $500 and was still going in 1986.[19] There are also minority newspapers in Canada to serve Chinese, Indians, Ukrainians and Asians.

Conduct

Newspapers in Canada rarely compete in terms of price in the reader market. Broadcasting is free from over 1,000 radio and television stations, so that there is broadcasting competition for Canada's apparently monopoly papers.

There is price discrimination in the advertising markets. National advertisers pay the most per million (one thousand column lines), local advertisers the least. The Canadian pattern in general is very similar to that of the US dailies in terms of pricing to both readers and advertisers.

Non-price competition by Canadian newspapers takes many forms. As in the United States, tabloid format, zoned editions, magazines, television guides, special sections and colour photographs have been employed in order to attract readers and hence advertisers. As in the United States, newspapers' share of total advertising revenues has been declining.

Duopolies are inherently unstable. Since 1981 Thomson had been sending satellite editions of its Toronto *Globe and Mail* to most major Canadian urban centres even if it owned the local daily too. When Southam's two Vancouver papers in British Columbia were on strike early in 1984, the *Globe*, within a week, introduced a four page British Columbia supplement. *Globe* circulation in Vancouver quadrupled. The move by Thomson reflected the adaptability of the latest technology and of the journalists too. The BC section was staffed by laid-off Southam employees and described as a 'temporary service' by a *Globe* vice-president. This example of newspaper competition in Canada in the 1980s showed that even when two chains have apparently split up the market, they are still rivals and prepared to take advantage of each other. They are therefore formidable potential entrants to each other's market, curbed as much in Canada by fear of government reaction as of each other.

To deter potential new entrants, existing newspapers adopt different strategies. In Vancouver, to prevent entry by the upstart Sun Publishing tabloid, publishers of the *Toronto Sun*, *Edmonton Sun* and *Calgary Sun*, Southam converted its morning paper in Vancouver, *The Province*, to a tabloid format in 1983 but continued its profitable *Vancouver Sun* as an all-day broadsheet. Southam also added colour and new sections.

Collusion against the public interest is always suspect in highly concentrated industries. An important test case of Canadian competitions policy involving newspapers took place in 1983. In the 1970s, both Winnipeg and Ottawa had had competing newspapers and the Jackal effect was in process in both cities. Early in 1980, Thomson bought out the Financial Post newspaper chain. As a result he acquired the money-losing Ottawa *Journal*, so that Southam and Thomson each had a loser and a winner in either Ottawa or Winnipeg. In August 1980 both chains closed their losers giving Southam a monopoly in Ottawa and Thomson one in Winnipeg.[20] The Canadian government claimed there had been a conspiracy against the public. They laid eight charges of anti-competitive conduct. The government eventually lost the case on every count. The newspaper chains' defence was that they had each independently made their decisions for good business reasons but had discussed the closures and had agreed together to shut down both papers at the same time. The closure of the two papers led to a Royal Commission, a case before the Supreme Court and a proposed new Newspaper Act. The proposed Act died on the Parliamentary order paper. It would have put a ceiling on corporate concentration in the industry, forced Thomson to sell some newspapers and provided government financial assistance to aid smaller newspapers and to subsidise foreign bureaus in order to recreate a more competitive press.[21]

Industrial organisation studies show that potential competition can have as big an influence on firms' conduct as actual competition. In the changing world of communications huge conglomerates wait on the sidelines observing all the media. In 1983, the telephone company, Bell Canada, created Bell Canada Enterprises which acquired printing plants, business paper publishers and city magazines. With a quarter billion dollars a year to invest, Bell Canada, or any other large conglomerate, might well be attracted to potentially profitable newspaper markets. In Canada the newspaper market is unusual in that it is still growing and could accommodate new entrants.

These observations raise one weakness in the proposed Canadian Newspaper Act. It would limit expansion by the major chains. Often small chains in Canada enjoy powerful local monopolies. The most likely challenge to them comes from the major newspaper chains. Should the proposed legislation ever be enacted, the potential competition of new entrants from this source, Southam and

Thomson, would be eliminated, so in effect not increasing competition but lowering it. Discouraging foreign investment in the Canadian media to maintain cultural independence also reduces potential competition. Likewise proposals in the Act to subsidise newspaper bureaus raise dangers of government influence and dependency. The Kent Report itself noted, 'The impulses to censor and control information run deep in the most benevolent of governments.'[22]

Legal restraints on the press in Canada are imposed by both federal and provincial governments. Libel laws, labour relations laws, official secrets acts and obscenity laws all constrain editorial content. A Freedom of Information Act was passed in 1983. Economic support in Canada takes the form of cheap postal rates, sales tax exemptions, income tax provisions discriminating against foreign publications and ownership of weak anti-combines and competition law.[23]

Performance

Canadian newspapers in terms of economic performance in 1986 do not merit the gloomy assessment of the Kent Report in 1980. Local daily newspaper competition is not viable in Canada in most markets which are too small to sustain competing dailies. Competition comes from the other media. Large chains have the resources to update capital, develop and underwrite new products such as *The Globe and Mail*, train journalists, offer job mobility to improve editorial content and use countervailing power to offset large advertisers' pressures on editorial content. They are also potential competitors in each other's markets. There is no evidence that the independent *Toronto Star* or the small Irving chain has any advantage over Thomson and Southam in terms of economic performance or contribution to open discussion and to freedom of information. The large chains have used their size to pressure unions to allow modernisation so contributing to progress, to save failing newspapers so contributing to employment, to target audiences for advertisers so contributing to efficiency, to combat actual and potential political and advertiser pressure on content, so contributing to equity. Inevitably a mixed blessing, local content and local feeling may have suffered, though the Kent Report produced little data to support this contention.

AUSTRALIA

Introduction

There are many comparisons between Canada and Australia. For these reasons, the Australian and Canadian newspaper industries are examined in the light of each other, Australia having developed in Asian isolation, Canada under the shadow of her huge effusive neighbour to the south.

Australia's population, however, is not only smaller than Canada's at 15 million, but very differently distributed. The bulk of the population lives in the six state capital cities. Other cities by comparison are small and there are few medium-size Australian cities.

Basic conditions

Demands

Australians are avid newspaper consumers. In 1984, 63 dailies had a combined circulation of nearly five million, about the same as Canada. There are also 470 non-dailies with a circulation of nearly nine million. Australia rates high on a daily newspaper per capita basis.

Unlike Canada, the general trend in per capita circulation in Australia has been falling for the last 30 years. As in other developed countries evening papers such as Melbourne's *The Herald*, Brisbane's *The Telegraph* and Perth's *Daily News* have been hardest hit.

There are several explanations for high consumption in Australia. First, Australia was settled later than Canada and America and many immigrants brought the newspaper habit from Britain. Second, radio and television competition for readers' attention and advertisers' dollar was slow to develop in Australia. In 1982 in addition to the National Broadcasting Service there were 134 commercial broadcasting stations, compared to 20,000 stations in the US and in Canada. Television broadcasting was also a late starter. In 1982 there were just 50 commercial television stations operating under licence from the Australian Broadcasting Tribunal. In other words, government restraint has tended to curb the degree of competition for newspapers from broadcasting. Though the bulk of Australian newspaper titles are rural publications, the greatest volume of

Table 8.4: Major Australian newspapers with circulations, 1985

Adelaide	The Advertiser (1858)	232,000
	The News (1923)	168,000
	Sunday Mail (1912)	252,000
Brisbane	The Courier Mail (1933)	218,000
	The Telegraph (1872)	140,000
	Daily Sun (1901)	140,000
	The Sunday Mail (1933)	351,000
	Sunday Sun (1901)	371,000
Melbourne	The Age (1854)	236,000
	The Herald (1840)	294,000
	The Sun-News Pictoral (1922)	562,000
	Melbourne Sunday Press (1973)	125,000
	Sunday Observer (1971)	101,000
Perth	The West Australian (1833)	233,000
	Daily News (1840)	103,000
	Sunday Times (1897)	251,000
Sydney	The Australian (1964)	124,000
	Australian Financial Review (1951)	59,000
	Daily Mirror (1941)	315,000
	Daily Telegraph (1879)	267,000
	The Sydney Morning Herald (1831)	256,000
	The Sun-Herald (1953)	606,000
	Sunday Telegraph (1939)	580,000

Source: Editor and Publisher Year Book, 1986.

newspapers in such a highly urbanised country as Australia are found in the metropolitan areas. Until very recently, distance prevented the development of newspapers with a genuinely national circulation, the exceptions being *The Australian* and *Australian Financial Review*. On a weekly basis *The Bulletin, The National Times* and *National Review*, qualify as nationals. For dailies, the costs of distribution, at least in the pre-satellite publication era, have made national newspapers non-viable.

Urban, affluent and middle-class therefore summarises demand for Australian newspapers. The market is dominated by the large-city dailies with a second tier to meet the requirements of smaller cities, rural areas and special interests. Such a description might suggest very little competition between newspapers, with local monopoly newspapers meeting local needs as in most smaller cities in North America or Britain, and the larger-city newspapers fragmenting the city market to create their own niche. In fact a somewhat homogeneous Australian society leads to newspapers which reflect this character. There are no newspapers to match the best or the worst of North America or Britain. Markets are too small and uniform for significant market niches to be worth exploiting. One consequence of this is that newspapers from different newspaper groups compete head-to-head in metropolitan areas to a degree not found in North America.[24]

Amongst the metropolitans, morning newspapers are usually home-delivered and tend to be more serious 'news' papers, whilst afternoon papers are sold on the street and emphasise entertainment and soft news. Tabloid formats have long been popular for both popular newspapers, as in Britain and recently in Canada, but also for more serious morning newspapers such as Sydney's *Daily Telegraph*.

In Australia the late start of television was preceded by a decline in the rate of growth of newspaper circulations which began in 1954. In other developed countries television was introduced earlier and has been blamed for the decline in newspaper readership and afternoon sales. The Australian case is unique and suggests that, even without the advent of television, newspaper circulation growth would have slowed.[25] It tends to strengthen the view that broadcasting and newspapers are complements as much as substitutes. Consumers want both. In Australia, the advent of television made little impact on the mix of quality and popular papers implying that if television whets the appetite for in-depth coverage, that in-depth coverage comes as much from populars as qualities. In fact, for analysis, Australians look to weeklies such as *The Bulletin* and *The National Times*, and not dailies.

Australia has one national daily newspaper, *The Australian*, established in 1964 and a money-loser until 1986. The *Australian Financial Review* also has pretensions to be a national but sells mostly in the two major commercial centres, Sydney and Melbourne. *The Australian* is a newspaper with many similarities to *The Globe and Mail* in Canada. Like the *Globe*, it seeks an up-market audience. Both have relatively small circulations even by their own national standards, *The Australian* had daily sales of 153,000 in 1974, 121,000 in 1979 and 124,000 in 1985. Both exert some influence amongst the country's leaders and elite. Both are owned by owners with reputations for only being concerned with the bottom line, Murdoch in Australia, Thomson in Canada, though both owners in the past decade have been prepared to lose considerable amounts running *The Times* of London. Power, influence, prestige and potential income justify the efforts.

Murdoch's *The Australian* was used in 1973 firstly to help the Labour government of Prime Minister Whitlam gain office and later to help undermine him. Some commentators ascribed the fall in circulation of *The Australian* in the mid-1970s to Murdoch's later opposition to Whitlam.[26] Such clear political positions in editorials can be interpreted as sound economic investments. For example, in 1980 Murdoch was allowed to purchase *The Times* in London without reference to the Monopolies Commission only because he had supported Thatcher strongly in 1979 in the tabloid *Sun*. Likewise in 1980, US finance for Murdoch's purchase of new Boeing 767s for Ansett Airlines in Australia was speedily forthcoming because of his support for Carter in his *New York Daily News*.[27] Clearly the Liberal Party in Australia was indebted to Murdoch for *The Australian*'s help in undermining Whitlam. In 1981 the debt was called.

Until 1974, Murdoch had been very supportive in his newspapers of the Australian Labour Party and of Prime Minister Whitlam. A year later, in 1975, he was active in the campaign to unseat Whitlam which led to the unprecedented dismissal of the Prime Minister by the Governor General. Murdoch claimed it was Whitlam's incompetence that cause his turn-around from supporter to opponent of Whitlam. Others reported that it was pique, that Whitlam had socially and politically distanced himself from the media including Murdoch and, more importantly, had refused to give Murdoch a licence to develop bauxite resources. As with oil and television, such licences are worth tens of millions of dollars and represent the pay-off for political support. Whitlam's refusal stemmed from the fact that Murdoch's application was for a joint venture with the American Reynolds Corporation and represented unwelcome foreign investment, contrary to the Whitlam mandate.[28]

Murdoch's shift from Whitlam-supporter to Fraser-supporter was so vehement that in 1974 there were strikes at *The Australian* and the *Sunday Mirror* by journalists and printers over alleged bias in the papers. In Australia there is no '*clause de conscience*' to prevent such editorial switches and Murdoch continued his support for the Liberals. It was six years before Fraser repaid Murdoch.[29]

Sixty per cent of all Australian advertising expenditures are made in Sydney and Melbourne. In Australia individuals are limited by law to holding two television stations. The two largest and most desirable cities to have stations in are Sydney and Melbourne. By 1979 two media firms, Fairfax and Packer already had stations in those cities. In 1979 Murdoch bought a television station in Sydney. A station in Melbourne was a desirable complement and Australia's largest private airline Ansett owned one there. So Murdoch bought

Ansett for its television licence. In 1980 the Australia Broadcast Tribunal rejected Murdoch as owner of the Ansett Channel 10 Station in Melbourne on the grounds that he was not appropriate. The Liberal government used its majority to change the Broadcast Act, reducing the criteria for ownership to financial, moral and technical competence. Murdoch got his Channel 10.

Supply

The Australian press is one of the freest in the world with no censorship. Libel laws are similar to those of Canada and the United States so that editors have considerable protection under the libel laws. Still there is generally benign government influence via government control of the broadcast media, labour laws including compulsory arbitration, limitations on cross-media ownership, anti-trust laws, subsidies and taxes.[30]

Australian labour law differs from that of Britain and North America. In terms of economic efficiency, the labour system seems to work relatively well for the Australian newspaper industry. Their disputes record compares favourably with that of most Western countries.[31] It is beyond the scope of this book to discuss the philosophical niceties of compulsory arbitration but Australia has not seen the mortal combats in the newspaper industry witnessed in Britain, Canada, France and the United States with the introduction of single-touch technology. Journalists belong to the Australian Journalists' Association. Journalists follow the British pattern of training, with long apprenticeship following high school rather than the North American system whereby journalists attend university.

Geography and history have affected the format of the news agencies in Australia. The Australian Associated Press (AAP) was created by the major daily newspapers and deals exclusively with the reception and distribution of international news. Internal news is transmitted by the Australian United Press (AUP) and the Queensland County Press (QCP) headquartered in Brisbane and responsible for northern Australia. The two agencies co-operate together. There is also a news bureau operated by the Perth newspapers which supplies Western news to the others. Because of the distances and small concentrated population of Australia these internal news agencies play a brokerage role unnecessary in other countries, where the international news agencies also handle national news. AAP is associated with Reuters.

Structure

Integration

In Australia newspaper distribution is carried out by independent newsagents. The Australian newsagents work under contract with the newspapers and are responsible for home deliveries. They also operate newsagents stores similar to those found in Britain.

There is vertical integration backwards into newsprint. Australian Newsprint Mills (ANM) is the sole Australian supplier of newsprint. Low import duties enable imports to make up for shortages of supply. ANM is part-owned by the major newspaper publishers except for Murdoch's News Ltd. News Ltd obtains newsprint from ANM but is large enough to enjoy some of the benefits of countervailing power. In fact, from 1972 to 1976 News Ltd. saved about $6 million as a result of long-term contracts made in 1966 over and above what ANM's shareholders-customers such as Fairfax would have paid for equivalent quantities.[32] Indeed Murdoch exploited his cost advantage in newsprint when he instigated a price war with Fairfax in Sydney in 1975 as discussed below.

Ownership

Ownership of the Australian newspaper industry is highly concentrated. Competition policy, as in Canada, has not been effective to offset the market forces working towards monopoly and the rise of media conglomerates. In Australia, three principal groups of newspaper owners have evolved and all have expanded into media conglomerates with non-newspaper interests. The groups are: The John Fairfax Group, headed by John Fairfax and based in Sydney; The Herald and Weekly Times Ltd Group (HWT), a public company based in Melbourne and better known as the Melbourne Group; and one of the world's most interesting and controversial newspaper and media companies controlled by Rupert Murdoch, News Ltd. Originally based in Adelaide, News Ltd was based in Sydney in 1986.

Whether measured in terms of share of total daily circulation or share of metropolitan markets or share of assets owned or influence, the Australian newspaper industry is highly concentrated as is the Australian media in general.[33] However unlike in Canada, in 1985 all major Australian cities had competition, usually from competing groups. In Melbourne, the Melbourne Group's *Herald* competed with the Fairfax's *The Age*. In Sydney, their *The Sydney Morning Herald* faces competition from Murdoch's *Daily Mirror* and *Daily Telegraph* whilst Murdoch's *The Australian* claimed national status and competed in all major cities.

No Royal Commissions similar to those of Britain and Canada have been established, although the Whitlam government of the early 1970s expressed interest in newspaper ownership and operations. This expression of interest spurred the formation of an industry-financed Australian Press Council. It seems that Australia's government, without commissions, has come to similar conclusions about the media as its commission-prone Commonwealth kin in Britain and Canada: basically, industry concentration has some unsatisfactory dimensions as regards the role of the 'fourth estate'. The industry has a natural tendency towards monopoly but government support via subsidies and intervention has possibly even greater dangers for freedom of speech. The Australian government therefore puts the problem, according to a general manager at Murdoch newspapers, in the 'too hard basket'.[34]

Like Canada's two major newspaper chains, the three Australian groups have found the home newspaper market too small. All have had to diversify into other media, publications and related activities within Australia or expand overseas.

Rupert Murdoch dominated the Australian newspaper industry in 1986. Worldwide revenues of News Corp. were $1.4 billion (US) in 1983 and $2.70 billion (US) in 1986. Since 1975 News Corp. has grown into one of the largest publishing companies in the world with nearly one hundred newspapers and magazines. Net income in 1986 was $169 million. In Australia its major newspapers were the *Daily Mirror* (Sydney), *Daily Telegraph* (Sydney), *Sunday Telegraph* (Sydney), *The Australian* (national), and the *Adelaide News* — his original family paper. In addition, in Australia Murdoch has oil and gas interests, half of Australia's largest private airline, Ansett, book-publishing companies and television stations. Murdoch has used his newspapers as cash cows to finance expansion into other fields.[35]

The roots of Murdoch's global empire go back 25 years to 1960. Duopoly can lead to intense rivalry. In Sydney in 1960 fear of competition from the Packer organisation led John Fairfax to take action leading to a restructuring of the Sydney newspaper market. Inadvertently, he gave Murdoch his chance. In Sydney, Fairfax had an advantage over Packer because Fairfax published a morning, an afternoon and a Sunday paper. Packer had just the *Daily Telegraph* in the morning and the *Sunday Telegraph*. When a family-owned evening paper, *The Mirror*, was put up for sale by the Norton family, Fairfax bought the paper. This kept Packer from gaining an evening paper and so gaining the economies of scale which had

Table 8.5: News Corporation; revenues, profits and margins, 1982 and 1984

		1982	1984
US:	Revenues ($US)	244	455
	Profits ($US)	4	24
	Margin (%)	1.8	5.3
Australia:	Revenues ($US)	477	586
	Profits ($US)	53	54
	Margin (%)	11.3	9.2
Britain:	Revenues ($US)	619	628
	Profits ($US)	12	59
	Margin (%)	1.9	9.5

Source: Business Week, 3 June 1985.

Table 8.6: Creative Accounting — News Corporation's balance sheet, 1985 (A$BN)

	pre-Metromedia[a] (30.6.85)	post-Metromedia (30.9.85)
1. Under Australian accounting rules		
Long-term debt	1.0	2.6
Other liabilities	1.0	2.5
Shareholders equity	1.3	2.9
2. Under US accounting rules[b]		
Long-term debt	1.3	4.3
Other liabilities	1.0	2.5
Shareholders equity	0.2	0.3

Note: a. pre-purchase Metromedia company.
  b. Treats preferred shares as debt and disallows revaluation of intangible assets (e.g. titles).
Source: The Economist, 15 February 1986.

heretofore been the Fairfax advantage. Fairfax should then have closed the paper. However, fear of government response to such a move and loss of public image led him to continue to publish *The Mirror* through a separate company. Circulation of *The Mirror* declined in the strange situation of two evening papers both produced by the same owner. Fairfax decided to sell *The Mirror*. Fairfax's managing director Rupert Henderson had known Rupert Murdoch's father, Sir Keith, who may have passed on his lack of

Figure 8.2: Simplified News Corporation structure, 1984

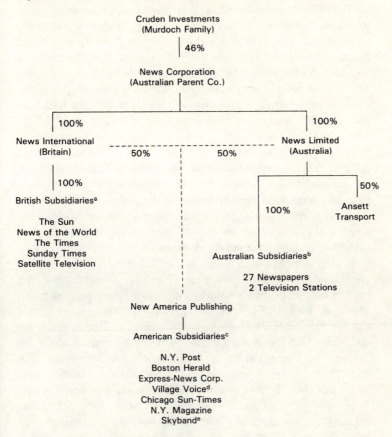

Notes: a. 28 operating companies.
  b. 51 operating companies.
  c. 10 operating companies.
  d. sold 1985.
  e. disbanded 1985.
Source: The Economist, 26 February 1984.

regard for his son's abilities. Rupert Murdoch appeared the ideal purchaser unlikely to have the ability to upset the market.[36] Henderson was wrong. Murdoch who had had a great regard for the *Daily Mirror* he had known whilst working in Britain in the 1950s, remodelled his Sydney *Mirror* on the Fleet Street *Mirror*. He moved it down-market, made it more sensational, and began to nibble at the

Fairfax *Sun*'s evening market.[37]

The Packer disadvantage in Sydney of not having an evening paper, and of not being able to buy one or start one without considerable risk and costs, led to their decision to sell the *Daily Telegraph* and *Sunday Mirror* in 1972. Not only did Fairfax have the *Sun* and Murdoch the *Mirror*, but Packer's downtown location made distribution of an evening in the return home rush hour a growing problem. They therefore decided to abandon newspapers for their television and magazine interests and to sell the *Telegraph* papers to Murdoch. He shrewdly paid $15 million for the titles and the goodwill, leaving Packer with their downtown real estate.[38] This freed Murdoch from obligations to the current Packer staff. Murdoch then started new printing and editorial operations at his own integrated headquarters where his own papers were already produced. Soon thereafter he merged the *Sunday Australian* and the *Sunday Mirror* into the *Sunday Telegraph* and produced all his four Sydney papers in one office so exploiting avaliable economies of scale.[39]

In 1979 when Murdoch sought to obtain a controlling interest in the Herald and Weekly Times company the Fairfax group bought a 14.9 per cent holding to prevent Murdoch dominating the Australian press. This made the John Fairfax Group the largest shareholder in Herald and Weekly Times. In effect Australia, again like Canada and at the same time, 1979, became dominated by two media conglomerates, the John Fairfax Group and Rupert Murdoch's News Corporation. The only other newspaper company of size was the Consolidated Press which was created out of part of Sir Frank Packer's former empire.[40]

In 1985, Herald and Weekly Times, with John Fairfax as majority shareholder, put out 16 metropolitan newspapers, 21 suburban newspapers and 20 country newspapers, more than a dozen magazines and had interests in six television stations and 14 radio stations. It also had interests in publishing, printing, property, insurance, transportation and newsprint. The John Fairfax Group, also owned 55 per cent of David Symes. John Fairfax published seven metropolitan papers, two country papers and in collaboration with David Symes, two metropolitans, five country and twelve suburbans. In collaboration with Consolidated Press, John Fairfax produced an additional five Sydney suburbans. John Fairfax's other interests included more than a dozen magazines, three television stations, seven radio stations, pulp and paper, newsprint, publishing, property, records, video and films.

Consolidated Press, also a conglomerate, published seven suburban papers, 14 county newspapers, and over two dozen magazines.

It had two television stations and five radio stations. Other interests included books, shopping centres, finance companies, publishing companies, video and sound productions, hotels and real estate. It covered the broad spectrum of entertainment, even owning the Australian Ski Co.

The international interests of Rupert Murdoch's News Corporation dwarfed the John Fairfax Group. In Australia in 1985, now just a minor part of his media empire, News Corporation was responsible for ten metropolitans, 40 suburban newspapers and 16 country newspapers. Two television stations, four magazines, books, films, publishing and records completed his media interests. News Corporation was diversified into transport, airlines, mining and lotto. Murdoch's overseas investments were mostly in the United States and Britain and are examined in the relevant chapters, but Figure 8.1 illustrates their extent. News Corporation also owned five newspapers and a radio station in New Zealand.

Conduct

I don't know any better than anyone else where the electronic age is taking us, or how it will affect a large newspaper company. But I do know it's going to have an impact. To prepare for that, and to have a position in that new industry, you want to be a major player in the production of entertainment programming.

Rupert Murdoch[41]

Biographies of both the life of Rupert Murdoch and of his successful newspaperman father, Sir Keith, emphasise a complex unsatisfactory relationship between the two. Whatever the psychological forces that motivate Rupert Murdoch, he has had a profound influence on newspaper industry conduct throughout the Western world.[42]

Murdoch's approach to selling newspapers has been controversial and often unpopular. The strategy was first applied to Australian newspapers. Basically he treats his newspapers purely as a business. Murdoch's approach is two-pronged. He cuts costs on the one hand. On the other, he makes no attempt to lead the reader. Instead he follows. He gives the readers what they want. He appeals to the lowest common denominator. This increases circulation. More readers generally mean more advertisers. Murdoch adopted the approach in 1955 at the age of 23, after Sir Keith's death, with the family's *Adelaide News* and by 1986 his formula had become familiar in cities around the world. Scandal, sports, news trivia and crime all packaged in a tabloid format.

Rupert Murdoch sought to identify other market niches within Australia. In 1964 he started Australia's first national newspaper, *The Australian* in Canberra. In 1967 he moved it to Sydney and began utilising facsimile networks to print first in Melbourne and later in Brisbane. Whilst other dailies used the AAP news service, *The Australian* also extensively used the Washington Post-Los Angeles Times service, AFT, stories from the quality English newspapers and similar sources. In 1983 *The Australian* still lost $4m but in 1986 profits were reported.

William J. Merrilees has observed that, in general, newspapers which compete, compete with product differentiation not price.[43] Typically rival newspapers compete in non-price dimensions. They use format, columns, supplements, special sections, special sports emphasis, business items, nutritional advice and the like to attract readers. In this area of non-price competition Murdoch has been an innovator with a daily nude (1969) and bingo (1981). Between 1975 and 1980 Sydney, however, witnessed the then unusual phenomenon of price competition between newspapers.[44]

The Sydney price war developed after News Ltd took over the *Telegraph* from the Packer Company in 1972. Prior to that Fairfax had been the price leader having papers in all three Sydney markets (morning-afternoon-Sunday) and the largest market share. For 31 years they had been the price leader. In 1974 a tougher Australian Trade Practices Act was passed making price agreements illegal. This may have explained Murdoch's failure to follow a 1975 price increase by Fairfax. Fairfax increased the *Sun*'s price to 12¢ from 10¢ and was not followed by the *Mirror*. In the post-OPEC cartel inflation period this amounted to an effective price cut by the *Mirror*. Observers, however, felt it was a challenge to Fairfax for price leadership, though Murdoch's motives are frequently unfathomable.[45] Furthermore, the evening paper would have been the obvious one to challenge since the evening products were less differentiated than the mornings and had more street sales, implying a higher cross elasticity of demand. The price war lasted for three and a half years until January 1979, by which time the *Mirror*'s cover price of 10¢ had remained unchanged whilst the consumer price index had risen 70 per cent. But Murdoch did not lose. It was estimated that the higher advertising revenue attracted to the *Mirror* as its market share increased brought Murdoch a net profit increase over the four years of $(A)2 million. Fairfax lost approximately the same amount. In 1979 Fairfax cut the *Sun*'s price to 10¢. Late in 1979 News Ltd increased the *Mirror* price to 15¢. Fairfax followed. In the summer of 1980 Fairfax increased price to 20¢. News Ltd followed. The next month the *Mirror* introduced bingo. Days later so did the *Sun*.

In other capital cities, even New York and London, only one evening newspaper has survived. This must be the prognosis for Sydney. The Sydney price war has illustrated the competitiveness that Murdoch has brought to the newspaper world. His price strategy brought him increased profits and market share. In 1981 he had 52 per cent of the Sydney evening market in what was a war of attrition.[46]

Content quality

Australian product quality is influenced not just by the owners but also by the legal environment.[47] Though Australia is acknowledged to be one of the freest presses in the world, editorial content is constrained by very powerful defamation laws and by the Trades Practices Act of 1974. The former curbs excesses of editorial content. The latter does not deal specifically with the newspaper industry but deals with false and misleading advertising in general and newspaper content falls under its umbrella. Fines can be as high as $275,000.

Australian press legislation varies from state to state. For example, Queensland has very severe obscenity laws and the 1954 Objectionable Literature Act includes a broad category of offences. Nationwide, contempt laws are powerful and judges may ban newspaper reports of trials until cases are over. Tough libel laws encourage newspaper self-censorship. Journalists prosecuted for defamation have to justify each part of the defamatory statement and journalist, editor, publisher, owners, even distributors may be held liable for damages which can be punitive. These laws contribute to the reputation for mediocrity that stigmatises Australian newspapers.

Performance

The Australian newspaper industry has served as a cash cow for the major owners, News, Fairfax and Consolidated, generating above-average profits. These have been used to finance other operations.

As in other countries, however, face-to-face competing newspapers and new entrants have been losers. In 1983 Rupert Murdoch made $8.5 million in Sydney from the *Daily Telegraph* which has a clearly established market niche. But his *Australian* after 20 years still lost money as did his *Daily Sun* in Brisbane. Likewise Fairfax has had to cross-subsidise the *Sun* in Sydney with profits from the *Financial Review*, the *National Times* and its television and radio subsidiaries.

NOTES

1. Culturally Canada is quite different from the USA. It has not been, unlike the USA, a 'melting pot'. It is a loose fragile federation held together particularly by fear of US annexation. It has a regional press.

2. *Canadian Dimension*, January 1982, p. 10.

3. In an attempt to rectify this the proposed 1981 Newspaper Act would have provided subsidies to Canadian news agencies.

4. In the future, satellites and the new information technology will overcome the fragmentation of the market caused by distance.

5. Canada, *Royal Commission, 1980*, p. 75.

6. This resulted from: (i) improved quantity and quality of live and syndicated news services; (ii) technological change causing the cost of labour-intensive local news collection to rise relative to the cost of non-local content; (iii) cost efficiency measures taken by chains; (iv) a lack of local newspaper competition; (v) a shift of function by local daily newspapers resulting in greater local coverage by such means as weeklies, freesheets and radio.

7. T. Kent, *Policy Options*, March 1982, pp. 2–34.

8. Data to test the desirability of alternatives is not available. How well the public is served depends partly on the qualities of individual owners, whatever their nationality, the firm's organisation and size.

9. T. Kent, *Policy Options*, pp. 2–34.

10. The Commission had been instigated by the simultaneous closures of Southam's *Winnipeg Tribune* and Thomson's *Ottawa Journal*. This gave monopolies to Southam's *Ottawa Citizen* and Thomson's *Winnipeg Free Press*.

11. *Editor and Publisher Year Book*, 1986, p. 183.

12. *Canadian Business*, June 1985.

13. Irving had been censured in 1969 by a Senate Commission on the Mass Media, and in 1975 by the Royal Commission on Corporate Concentration.

14. Canada, *Royal Commission, 1980*, p. 61.

15. Péladeau's Montreal *Sunday Express* closed in 1985, a Philadelphia tabloid closed in 1978 and the Winnipeg *Sun* in 1986 still lost money. For 1987, he announced plans to launch a new English daily in Montreal.

16. *Editor and Publisher Year Book*, 1985, p. 186.

17. Southam began in 1877 with the daily *Hamilton Spectator*. Until 1960 it was purely a newspaper chain. Since then it has doubled its number

of newspapers to 16, and has also established itself as a major Canadian printer, as a publisher of 75 business and professional journals, as the largest book retailer in Canada, and acquired interests in the broadcasting media in both Canada and Britain. Through its share-holdings in Selkirk Broadcasting, it has interests in five Canadian television stations, 11 radio stations, cable television and film productions. It has broadcasting interests in both the US and Britain. Newspapers remained the major source of revenues for Southam in 1985. Compared to Thomson, Southam is a small company.

Thomson began in 1934 when Roy Thomson, later Lord Thomson, bought the *Timmings Daily Press*. To many people the late Lord Thomson epitomised the commercial or profit-motivated press baron. His formula was in principle simple. Buy small monopoly newspapers, rigidly monitor costs, and allow editors total independence so long as they keep within budget. Since World War II, the formula has enabled his son Kenneth to become Canada's first billionaire and to create one of the great newspaper empires of all time and, as described in Chapter 5, grow spectacularly since 1960. The Canadian newspaper market proved too small for Roy Thomson's ambitions. Emulating another Canadian, Maxwell Aitken, later Lord Beaverbrook, he expanded into Britain (eventually to earn a peerage) and then into the United States. Lord Thomson died in 1976. By 1985, Thomson Newspapers Ltd owned 52 newspapers in Canada and 76 in the United States.

As with Southam, Thomson diversified using newspapers as a cash cow. Even before World War II, Roy Thomson had investments in radio. He was one of the initial sponsors of British commercial television (STV) in the 1950s. By 1986, Thomson had become a huge conglomerate with interests in North Sea oil, US oil and gas, Canada's three major department stores, real estate, electronic communication systems, radio and television, travel and insurance companies. Unlike Southam, for Thomson newspapers are no longer the principle business.

18. *Editor and Publisher Year Book*, 1985, p. 186.

19. CBC Radio, 'Good Morning Radio', 11 February 1986.

20. *Macleans*, 19 December 1983.

21. *Financial Post*, 26 September 1981.

22. Ibid.

23. Ibid.

24. There are no equivalents to the reputable *New York Times* nor the tabloid *New York Post*.

25. Inferior goods are goods which experience a decrease in demand as incomes rise. In the case of newspapers which are a time-consuming leisure activity, with higher income consumers can afford to spend their leisure on more enjoyable, if expensive, activities such as golf, boating, spectator sports and so on.

26. M. Leapman, *Barefaced Cheek*, p. 142.

27. Ibid.

28. Ibid., p. 153.

29. This time gap reflects the long-term nature of propaganda demand. That demand is like a long-term investment which may never pay off, but if it does may provide an excellent return.

30. *Macleans*, 26 September 1963.

31. Australian industrial agreements if successfully negotiated are ratified by the Commonwealth Tribunal. Where an agreement is not reached an award is imposed under compulsory arbitration.

32. William J. Merrilees, 'Anatomy of a Price Leadership Challenge', *Journal of Industrial Economics*, March 1983, p. 310.

33. Ibid.

34. *Macleans*, 26 September 1963.

35. *Fortune*, 20 February 1984.

36. M. Leapman, *Barefaced Cheek*, p. 162.

37. Reflecting his ambition he also began to buy shares in International Publishing, then owners of London's *Daily Mirror*.

38. In 1980 when Murdoch bought *The Times* from Thomson he tried to buy the titles only to avoid the union's stranglehold on the papers.

39. In 1980 Murdoch hoped to do the same thing at *The Times* by buying just the title and goodwill from Lord Thomson. However, in 1986 he achieved a similar result when he walked away from his Fleet Street premises and offered to give them to his former union employees.

40. M. Leapman, *Barefaced Cheek*, p. 162.

41. *Fortune*, 20 February 1984.

42. Murdoch had been lucky. He nearly stumbled at the outset. In 1962 Murdoch gambled on buying up £3 million worth of American television programmes for his Wollongang television stations outside Sydney. He then hoped to recoup the money by attracting more of the Sydney viewer and advertising to his station. Fairfax and Packer in Sydney thought he had overstepped himself. But Frank Packer decided to play it safe and bought a 25 per cent share in Murdoch's venture. Like Fairfax and the sale of the *Mirror* in 1961, Murdoch's success in television resulted from a tactical mistake by a rival, in this case Packer.

43. William J. Merrilees, 'Anatomy of a Price Leadership Challenge', p. 291.

44. In Fleet Street from 1982 onwards Murdoch has held down prices at the *Sun* and *The Times* to the financial discomfort of the *Mirror* and the *Guardian*.

45. William J. Merrilees, 'Anatomy of a Price Leadership Challenge', p. 291.

46. Murdoch's competitiveness has been all-embracing, extending to greenmail. In 1979 in Sydney when the block of HWT shares discussed above came up for sale Fairfax put in an offer. Murdoch made a better offer until eventually the share price had risen considerably. Whilst Fairfax was successful in obtaining a 14 per cent holding in HWT, Murdochs' intervention forced Fairfax to pay $20 million more than they would otherwise have had to pay. It reaped a $3 million gain for Murdoch as he unloaded his overvalued shares in the process.

47. *Europa Year Book*, (Europa Publications, London, 1985), p. 1143.

9

Communist World

Although the Communist newspapers as physical products are not very different from Western newspapers, they do have a very different function.

The term newspaper tends to convey a false image. News implies something previously unknown, not the columns, features, comics and entertainment that make up the bulk of modern Western papers. Communist newspapers likewise carry little real news. Their mission is not to attract readers to then sell to advertisers but rather to help mould public opinion in support of Party policy.

USSR

Supply

In the USSR all newspapers are supplied by state organisations of some sort such as trade unions, the Party and youth groups. For them, the capitalist concept of economic viability makes little sense. First, in the planned environment of a Communist system, prices for both productive inputs and outputs of final goods and services are arbitrarily imposed by state plans. Second, newspapers are produced for control and propaganda, not to generate revenues and make profits. In terms of the economics and opportunity costs of newspapers, the ends, social control, justify the means at almost any cost. Lenin said, 'The Press is the most strong and powerful weapon of the Party.'[1] Newspapers are a powerful means by which the Party can guide society. The newspaper supplies a service for the Party rather than the individual. It is the Party not the consumer who decides whether a particular newspaper is worth buying. The Party 'buys' the newspaper by permitting it to continue in publication, assuring the availability of inputs and underwriting it financially. Just as consumers in the developed world buy newspapers for entertainment, education, opinion and news, if they think the price worthwhile and advertisers buy it for reach, so the Party 'buys' the newspaper. It is a means to disseminate the ideas of Marxist-Leninism, to present information about the Soviet Union and other countries, and to encourage proper attitudes to the state, to work and to society. If the paper does not 'buy' adequate propaganda then the Party does not support the paper, just as advertisers do not support a Western paper with inadequate reach. Since much of what is popular and sells newspapers in the West — sex, scandal, crime, personalities, lifestyles — is of no use for propaganda and social control, they are not supplied however much Soviet people might like and be willing to pay for such things. There is no equivalent to the *Daily Mirror* in Britain or *USA Today* in the United States.

Since the Party trains and hires editors, they act as gatekeepers to ensure nothing harmful to the state is published. Newspapers accordingly are serious in tone, biased to support the Party and, according to a *Pravda* editorial in 1985, dull.[2]

In terms of physical inputs such as newsprint, presses and inks the state ensures these are available as part of the five-year plans at appropriate prices. News content comes largely from the news agency TASS. TASS was set up in 1925 as the central organ of information for the USSR. There are other news agencies which collect and distribute features, but features that are non-controversial and which in any case make up only a minor proportion of content. In each of the republics that make up the USSR there is a news agency, but these operate as extensions of TASS.

As one of the five international news agencies, TASS, had in 1985 over 200 overseas correspondents. It exchanged news with Reuters, AFP, UPI and AP and with 50 national news agencies. TASS distributed only what it considered appropriate content. Its gatekeeper function is a vital part of USSR security. Its value to the state is incalculable. It determines what information goes out and who gets what of what comes in. It uses security classifications for distribution similar to those used by the military. As part of the paraphernalia of state security and control, the total costs of TASS are unavailable, and probably incalculable and meaningless.

Editorial input for USSR newspapers is provided by so-called journalists. Their job is to support the state, not investigate, expose and report. There are legions of journalists. *Pravda* alone claims

40,000 correspondents, but few of these are professionally trained, full-time, or even paid. Lenin's theory of the press encourages involvement of the masses, so that submissions and letters from correspondents in other occupations are encouraged. They provide a source of newspaper content, information about USSR society and a means of social control. There are some professional journalists, many of whom are trained to university level and a five-year course is provided by Moscow State University for students from both the USSR and developing countries. They are taught that capitalist journalists are financially supported by capitalists and advertisers, therefore, Western journalists serve their capitalist masters' interest. Objectivity in the West is a sham, they are told. By contrast, Communist journalists are taught to believe they work for the benefit of society. This means selectively manipulating and presenting only that information which will achieve the Party's goals.[3]

It means preparing and maintaining support for events like the Afghanistan War, the Olympic boycott and the invasion of Hungary. It means encouraging suppport for Andropov's economic reforms and Gorbachev's anti-alcohol drive. It can mean suppressing the truth. It can mean not reporting airline crashes, ignoring Khrushchev's death and suppressing the details of the Chernobyl disaster. Lenin said 'objectivity is objectionable'.

Demand

Like Western newspapers, the USSR paper also serves two markets. First, there is the Party. Second, whilst there are no advertisers and no advertising market there is a huge reader market hungry for information.

USSR citizens are reported to spend up to three hours per day in queues or line-ups just to buy the necessities of life and the occasional luxury. They are consequently avid readers. Popular novels are in short supply, until 1984 the state planners, not the market, decided how many of each book should be produced.[4] In this environment of restricted supply there is an eager ready market for the 640 daily newspapers published in the USSR. Paid circulations in the USSR are impressive by any standard and newspapers reportedly cover their costs.[5] This apparent success of newspapers in the USSR reflects not the quality of the press, but the failure of the USSR media to meet consumer demand as defined in the West. Nothing better is available, there are few substitutes.

Table 9.1: Major USSR newspapers with circulations, 1984

Name	Founded	Daily circulation	Related organisation
Pravda (Truth)	1912	10.7m	Communist Party
Trud (Labour)	1921	10.5m	Trade Union
Komsomolskaya Pravda (Youth Truth)	1925	10.0	Communist Party
Izvestiya (News)	1917	8.6m	Supreme Soviet
Selskaya Zhizn (Country Life)	1918	8.5m	Communist Party
Sovietski Sport (Soviet Sport)	1924	3.9m	Trades Union
Sovietskaya Rossia (Soviet Russia)	1956	3.2m	Supreme Soviet
Krasnya Zvesda (Red Star)	1924	2.4m	Defence Ministry

In the USSR much demand for news and entertainment is not met. Whenever demand for any commodity is restricted, people seek to get that news and information elsewhere. Whilst unofficial publications meet part of that suppressed demand, it also emerges in less easily traced ways like listening to shortwave broadcast radio from other countries. Jamming these foreign broadcasts imposes considerable cost to the state. In 1985, the USSR spent between $100 million and $300 million, according to the US Information Agency, employing up to 15,000 technicians just to jam shortwave broadcasts of news and information from the United States, Britain, West Germany, Israel, South Korea and China.[6] It required 2,000 jamming transmitters in 100 cities to block foreign transmissions partially. The jamming emphasises that the money value placed on information control by the USSR state is very high. Whether *Pravda* or *Izvestiya* make profits or are cost effective, therefore, is not really important. Their propaganda value to the state would justify huge subsidies if necessary. The state puts a high value on a monopoly supply of their own information. If they did not, they could simply ban the sale of shortwave radios and deprive USSR citizens of all shortwave broadcasts. But for the thinly populated two-thirds of the USSR east of the Ural Mountains, the only means to reach them, educate them and control them in 1985 was by shortwave radio.[7] To this end there were 45 million receivers. The new information technology, of satellites, videos and computers will make it even harder and much more expensive in the future for the USSR to isolate its citizens. In 1983, 20 million Russians were thought to listen to illegal broadcasts.[8] The official line was that whilst broadcasting may confuse, the control of print is the key to information control, hence the importance of newspapers.[9]

Poland

On 13 December 1981, Poland declared martial law and the Solidarity era ended. This provided some economic insights about the Polish press and Eastern Bloc journalism.

First, despite news censorship laws and the closure of many publications for 'financial reasons', the majority of Polish journalists stayed at work. They had to be 'verified' by review boards as recognising the errors of Solidarity to do so, but it meant pay and position. Sixty journalists were sent to internment camps, 2,100 were fired or resigned but 80 per cent remained at work. During the Solidarity era membership in the Association of Polish Journalists had exceeded 10,000. Some journalists after martial law even joined the government, most notably the editor-in-chief of the liberal *Polityka* who became deputy prime minister.[10] What this reflects, though it looks like opportunism, is that many journalists in Communist countries see themselves as quasi-public servants. It reflects the different perspectives which journalists can have as to what constitutes good journalism. Whilst some resigned as a protest against martial law, others continued to serve the state just as civil servants in the West serve a change in government. It did not mean they condoned martial law.

Second, even in Communist countries people cannot be forced to read newspapers. After martial law was invoked it was reported that the major dailies experienced a fall in sales with many copies remaining unsold. By 1983 it was claimed there were 700 illicit publications in Poland and that Radio Free Europe was practically a second channel. Third, for the Roman Catholic Church, martial law led to the elimination of entry barriers. In return for accepting martial law the Church was allowed to start new publications. At the same time the Roman Catholic Church became a legal cover for Solidarity supporters' activities. Five years after martial law it was estimated there were 1,000 Polish underground publications.[11]

Structure

All newspapers in the Communist world, even the more individualistic Polish press in the 1980s, are strictly controlled. The newspaper industry in the USSR is part of a state-controlled information system which extended in 1984 to include:

(i)   640 daily newspapers.

(ii)   8,000 newspapers published in 55 languages.

(iii)   TASS news agency.

(iv)   Radio broadcasts to all the republics in 68 languages totalling 1,040 hours daily.

(v)   Radio broadcasts to all five continents in 64 foreign languages.

(vi)   Television telecasting totaling 1,900 hours per day to four-fifths of the population. In 1982, 81 cities had two or more stations and Moscow had six stations with Moscow I operating twelve hours per day.

(vii)   A monopoly of publishing extending to 236 publishing houses under the control of the State Committee for Publishing, Printing and Bookselling. The publishing houses specialise by subject; for example, medicine, science and education. Directly or indirectly the Committee controls every aspect of the publishing industry from inputs such as newsprint to printing, content, format and final distribution. All aspects of publishing are integrated both horizontally and vertically under the Committee.[12]

As in the West, newspapers operate in an environment where close substitutes compete for the readers' limited time and income. But the structure of that environment in the USSR contrasts with that of the West. The state decides on the quantity, content, quality and prices of all newspaper substitutes. This serves to strengthen demand for print in several ways:

(i)   USSR broadcast media content lacks the variety and popular entertainment content found on Western television and radio.

(ii)   The use of queueing as an allocation device provides people with more time to read.

(iii)   A good public transport system and few private cars encourages reading by commuters.

(iv)   Widespread apartment living in urban areas encourages small families and limits household obligations, so releasing time for reading.

(v)   Russia's northern climate necessitates indoor activities for much of the year.

(vi)   Low incomes combined with limited spending opportunities reduce competition for the Soviet consumers' time.

All in all, these factors mean enormous demand for reading material of all sorts.

The Soviet Union produces one-quarter of all books produced in the world. In 1980 1,760 million books were published. There were over 80,000 titles in the 89 different languages spoken in the USSR as well as in 56 foreign languages. These were sold through 14,000 bookstores and 34,000 kiosks located in the workplace. Despite this vast output, demand as understood in the West, was not met. Though price discrimination of sorts is practised with higher prices for adult fiction and lower prices for educational and children's books, markets are not cleared and there are shortages of novels and surpluses of many ideological and philosophical works. In 1984 for the first time, it was announced that if shortages of certain popular works occurred, including in 1986 those of Pasternak, further printings would be made.

The major daily newspapers are listed in Table 9.1 with 1984 circulations. The table reveals who is persuading whom. Product differentiation takes the form of identifying a particular market such as youth, military, industrial labour, agricultural works and then attempting to meet that market's requirements — as seen by the state.

Conduct

USSR newspaper content is carefully planned. In terms of product strategy there is much caution. Content and presentation is carefully discussed before publication by newspaper editors, themselves vetted by and working for the Party. Content is dissimilar to that found in the Western paper. The emphasis is on good news, more like advertising messages in the West, with reports of inspiring speeches, economic achievements and stories about outstanding workers. Pessimism, bad news, unless about capitalism, insoluble problems, and anything of a destabilising nature to society are excluded. News about personalities, gossip, comics, advertisements, travel, sports, crosswords are all largely ignored. And all is packed into a few pages. *Pravda*, for example, typically has six pages, other newspapers four.

Newspapers are more important than broadcasting in instructing the people about what to think, and also as a medium by which the Party is informed about what the people are thinking. Over half a million letters to the editors of the major newspapers are received each year and *Pravda* has 50 staff members whose sole jobs are to investigate letters. Since there is no competition for readers there is little incentive for scoops or even any urgency to report those events which it is in the state's interest to inform the people about. News as generally understood in the West, 'fresh information of something that has lately taken place' is replaced by news as 'something before unknown'. News is a privilege, not a right.[13]

The product strategy described above applies at all levels: national, regional and local. Newspapers in the republics as well as city and district newspapers and weeklies use the material received from TASS to comment, persuade and generally further the interests of the Party.

Prices are set by the state. In 1983 *Pravda* cost three kopecks or four cents at official exchange rates. Such figures have little meaning since the official exchange rate does not reflect purchasing power parity, nor does it tell one anything about USSR incomes. A more meaningful comparison is between what work time a typical Westerner takes to earn a paper in contrast to a USSR worker. In 1984 most US newspapers cost 25 cents. In 1984, the average US industrial wage was $21,000. In other words it took less than five minutes to earn enough to buy a newspaper, often with over 200 pages, mostly advertisements. In the USSR it took about the same, for six pages, with no advertisements.

In many ways the economics of USSR newspapers is simpler than that of Western newspapers. As essential parts of the state apparatus, they are funded by the government in a manner similar to defence or police funding. They are necessary, therefore the funding will be found; and like many government programmes worldwide, once in place there is an inertia to change them. As Table 9.1 shows, all but one Russian newspaper were started in the years immediately after the revolution. A lack of competition means that many of the product strategies incumbent on Western newspapers do not have to be followed. The pursuit of advertisers, keeping up with readers taste changes, timeliness, identifying potential new entrants, research and development, legal ramifications of firms' behaviour and maintaining cash flow are not relevant. So long as a Russian newspaper continues to meet state economic goals, its own economic survival is secure.

USSR economic goals are similar to the goals of Western economies: full employment, equity, economic growth, efficiency and a satisfactory balance of payments. To some extent the two economic systems, planned and market, are reflected in their respective newspaper industries. Both systems have their weaknesses.

Planned economic systems like the USSR's, hide unemployment as underemployment, and instead of the excess profits and failure to internalise all social costs of capitalist systems there are planned prices resulting in shortages and surpluses. Likewise, in economic terms, the ability of the Communist press to suppress bad news, violence, crime, glorification of the individual and material success, which in the West can demoralise readers, and instead to motivate USSR society to a greater economic contribution might add to economic performance. The price obviously is press freedom, freedom of speech and individual freedom. In any case, it is unclear that the sex and violence reported in the decadent Western press does lead to imitation, demoralisation or external costs. Compared to Communist workers, Japanese workers are models of productive efficiency in spite of a free press. In terms of content, the worst of Murdoch's American tabloids is equalled by the worst of his British, yet America is a much more violent society. And Britain is less violent than she was a century ago, before the popular press existed. A brief examination of the press and society suggests that the press is not omnipotent in its ability to motivate society to work harder, Russia's economic performance being a case in point, nor to degenerate into costly lawlessness and social disregard, as illustrated by Japan.

CHINA

Demand and supply

The Chinese claimed a total annual circulation in 1983 of 14 billion, about 45 million a day. As an 'important educational medium for the people and a channel to guard against moral pollution', the Chinese Communist Party is concerned about who does and does not have access to various newspapers.[14]

To monitor distribution, Chinese newspapers are sold by subscription and delivered by post. There are three distribution categories: 'public' or open to anybody, 'domestic' which are restricted to distribution only in China but with few restrictions and 'internal' which are very restricted and foreigners and most Chinese citizens cannot see them.[15]

Party attitudes are voiced in the *People's Daily* which is the official paper of both the Communist Party and the government. This contrasts with the USSR where *Pravda* is the voice of the Party,

Table 9.2: Major Chinese newspapers with circulations, 1985

City	Title		Circulation
Beijing	Beijing Ribao	Peking Daily	1,000,000
	Cankao Xiao		8,500,000
	China Daily (1981)		70,000
	Gongren Ribao	Workers Daily	1,700,000
	Economic Daily		1,500,000
	Guangming Ribao	Brightness Daily	1,500,000
	Jiefang Ribao	Army Daily	100,000
	Renmin Ribao	People's Daily	7,000,000
Changchun	Jilin Ribao		500,000
Chengdu	Chongoing Ribao		500,000
	Sichuan Ribao		1,350,000
	Fujian Daily		600,000
Guanshou	Guangxi Ribao		650,000
	Guandong Ribao		500,000
	Nanfang Ribao		1,100,000
	Yangcheng Wanbao		1,600,000
Guiyang	Guizhou Ribao		300,000
Hangzhou	Zhejiang Ribao		700,000
Harbin	Heilongjaing Ribao		500,000
Jaingsu	Hsinhua Ribao		900,000
Jinan	Dazhong Ribao		300,000
Kumming	Yunnan Ribao		300,000
Nanjing	Xinhua Ribao		900,000
Nanning	Guangxi Ribao		800,000
Shanghai	Jiefang Ribao		1,000,000
	Wen Hui Ribao		1,500,000
Shengyang	Lioniug Ribao		600,000
Tianjin	Tianjin Ribao		700,000
Urumqi	Zheiyang Ribao		700,000
Wuhan	Hubei Ribao		700,000
Xi'an	Shaanxi Ribao		500,000
Zhengzhou	Hainan Ribao		100,000

Source: Editor and Publisher Year Book, 1986.

and *Isvestiya,* that of the government. Other Chinese papers at the local and regional levels then follow the line of the *People's Daily,* as do the broadcasting media. Distribution figures are a poor indicator of Chinese demand. *Renmuir Ribao (People's Daily)* had a distribution of 6.9 million in 1985 but this included arranged distribution and office issues. It is, like *Pravda,* very boring and is not widely read but is important in that, as in the official Party paper, it sets the official line for the rest of China's press. This amounted to 103 newspapers and 1,433 periodicals in 1983. On the other hand *Cankao Xiao (Reference News),* with a circulation of 8.5 million, is thought to have 30 million readers, largely on account of its foreign news content. Distribution figures for Chinese papers therefore largely reflect government demand for propaganda, not reader demand.[16]

Lenin stated that the press had three roles: collective propagandist, agitator and organiser. Mao Tse Tung said it must be 'loyal eyes, ears and tongue' to the Party.[17] It must publicise Party decisions, educate the masses and link the masses to the Party. The function of the Chinese press fits the traditional Leninist-Marxist Communist mould notwithstanding the rift with Moscow. It is to propagate the official party line and encourage the pursuit of social goals rather than individual goals. To achieve this vital goal for one-quarter of the world's population, (greater than the USSR, Europe, Canada, Japan, Australia and the USA combined), might suggest a large newspaper industry. Yet in comparison to the other major powers the Chinese newspaper industry is small. (See Table 1.1). Many papers are just wall sheets or single sheets.

The Party view affects how Chinese journalists function. As a good press officer in the West is expected to be loyal to the government or corporation he represents, and to its policy changes, so a Chinese journalist is expected to be loyal to the Party and its policy changes. The why, when, where, who and how of Western news gathering is seen by the Chinese as superficial. Observation and interviews without involvement, it is believed, leads to inaccurate and incomplete reporting. A full picture requires input from the masses, hence the heavy reliance in China on reader input.

Chinese newspapers, like USSR newspapers, have a certain timeless quality. Content is carefully considered by Party officials before being printed and is often still relevant days and weeks after being received and being published. In this respect, it is like much soft news content in Western papers.

Since 1979 and the four modernisation programmes, China has wished to buy a better image overseas. Since foreign newspapers are prepared to buy, or pay for, the right to report on China, China has not had to pay the full cost of informing foreign correspondents. Rather, China has shown her commercial acumen by collecting an excess profit on each interpreter assigned to the foreign press. By 1983, the government had allowed 26 countries to send over 100 correspondents to China.[18] Given China's view that spot news is superficial and unrepresentative, she has not allowed foreign correspondents free access to collect news. Instead correspondents are isolated. They live in special compounds, must rely on interpreters, have limited contact with state officials and ordinary citizens and experience travel restrictions. The role of the interpreters is vital in filtering the news, acting as gatekeepers, and generally providing a subtle form of censorship. Provincial and local newspapers are not available to foreign correspondents so much background information is not available. What news foreign correspondents can gather tends to be accurate but incomplete and therefore misleading.

In fact, all the financial costs of reporting are born by the foreign press and China makes a profit on the assigned interpreters for whom it charged each correspondent $275 per month in 1983, yet paid them a little over $50. In 1983, keeping a correspondent in Beijing cost about $250,000 annually. The USA maintained 22, Japan 20, the USSR 2 and Canada, Britain, France, Italy, West Germany and Yugoslavia between 4 and 6 each.

The Party wants certain work units and individuals to have a genuine newspaper with authentic information and opinion from around the world.[19] *Reference Material* (Cankoa Zilia) provides this. Twice daily 80 to 90 pages are printed with translations from foreign wire services and newspapers. The paper cannot be bought nor can individuals subscribe to it. It is the basic sourcebook from which propagandists derive their information and only about two million Chinese qualify to see the paper.

Structure and conduct

Reference News (Cankoa Xiaoxi) had a reported circulation in 1982 of over eight million, one of the world's highest, and a readership several times that. *Reference News* is a four-page daily which might not be anticipated to circulate in a Communist state. Mao Tse Tung described its function as a 'vaccination to increase the political immunity of the cadres and the masses'. It consists entirely of translations from the foreign press.[20]

Until 1980 *Reference News* circulation was limited to middle-level Chinese officials. In 1980 *Reference News* announced:

Readers who have not been able to obtain subscriptions to *Cankoa Xiaoxi* may, in accordance with the subscription procedures, go to their local post offices for subscription upon presentation of a letter of certificate from the leadership organization at the people's commune for local (rural) units; or from the political organization at the regiment or above for military units.[21]

Although no longer restricted, the state still knows who buys the paper.

The four pages of *Reference News* carry in order: foreign news reports about China; political and economic news about the West; Third World news; science, sports and features. More than half the content in 1983 came from AP, UPI, Reuter and AFP, nearly one-quarter from European and Japanese publications and just two per cent from TASS. Though translations were verbatim, they were selective and served the Party's goals. Page two emphasised the US which was compared favourably to the USSR. Americans were termed 'foreign friends'.[22] With careful selection *Reference News* has become a powerful propaganda tool. Accurate but incomplete news can misinform.

The Chinese press in 1985 propagated the Party message and attempted to create certain attitudes. To that end, false information, partial information and innuendo were used.[23] Taiwan, which in the early 1970s had been ruled by 'a bag of thieves', was ruled by 'Mr' Chiang Kai-Chek after 1978. In *Reference News* Taiwan's high standard of living was still ignored and her problems magnified 'Prostitution is . . . a major industry'. Taiwan's 'progress' was translated as 'malpractice', China's own 'primitive' transport became 'uncomplicated', 'in almost everything' became 'in some respects' and so on.[24] The intent was to distort. The selective use of quotations to create a favourable image has its parallels in the Western press, noticeably in the field of advertising. A different parallel can also be made to Western quality papers. *The Times* of London is not very interested in CDE income group readers because *The Times* advertisers don't want to reach CDE readers. Likewise the Chinese Communist Party only wishes to educate certain cadres with *Reference News*. In both cases non-target groups may, but are not encouraged to, read the newspaper.

The Chinese press serves two markets: first, the Party and government's demand for propaganda and for information, particularly from letters: and second, the reader market for news information and to a limited extent entertainment. As in the USSR, there are limited entertainment alternatives. The central role of the press means demand in the first category is inelastic. The paper is an essential propaganda weapon for the government who will pay whatever price (subsidy) is necessary. Demand in the second category is limited by low incomes, low literacy rates and distribution difficulties. It is also limited by competition from the other broadcasting media which are also owned by the Party. In 1985 it

229

was too early to determine whether China would follow the pattern of other developing countries and leapfrog the newspaper phase as a means of providing information and entertainment for the masses. Clearly the Communist press in general does not supply the market for soft news and entertainment. The market demand is, however, there. In 1983, during its programme of increasing the use of markets, China introduced a more popular paper *Story* which was warmly received.

In 1985, Associated Press reported that 600 million Chinese lived in areas which had access to television on China's 40 million television sets, up from 200,000 sets in 1975 and three million in 1981.[25] In 1985 China claimed production of ten million sets with pent-up demand for colour sets. As a result imported sets at $350, or one year's salary for an average worker, sold well. Programming came under the authority of the Ministry of Radio and Television which operated two state networks and 52 local stations. There was about ten hours per day of programmes; news, sports, lectures, plays and cartoons were typical content. Since 1979 there have been commercials aimed at promoting a variety of products from shampoos to computers.[26]

Prices are generally an effective means of rationing worldwide. *Reference News* sold for six yuan per month in 1982 at a time when average per capita income in China was 35 yuan per month.[27] Still millions subscribed to the four-page daily. *Cankoa Xiaoxi* met a demand for news and entertainment unavailable elsewhere in China. In the West in 1985 an average worker would pay about one-half to one per cent of his income for perhaps 15 pages of editorial. In China he paid about ten per cent for four pages of *Reference News*, or about 30 times as much, allowing for the space-saving efficiency of Chinese script. Since 81 per cent of *Reference News* content came from the major wire services, Reuters (22%), AP (22%), AFP (20%) and UPI (17%), the conclusion must be that the Chinese charged what the traffic would bear given the state's desired circulation.

China's shrewd pricing policy can be seen elsewhere, for example in its heavy mark-up on translators for foreign press correspondents in China discussed above and the hefty prices it set for an advertisement in the English-language paper *China Daily* established in 1981 and distributed in North America as well as China. The opening of China's economy in the 1980s opened up many new markets including a new newspaper market. With *China Daily*, the party planned to reach three groups. First, English-speaking Chinese in China where 25 million people were claimed to be learning English; second, the non-Chinese resident group; third, foreigners abroad.

China Daily's inception involved the publishers of *The Age* in Melbourne, David Symes and Co. Ltd.[28] They provided editorial, managerial and technical advice and arranged the purchase of four state-of-the-art web-offset presses capable of producing 40,000 copies hourly. In 1983 circulation in China of the eight-page paper was 70,000. As a product it was more like a Western paper. It avoided the traditional Chinese journalistic style which interprets news and commentary and instead offered shorter stories and more foreign news. Content came mainly from Xiaoxi news agency. Having a well-targeted audience, the Chinese charged a respectable $2,625 for a full-page advertisement. Advertisers included both Western companies wanting to crack the Chinese market and Chinese firms wishing to create an image in the West.

In the 1980s, China's emphasis on economic progress and the decision to open China to foreign capital, technology and ideas brought rapid change. Late in 1983 China's leaders decided not all the changes were beneficial and a campaign to eliminate 'spiritual pollution' was introduced.[29] One victim was the newspaper tabloid *Story*. *Story* had been introduced earlier that year as part of the four modernisations to meet demand for 'soft news'. *Story* proved too successful. It quickly achieved a circulation of two million. Readers wanted the product but the main buyer, the state, did not. *Story*, therefore, was closed. Parallels to Western newspapers such as *The Washington Star*, which closed in 1982 though it had a good readership, can be drawn. In the case of *The Star*, the paper did not satisfy advertisers' requirements. The dull unwanted *People's Daily*, meanwhile, responded to the ideological shift with a number of self-critical articles but continued production.

Whereas only about five per cent of American or British workers work in agriculture, the majority of Chinese still do, and 79 per cent of the population is rural. In 1980, *Zhanguo Nongmin Bao* (The Chinese Peasant Paper) was launched as a bi-weekly to explain the government's economic policies for rural areas in simple terms. Within a year circulation was 700,000, twice that of *The Times* of London. The paper's role was two-fold. First, to educate the peasants; second, to inform the government. Each day the paper received 700 letters from peasants. Many were for information, or education, about production, cultural and Party matters. Other letters request counselling on family and moral questions. But they also informed the central Party about rural affairs. Demand for *Zhanguo Nongmin Bao* reflected higher peasant incomes and literacy levels. It was the first peasant paper with individual subscriptions, previously only production brigades or people's communes had subscribed.[30]

Up until the mid-1960s many local newspapers of both a general and special nature were published in China. In the 1960s the state decided many local county newspapers were not worth the price to them, the state. Despite reports of considerable dissatisfaction from readers over closures, the government decided that local broadcast radio was a cheaper and more efficient way for the state to inform, educate and control peasants. Remaining local newspapers became more special interest in nature and provincial newspapers increased circulation. By 1980 in Hunan province, for example, no country newspapers at all were published. Only four local newspapers in the province remained, all municipal papers. However, during the 1970s circulation of the four-page provincial daily *Hunan Ribao* tripled to 700,000.[31]

Hunan Ribao employed 240 editors and correspondents, 50 clerical staff and 200 printers who worked for various propaganda (public relations) departments of various units in the province. Readers sent it 100 letters per day. About 50 per cent of the four pages of the daily were devoted to reports from the national news agency Xiaoxi. It claimed a total readership in 1980 of over three million. Advertisements were included in the provincial *Hunan Ribao* but contributed approximately five to ten per cent of space and five per cent of total income. In selling space for advertisements price discrimination was used with lower rates for cultural announcements such as notices about books, sports and films.

The municipal or city paper *Datay Bao* in Shiaxi province reflected the financial difficulties of remaining local papers as they faced competition from radio. Representatives of *Datay Bao* stated that one copy sold for two *yen* but cost four to five *yen* to produce. However, as in the USSR, costs are a nebulous term. At *Datay Bao* they paid Y20,000 to Y30,000 per year for approximately 30,000 tons of newsprint and Y300 per day for printing. Thirty editorial staff and clerks received Y720 per annum each or Y21,000 per annum. Printing three hundred days per year, newsprint, print and labour alone cost over Y140,000. Yet they claimed the Party subsidy of Y75,000 covered more than half their costs. Wire services, distribution, capital costs and the like were not apparently to be included as costs.

Datay Bao received less Party support than provincial papers. Whilst state plans guaranteed newsprint allocations for provincial papers, *Datay Bao* had to negotiate with paper mills for their above and beyond plan surplus output. Though they paid the state price for newsprint, quality was lower, and transport and negotiation costs higher. Furthermore, the content of local broadcasting meant radio was closer to local papers than to provincial papers, so increasing competition.

In China, therefore, newspapers emphasise national, provincial and special interest propaganda requirements. Radio meets the needs of the Party for local propaganda. It is cheaper and more efficient than local newspapers for state purposes. A typical, simple broadcasting network to serve 750,000 cost Y100,000 a year to run and required a staff of under 30. Local radio broadcasting also has the advantage that it can be heard by illiterates, adapt to local dialects, be imposed in the factories and fields and be used as a mass address system.

In the West, broadcasting and newspapers compete, but also complement each other, at all levels from local to national. In China, radio is used to meet local general propaganda needs. From the state point of view, such a fragmentation of the market is efficient. In terms of meeting consumer demand it is a failure, and emphasises once again that in Communist countries the media primarily serves the Party.

NOTES

1. Marshall MacLuhan, *Understanding the Media* (McGraw Hill, New York, 1964), p. 156.

2. *The Economist*, 11 January 1986.

3. Assertions both that capitalist and Marxist journalists serve the interests of their masters and not their readers have a ring of truth. At all newspapers in the free world as well as the Communist world, hiring, promotion and rewards depend upon performance and that means working within the system and not offending the paymaster.

4. CBC Radio, 11 August 1984.

5. M. Walker, *The Power and the Influence* (Quartet Books, New York, 1982), p. 64.

6. *Los Angeles Times*, 15 December 1984.

7. Ibid.

8. Ibid.

9. Information control is used for both political and economic reasons. It prevents USSR citizens knowing how low their standard of living is when

compared to those of the West and other Eastern Bloc countries.

10. *Columbia Journalism Review*, October 1984, p. 36.
11. Ibid.
12. *Europa Year Book* (Europa Publications, London, 1985), p. 899.
13. *The Economist*, 11 February 1986.
14. *Journalism Quarterly*, Summer 1982, p. 240.
15. *Problems of Communism*, July 1984, p. 59.
16. *Nieman Reports*, Winter 1980, p. 32.
17. *Journalism Quarterly*, Summer 1982, p. 240.
18. *Gazette* (33), 1984, p. 87.
19. Ibid.
20. *Journalism Quarterly*, Summer 1982, p. 240.
21. Ibid.
22. Ibid.
23. *Problems of Communism*, July 1984, p. 65.
24. Ibid.
25. *Time*, 28 November 1983.
26. *The Economist*, 8 July 1985.
27. *Problems of Communism*, July 1984, p. 62.
28. *Macleans*, 13 June 1983.
29. *Time*, 28 November 1983.
30. *The China Quarterly*, June 1981, p. 322.
31. Ibid., p. 330.

10

Third World Countries

It is hard to generalise about a potential audience of three and a half billion readers but Third World newspapers are characterised by poor circulation, low advertising revenues, considerable regulation and slow growth. As economic enterprises most Third World newspapers are barely viable. The basic market conditions, to say nothing of political and social conditions, are hostile to the development of a broad-based mass-circulation newspaper industry. Before examining specific cases, some general comments are made about the nature of the Third World newspaper industry.

AN OVERVIEW

The newspaper industry of the Third World in terms of size and circulation is an industry in its infancy. Whether it will ever grow up and, if so where, is debatable. The Third World newspaper industry in the 1980s faces obstacles to growth similar to those of the nineteenth-century Western press, but compounded by further difficulties which the nineteenth-century Western press did not face. These include low literacy,[1] high prices relative to incomes,[2] high input prices[3] and low advertising expenditures.[4] In the West these obstacles to growth were largely overcome by 1900. They create a vicious circle. High prices and low literacy lead to low circulation, and low circulation means limited advertising revenues to subsidise newspaper costs. Newspaper prices therefore remain high for the number of pages and content since circulation revenues have to be the main income source.

In the Third World, however, there are many other problems which did not face the early Western press and are not easily

235

overcome even if the other obstacles are removed. These include:

(i)   Government opposition. In much of Asia, Africa and South America, democracies have been overthrown. Newspapers and a free press were associated with the former elite and former colonial powers. There is often a negative legacy effect, a state bias against newspapers.

(ii)   Language diversity. In Africa there are 1500 different native tongues, in India 1600.

(iii)   Inadequate transportation and distribution facilities.

(iv)   Alternative methods to inform and influence. Radio, and television which was vastly extended in the 1980s with satellites such as Intel 83 reaching nearly half a billion people in India, have pre-empted the newspaper. The mass-newspaper stage in economic development has been leapfrogged.

(v)   Alternative vehicles for advertisers. Foreign magazines such as *Time* and *Reader's Digest*, domestic weekly publications and broadcasting divert potential advertising from daily papers.

(vi)   Low total advertising expenditures.

(vii)   A great variety of consumer goods which did not exist in the nineteenth century. Items such as watches, ballpoints, cheap fashion goods as well as transistor radios compete for the potential newspaper dollar.

(viii)   Censorship, a lack of a free press tradition and the risk of harsh arbitrary penalties for antagonising the powerful.

(ix)   Inadequate access to financial capital and alternative safer venture opportunities for available capital.

(x)   Import restrictions on newspaper capital equipment and supplies.

(xi)   A lack of capital equipment suitable for non-Roman scripts.

(xii)   A lack of skilled labour able and willing to work in the vernacular languages.

(xiii)   Social and cultural obstacles. Feudal, tribal and non-verbal traditions all work against newspaper demand.

Since non-Communist Asia (less Japan) and Africa accounted for two-thirds of the world's population in 1986, not all these generalisations apply to every country. Even within one country, for example India, there is great diversity in the basic conditions of the press. India has a huge middle class. Statistics about the African and Asian press are unreliable and so many aspects of market conditions are impossible to quantify. Still, common themes can be identified and illustrated.

Much of the Asian press can trace its origins back to the Western colonisation and Western missionary work in the nineteenth century. That influence is still strong. Not unrelated to the former role of a colonial press, the press is often still regarded as a vehicle to support the state and to provide propaganda in pursuit of stated social, economic and political views, as did the colonial press. In other words, the Third World press frequently fits into the authoritarian model. Furthermore, radio and television have already been introduced to most of the Third World. Broadcasting media have preceded the widespread circulation of newspapers and the development of a newspaper habit. In fact they may have pre-empted it. Newspapers as a means of mass communication have experienced a leapfrog effect. Also, most news now comes from Western news dominated wire services. They supply 80 per cent of news to India.[5] Governments tend to oppose these news imports because of their potentially disruptive effects on society and their potential to be used against the government interest.[6] Also the broadcasting option creates an economic constraint by providing a close substitute and so diminishing the potential audience, profitability and influence of the press. A year's subscription for an average Indian to a newspaper in 1986 would take about a month's earnings, for a Westerner about a day for a superior product. Few Indians make that financial sacrifice when free radio, albeit a government monopoly, is available.

In the Third World, there is an important distinction between the vernacular press and the English-language newspaper. The latter has an influence far in excess of the proportion of English-speaking people. The reasons for this are partly traceable to the colonial heritage, the fact that English is the international language of business and technology, and the high correlation between the English speaking and the wealthy. English is the bridge between the educated, government elites and business. The English-language newspapers attract the bulk of advertising because of their high income audience. Inputs of capital, machinery, newsprint, news and labour also favour them. English is the language of the major news agencies and capital markets. Much machinery comes from the English-speaking countries and is designed to use the Roman alphabet. English is an economical language in terms of the space

237

it needs to convey a message. The most educated and qualified editors and journalists often speak English. English-language newspapers can attract the most able. Finally, distribution tends to be easier for the English-speaking newspapers whose market is largely in the larger metropolitan areas. Given the poor transportation infrastructure of many Third World countries, distributing newspapers to rural areas is, in itself, a major problem. The following case histories illustrate the range of obstacles facing many newspapers in the Third World in the late twentieth century.

INDIA

India accounts for 20 per cent of the world's population 30 per cent of the Asian population (less Japan) and only four per cent of the world newspaper market. Of that, the circulation of English-speaking newspapers constitutes 35 per cent of the market, Hindu newspapers 45 per cent, and the other 12 major languages (over 800 dialects) 15 per cent. Total newspaper circulation in 1985 was less than that of Japan's single largest newspaper *Yomiuri Shimbun*. Total newsprint consumption would have been inadequate to meet the total requirements of the *New York Times*. Such statistics, however, tend to underestimate the influence of the press in India where a single copy of a newspaper may be passed along and read by many people. In addition the overall statistics hide the diversity of the newspaper industry in India where newspapers are produced in many languages and where quality varies from that of *The Times of India* to amateur mimeographed one-man operations.

Culture and language constraints act to diminish demand for newspapers in India. In contrast to Hinduism, Christianity, Judaism and Islam are all historical religions and instruct man as to how he should live in this world. Most Westerners are bewildered by Hinduism's teachings, its passivism, fatalism and karma mentality. Mahatma Ghandi said, 'Turn the spotlight inward'.[7] To Hindus the infinite is more important than the finite, and the outer world as perceived by Westerners is only provisionally real. Also words are seen as inadequate to describe reality. To many Hindus therefore, newspapers cannot fulfil a very useful function. In terms of a Hindu's life purpose newspapers are largely irrelevant.

Table 10.1: Major Indian newspapers with circulations, 1985

Title	Founded	Language	Circulation
Bombay (population, 6 million)			
Bombay Samachar	(1822)	Gujarati	144,000
Economic Times	(1961)	English	72,000
Indian Express	(1940)	English	143,000
Lokasatta	(1948)	Marathi	204,000
Maharashta Times	(1962)	Marathi	178,000
Navbharat Times	(1950)	Hindi	368,000
The Times of India	(1838)	English	281,000
Calcutta (population, 7 million)			
Amrita Bazar Patrika	(1868)	English	139,000
Ananda Bazar Patrika	(1922)	Bengali	396,000
Economic Times	(1961)	English	72,000
Jugantar	(1937)	Bengali	325,000
Statesman	(1875)	English	205,000
Vishwamitra	(1917)	Hindi	80,000
Delhi (population, 3.6 million)			
Economic Times	(1974)	English	72,000
Hindustan	(1936)	Hindi	161,000
Hindustan Times	(1924)	English	268,000
Indian Express	(1953)	English	160,000
Navbharat Times	(1950)	Hindi	368,000
Sandhya Times	(1979)	Hindi	71,000
Saptahik Hindustan	(1950)	Hindi	101,000
The Times of India	(1850)	English	171,000
Madras (population, 2.5 million)			
Daily Thanthi	(1942)	Tamil	320,000
Dinamini	(1934)	Tamil	188,000
Hindu	(1878)	English	366,000
Indian Express	(1959)	English	292,000

Note: In Bombay there are small circulation newspapers (5,000–50,000) published in English, Sindhi, Urdu, Gujarati, Marathi and Hindi; in Calcutta in English, Bengali, Hindi, Punjaki and Urdu, in Delhi in English and Hindi; in Madras in Tamil, Teluju and English.
Source: Editor and Publisher Year Book, 1985.

Demand

Total advertising expenditures in India in 1985 were under one-quarter billion dollars, or less than one-quarter of Proctor and Gamble Corporation's 1986 advertising budget. India has perhaps 3,000 newspapers for its population of 800 million.[8] It has about as many literate people as the USA, although literacy is not necessarily the same as newspaper literacy and the ability to understand a newspaper. Fewer than 50 daily newspapers in 1985 had sales exceeding 50,000. Nearly half of all newspapers were published in Bombay, Madras, Delhi and Calcutta.[9] The so-called rural press was particularly poor in terms of capital and labour inputs. Much of the equipment was ancient and most of the journalists had limited skills. There are no satisfactory statistics available but the majority of the Indian people, in 1985, who lived in the over half million villages and small towns of India were poorly served both in newspaper quantity and quality. Half a billion people shared under ten million (usually two- and four-page) papers daily. In 1968, circulation of English-language newspapers was 1.9 million for 17 million English-speaking Indians, a ratio of 9.1 and comparable to some Western levels, for example, Spain and Italy. The English-language press in 1986 remained the most commercially viable.[10]

Less than a quarter of a million Indians claim to be proficient in English as their mother tongue, in contrast to over a quarter of a billion, 40 per cent, who speak Hindi as their mother tongue. Yet English-language newspapers dominate the press in terms of size and newsprint consumed and this makes Hindi newspapers unattractive to advertisers who therefore tend to shun the Hindi press. The Hindi press consequently suffers from inadequate income from both readers and advertisers. As a result the quality and circulation of the Hindi press is low. In the vernacular press, poorly-trained journalists are poorly paid for poor editorial content. Total newspaper circulation exceeds half a million in the following languages: Bengali, Gujarati, Malaysian, Marthi and Tamil. Despite the fact that in 1985 over half the population spoke neither English, nor Hindi (over 2000 different dialects are spoken in Bombay alone), no other language provided a viable newspaper market.[11]

The vernacular press tends to be parasitical on the English and Hindi press, taking from them the national and international news that those papers have obtained from the wire services.[12] For local and regional news they tend to rely on handouts from local governments and public agencies. Small wonder that a typical labourer is ill disposed to part with two hours' earnings for four pages of second-hand news, much of which can be obtained from radio in any case. A study by the Registrar of Newspapers in 1975 found that 80 per cent of daily papers had sufficient advertising for just one-quarter to three-quarters of a page and for many of these papers government advertising was the main source of advertising.

Seventy per cent of the Indian population is illiterate and therefore incapable of reading a newspaper, although many illiterates will listen to newspapers read to them. This still leaves a potential audience of over 200 million, the same as the USSR population. Low incomes, even amongst literates, are only part of the explanation for low demand. Income is very unevenly distributed in India and the vast mass of 300 million rural illiterates pulls down the overall average income and masks sizeable amounts of considerable affluence and potential markets. There is a middle class of 50 to 100 million. Only the USA and USSR have more scientists. There are twelve million shareholders, only Japan and the US have more. Neither does an inadequate transport and distribution system fully explain such low levels of circulation. The majority of illiterates live in rural areas and are excluded by their illiteracy rather than by distribution problems. Literates are more heavily concentrated in the cities where distribution is possible, though traffic congestion in places such as Calcutta and Delhi is as formidable an obstacle as anywhere in the world. Low formal education levels even of those who are literate and live in urban areas again does not fully explain very low circulation. Circulation in Britain and in the United States at the turn of the century, when the school leaving age was twelve, far exceeded that on a per capita basis per literate in India in 1986. Very low circulation in India is explained, as in other Third World countries, by radios and, since 1985 in India by satellite television, which had pre-empted the development of a newspaper habit. Most of those on low incomes have access to news and information at no cost. Those who would have bought a newspaper when newspapers had a media monopoly as in the West in the late nineteenth century have, in India in 1986, a free substitute.

There is no commercial radio in India. All India Radio has a monopoly of radio broadcasting. It does carry commercials but is largely financed by government grants and licence fees for radios. In 1969 there were seven million licensed radio sets and 50 million people had access to radios. The impact of television was negligible. By 1985, the Insat '83 satellite had extended television to reach 400 million.[13]

Since the monopoly broadcasting media is controlled by the Ministry of Information, alternative substitutes to radio and television play a vital role in India's democratic system. Weekly newspapers and magazines attempt to meet local demands and the multitude of special interests that exist in India's huge heterogeneous market. Since weeklies and magazines are less perishable than dailies, can be shared, appeal to special interests and take a smaller

241

share of annual incomes, an economically viable market can be found for them despite the general poverty of the country. Many of the weeklies and magazines are published in English. Government control of broadcasting and the small volume of advertising allowed on radio and television help support the Indian press by minimising potential competition. So do restrictions on foreign-owned periodicals.

Government influence

Since independence from Britain in 1947, India has been plagued by internal conflict so that although the Indian constitution guarantees freedom of the press the Indian Parliament has power to impose 'reasonable restrictions', which in the face of famine, wars with China and Pakistan, internal religious conflicts between Muslims, Hindus and Sikhs, and assassinations, including that of Mrs Gandhi in 1984, have meant considerable limitations.

To keep the press under control in the 1980s the government used economic measures. Newsprint, most of which must be imported, is kept in short supply and there is a blackmarket in newsprint. Cover prices have been pegged, and official advertising kept undependable. As a result newspapers must cut costs. They cannot afford many staff reporters and even *The Times of India* in Bombay and the *Statesman* in Calcutta must rely heavily on the national news agencies, UNI and PTI, and on the international news agencies for input.

One argument in favour of newspaper chains everywhere is countervailing power, usually against big advertisers, but also against powerful suppliers of labour, newsprint, news and in India against big government. In India, The Indian Express is the biggest newspaper chain. In the 1980s it was the leader in exposing the Congress Party's abuse of power, despite government retaliations. In one case in 1980, the chief minister of Maharashtra state (pop. 62 million), the *Indian Express* revealed, had allocated scarce materials in return for 'charitable donations'. In response to the revelations the minister called in a political debt owed to him by Bombay's most powerful union leader. Excessive wage claims and other labour troubles at *Indian Express* followed. *Indian Express* then attempted to close and move to another city. The minister responded by invoking a law allowing him to forbid closure of any factory, so imposing additional costs for *Indian Express* in the form of legal expenses.[14] The message was clear. In India, investigative reporting is uneconomic.

In 1975 media censorship was imposed. Mrs Gandhi later said censorship was a costly mistake since her government, as a result, became misinformed. Another legacy of censorship, it was said, was to make the public more appreciative of a free press when the Emergency ended. Censorship modified the attitudes of government, owners and readers.

From 1969 to 1975 Gandhi's Congress Party had sought to weaken the press using economic measures. In 1969 newsprint quotas and licence requirements to import printing machinery were introduced on the economic grounds of helping the balance of payments. In 1971 the state redefined the role of the press: 'to report to the people and not advise the government'. It also sought to impose a scheme whereby the government would have a half vote in management on all papers with over 15,000 in circulation. In 1972 it used import controls to limit newspapers to ten pages, again supposedly to help the balance of payments. Increasingly too, the state gave favoured journalists and proprietors preference in the allocation of scarce cars and scooters as well as nominal rents on residential accommodation. In a poor country with no social security, the economic incentive to journalists to curry favour with the government and so join the privileged is powerful. Thus, in 1975, when censorship was imposed, some journalists even supported it.[15]

After the Emergency ended in 1977, state power to control the press remained considerable. Under a post-Emergency amendment to the Industries Act, the state can take over mismanaged printing establishments, control quality, set cover prices, set advertising rates, control raw materials allocation, take over distribution and withhold government advertising. Control also takes two psychological forms. One is to create an atmosphere of fear of economic reprisal, the other, perhaps more powerful, is the threat to withdraw economic privileges like cheap rents already granted.

Supply

English is a relatively compact and efficient language for printing. The Indian-language papers are not only more difficult to set but require more space for equivalent messages, so increasing costs. Given the small circulation of Indian-language papers, collecting local news is prohibitively expensive. They therefore tend to depend heavily on government handouts. In fact, many small newspapers take all their national news from All India Radio which transmits the news after midnight at dictation speeds so that small newspapers can take down the news.[16]

For major news service Indian newspapers rely largely on Reuters as an international news agency and devote much space to international affairs. In addition to Reuters, the principal news agencies are Hindustan Samachar, Samachar Bharati, United News of India (UNI) in New Delhi and Press Trust of India (PTI) in Bombay which transmits news in up to nine different languages. There is also an internationally funded Press Institute of India which monitors the press and the India Press Commission which examines issues of concern and makes recommendations.

Staffing Indian newspapers is a nightmare away from the four big cities. Papers cannot afford high wages. They therefore fail to attract any talent, and any they may attract or create is quickly recruited by public relations and similar better-paying occupations. Translators, particularly competent translators, are hard to find. Communications make it difficult to ferret out what is happening in the villages, and in any case there is limited interest in what news is collected. School teachers are frequently used as part-time reporters and stringers.[17]

Most newspapers are not unionised. About one-quarter of India's 20,000 journalists belong either to the Indian Federation of Working Journalists or to the National Union of Journalists. As in China and the USSR, newspapers rely on letters as input and to some extent as substitutes for stringers. The difficulty is that letters tend to include bias and misinformation and are a far from satisfactory source of news even if the price is right.[18]

Technologically many Indian newspapers are museum pieces, using treadles to run outdated and worn out presses for which spare parts are unobtainable. Investment funds to update are not generally available. In any case the government is loathe to authorise the import of capital machinery that will eliminate jobs and cost foreign currency. Most newspapers are still set by hand and the process is made even more inefficient by the fact that the vernacular languages are both less efficient and more difficult to set. Bengali, for instance, has not 26 characters but 120 characters.

The problem of newsprint is particularly important in India. Since labour is cheap and capital equipment old and labour-intensive, the proportion of costs devoted to newsprint runs at around 40 per cent compared to a little over 20 per cent in most Western countries. India produces its own newsprint but the quality is poor and imported newsprint is preferred. The government grants licences to import but to save scarce foreign currency this is restricted and newspapers are granted quotas. Some newsprint is imported by the government's State Trading Corporation and then sold at a mark-up above world prices.

The small size of the market means that newspaper enterprises are small in contrast to those of developed countries. The largest firms are Express Newspapers and Bennett Coleman. The small scale is illustrated by the fact that the English-language *The Statesman* in 1984 employed fewer than 100 journalists. This contrasts with several thousand on the staff of the large Japanese and British newspapers. Therefore, despite the huge size of India and the large potential audience, the press, and particularly the Indian-language press, is small and fragmented.

Performance

In terms of conduct and performance, the Indian newspaper industry can be judged on different levels. It is largely free. It does perform the watchdog function. Independent firms and chains do survive in the market place. Product quality levels of most Indian-language papers is low. But the press has survived. Given the alternative possible scenarios of a poor developing country, survival must be judged a success in itself.

AFRICA

Africa provides a small, but potentially large, market for many of the products of the developed world, but the prospects for newspapers are poor. Just about every conceivable obstacle to an economically viable press discussed earlier in the chapter exists in Africa. Though Swahili is the major language spoken by 50 million people, there are another 1500 native languages.

Since independence, the majority of African countries have had a tragic history in the areas of economic growth, human rights, freedom, justice and equality. As tyrants such as Idi Amin and Jean-Bedel Bokarsa took over and as one-party rule has emerged, democratic institutions inherited from the colonial era, such as an

245

Table 10.2: Circulation of major Nigerian and South African newspapers, 1985

Nigeria

State

Oyo	Daily Sketch (1904)	64,000
Lagos	Daily Times	200,000
	National Concord (1980)	200,000
Jos	Nigeria Tribune (English)	109,000
	Nigeria Standard (1972)	100,000
Kaduna	Democrat (1983, English)	70,000

South Africa

Capetown	The Argus (1857)	102,000
Durban	The Daily News (1878)	87,000
	Ilanga (1903, Zulu)	106,000
	Sunday Tribune (1937)	120,000
Johannesburg	The Citizen	104,000
	Rand Daily Mail (1902)	119,000
	Rapport (1970, Africaans)	416,000
	Sowetan (1980, English)	96,000
	Star (1887)	185,000
	Beeld (1974, Africaans)	100,000
	Sunday Times (1906, English)	470,000

Source: Editor and Publisher Year Book, 1986.

independent judiciary and a free press have disappeared. So, for the most part, has the free enterprise system, upon which a free press depends for advertising support, collapsed.

Recent events in Nigeria reflect the dynamic interplay of these obstacles. Nigeria has the largest population in Africa, perhaps 100 million. It also had, until the 1986 oil price plummet, one of the highest standards of living in Africa. Until 1983, it had one of the most free media in Africa. It was reasonably successful by Third World standards with many newspapers, magazines, television and radio. Events since 1984 suggest that the Nigerians' earlier modest success will not be repeated anywhere in Africa in the near future.[19]

Since independence from Britain, the Nigerian press had operated within an authoritarian framework. Although the Nigerian constitution declares 'Every person shall be entitled to own, establish, and operate any medium for the dissemination of information, ideas and opinion', in fact government involvement in the media had been extensive. Many newspapers were started by the government; others, such as the case of New Nigeria Newspapers Ltd's *New*

Nigerian in 1975, were taken over by the government. The government rigidly controlled broadcasting, operated the Nigerian News Agency, and set up Ministries of Information. The independent newspapers by 1982 accounted for only twelve per cent of the press, and most of them were partly-affiliated and either directly or indirectly party-financed.[20]

With those basic conditions and industry structure, conduct and performance by world newspaper industry standards was inevitably disappointing in Nigeria by the early 1980s. Taxes were used to subsidise the government media. Content came largely from government sources, therefore was biased, inadequate and lacking in credibility. Consequently, demand for newspapers was limited. Finally, intimidated and fearful, newspapers failed to criticise. Journalists became sycophants. Promotions and rewards depended on pleasing the politicians. Even then, to be a journalist was a high-rank occupation. They had to support the right politicians and parties. In unstable, bloodthirsty, tribal Africa the repercussions from writing and putting on record the wrong view could be severe. This was brought home clearly in Nigeria. Late in 1983 military officers threw out the civilian government. In March 1984 they issued a decree with formidable implications for the press throughout Africa. For acting against the government's interests, newspapers could be closed and journalists imprisoned. The decree was retroactive with the onus of proof on the accused. There was no appeal against the special press tribunal made up of three military officers and one higher court judge.[21] Military coups and retroactive legislation, torture and murder are strong disincentives to putting anything in print that could later be held against one. The Nigerian experience was not unique and served as a warning to journalists throughout Africa's single-party democracies. A further *coup* in 1985 reinforced the message.

The intervention in 1984 by Rowland in *The Observer* of London's reporting of atrocities in Zimbabwe, discussed in Chapter 5, gave prominence to the African philosophy of leadership. Unless Rowland suppressed information about tribal atrocities against Joshua NKomo, the economic privileges of his Lonrho conglomerate in Zimbabwe would be withdrawn.[22] For an indigenous newspaper the penalties would be worse. In such violent, unstable and tragic climates, economically viable free newspapers have little or no future.

South Africa

South Africa with its apartheid and abundant mineral resources has a unique social and economic structure. Readership amongst the four million whites matches European levels, amongst blacks, African levels. Circulation in 1985 was under 1.5 million spread over 23 dailies. It totals much the same as London's *Daily Telegraph* or New York's *Daily News* but represents one-third of total African circulation.

South Africa's newspaper industry structure has much in common with Australia's or Canada's. Large distance and low population density has meant no national newspaper tradition. As in Canada, there are two dominant white languages. As in Canada and Australia, national chains dominate. Since 1985, four chains, two in each language, controlled 90 per cent of circulation. As in Canada, there was very limited competition, only in Johannesburg did the morning *Rand Daily Mail* and *The Citizen* compete.[23]

Increasing racial conflict affects basic conditions, structure and performance. Existing newspapers may be intimidated affecting product quality and reader demand. A barrier to entry for would-be entrants is created by threats of press controls and sanctions. Both foreign firms and domestic firms must be discouraged by the risks involved. For foreign firms mere association, even just through advertising, with South Africa could prove costly elsewhere. The advertising base becomes eroded. The events of 1985 and 1986 when many firms divested from South Africa reflected the undermining of the finances of South African newspapers.

With the introduction of draconian censorship in 1986, with the prospect of ten-year jail terms for journalists simply being at the site of unrest and with the establishment of a Media Operations Centre to examine all news copy before publication, the long-term prospects for a viable commercial press became exceedingly bleak.

FAR EAST

In the mid-1980s the economic miracle of the world has been the performance of South Korea, Hong Kong, Singapore and Taiwan. Newspapers there are expected by their governments to do their part to further the economic growth of these areas where economic growth is prized above the alien concepts of freedom of speech and a free press.

Table 10.3: Major Far Eastern newspapers with circulations, 1986

Hong Kong[a]

Ching Po Daily News (1956)		105,000
Fai Pao (1963)		150,000
Hong Kong Commercial Daily		100,000
Hong Kong Daily News (1959)		145,000
Hong Kong Economic Journal		72,000
Ming Pao Daily News (1959)		118,000
Oriental Daily News (1969)		600,000
Sing Pao Daily News (1939)		360,000
Sing Tao Wan Pao (1938)		165,000
Tin Tin Yat Pao (1960)		110,000
Wah Kin Yat Pao (1925)		120,000
Wen Wei Po (1948)		100,000

Singapore

Sunday Times (1931)	English	291,000
The Strait Times (1845)[b]	English	266,000
Nanyang Xingshon Lianhe Zaobao	Chinese	187,000
Shin Min Daily News (1967)	Chinese	91,000

Malaysia

Benta Hanyan	Malay	161,000
Nanyang Sian Pan (1923)	Chinese	120,000
New Strait Times (1845)	English	199,000
Iltusan Malaysia	Malay	206,000
The Star	English	136,000

Philippines

Balita (1972)	Filipino	137,000
Bulletin Today (1972)	English	273,000
Manila Times	English	N/A
People's Journal (1978)	English	500,000
People's Tonight (1978)	English	250,000
The New Philippines Daily Express (1972)	Filipino	260,000
Times Journal (1972)	Filipino	260,000

Notes: a. There are another 20 newspapers with circulations over 50,000.

b. Several other local-language dailies are all owned by the Strait Times Press.

Singapore

Singapore, in 1985, was a very tightly-controlled society. Whilst privately-owned, the press was far from free. It fitted the authoritarian model.[24] Government regulations have included licensing newspapers, restructuring the newspaper industry and 'recommending' senior newspaper executive appointments.[25] The dominant People's Action Party (PAP) expects newspapers to be their lackeys and the financial incentive to be so is strong. This was demonstrated at the renowned 140-year old *The Strait Times* in 1984.

Since the 1970s, *The Strait Times* had been one of the most profitable papers in Asia. With rapid economic growth advertising expenditures soared and the *Times* with an English-language monopoly benefited accordingly. Since the early 1970s the paper had followed the official line on all major issues but still had upset the government for being 'critical' and 'negative'. Government control took the form of issuing a licence to a local afternoon tabloid the *Singapore Monitor* to publish a morning paper starting in 1985. Three Singapore banks were then pressed into financing the new paper. In addition, *The Strait Times* was encouraged to appoint a former top civil servant as executive group chairman. Prior to this, in 1982, a government rationalistion of the industry had forced *The Strait Times* group to close their afternoon tabloid so creating a monopoly for the favoured *Singapore Monitor*.[26]

The Strait Times' experience in Singapore is all too familiar. Papers that toe the government line and exercise self-censorship may make substantial profits. Even mild criticism can jeopardise that relationship and prove highly expensive. The economic incentives to comply are strong for owners and journalists. The price of opposition is exhorbitant. In Singapore, the local press is tightly controlled but the foreign press is also pressured to self-censorship. In 1985, the *Asian Wall Street Journal* made an apology in the High Court of Singapore for contempt of court, an offence which can lead to imprisonment. The paper's offence was that it had reported that Singapore's courts were used against opposition politicians.[27]

Malaysia

Malaysia illustrates many of the problems for newspapers in the developing countries which experience economic growth. There is ethnic diversity with Malays, Chinese, Indians and East Malays making up the bulk of the population, and language diversity with Malay-, Chinese-, English- and Tamil-language papers. Radio, television and video, self-censorship and government control have all inhibited newspaper growth. Those newspapers that were produced, 1.4 million in 1984 for 15 million people, had business and political ties, but the leapfrog phenomenon was apparent with rapid growth in demand for broadcasting and slow growth for newspapers.

Amongst the major English-language papers in 1984, *The Star* (170,000) had former prime minister and 'father of Malaysia', Tunker Abdul Rahman, as chairman. He also wrote a column for the paper. *The Star* was a subsidiary of Hua Ren which was effectively a commercial arm of the Malaysian Chinese Association (MCA). MCA in turn was a leading member of the ruling National Front Coalition government. MCA provided advertising, guaranteed loans, put up collateral and vetoed senior appointments to *The Star*. The best-known English-language paper was the *New Strait Times* (192,000) which was owned by the Fleet Group. Since the finance minister had a controlling interest in Fleet Group, both *The Star* and *New Strait Times* were effectively government-controlled. The leading Malaysian-language papers had similar close ties to business and politics.[28]

The Malaysian Prime Minister, Dr Mahathir Mohamad made a speech in September 1985. Discussing political instability and uncertainty and the role of journalists he said, 'Where a false, or even true [sic], word can lead to calamity, it is a criminal irresponsibility for that one word to be uttered'. Reflecting this authoritarian philosophy, a report in the *Far Eastern Review* was condemned for violating the official secrets act in 1985 when it reported on the prospects of Malaysia's trade with China. The reporter was fired. At the *New Strait Times*, a report about Malaysia's plans to import American defence equipment led to charges, also under the official secrets act.[29]

In 1986 the *Asian Wall Street Journal*'s two correspondents were expelled and the paper barred from Malaysia for three months. The paper had reported that a government attempt to corner the tin market had cost $253 million.

Whilst the government's actions hurt and possibly curbed the newspapers involved, the government's attacks created a less favourable environment for the foreign investment required for the future in Malaysia's economy.

Hong Kong

The point has been made that the Chinese have no tradition of liberalism and individual liberty.[30] They are conservative. Opposing views are not tolerated. Freedom of the press is therefore an alien concept and irrelevant. In Hong Kong, in 1985, 60 Chinese-language papers with a circulation of 1.5 million were published daily. Highly competitive, their goals were openly and admittedly to exert influence and make money. In 1985, the former editor-in-chief of the Jing Tao Group of Newspapers, a major Chinese-language newspaper chain in the Far East, said any loss of freedom to the press after 1997 did not matter. Few people, he declared, would even miss it in Hong Kong. The reader public was uncaring about freedom of expression and journalism. Prosperity and stability were society's main objectives.[31] Even to many newspaper editors the repressive but effective regime of Lee Kuan Yew of Singapore was not just acceptable, but desirable. Limits on personal and press freedom in Hong Kong, Taiwan and South Korea were generally accepted as a fair price to pay for prosperity. Self-censorship to please the authorities whatever their colour was the norm in markets where the reader public was uncaring and journalists were overwhelmed by the sheer task of earning a living. A Hong Kong journalists earned just $256–$640 US monthly in 1985 necessitating moonlighting and compromise just to survive.[32]

In 1986 Rupert Murdoch entered the Hong Kong newspaper market when he paid $105 million for a 35 per cent share in the *South China Daily*. With the opening up of China to increased trade and with the rapid growth of the Far Eastern economy it made sense to expand his news empire to Hong Kong.

The Philippines

As have Germany and Japan, the Philippines has a press system rooted in the American tradition of press freedom. The transplant has been unsuccessful. Up until 1971, the Filipino press was the most vital in Asia with 19 daily papers in Manila alone. The leading papers such as the *Manila Times* were owned by businessmen with interests in sugar, television and mining. They had mostly opposed Marcos since he became President in 1965. They used their papers to extend their economic and political influence. Their vitrolic attacks on Marcos included the business projects and economic policies of Marcos and his wife Imelda and were one reason why Marcos imposed martial law in 1972. The pro-Marcos newspaper structure sustained until 1986 dated from then.

Immediately after martial law was declared, many newspaper journalists and publishers critical of Marcos were jailed. Their papers were closed, taken over by the government, and later transferred to Marcos' own business supporters and cronies. The usual panopoly of measures followed martial law to guarantee direct censorship as well as self-censorship. There was an Office of Media Affairs to issue directives to editors and vague libel laws were used to coerce the more courageous or foolhardy to comply. Libel suits, licensing, military interrogation and even charges of subversion with a maximum penalty of death was used to control the press. Moderates were bought off with jobs such as government public relations officers. Many of these measures remained after martial law ended in 1981.

In 1983 Benigno Aquino, a former *Manila Times* correspondent for 18 years was assassinated. Like other journalists, Benigno Aquino had used newspaper columns as a vehicle to achieve position and political power. His murder created worldwide outrage. Initially the captive national press played down the affair but the internationally-supported powerful Catholic Church did not. In the following days the small Catholic radio station *Ventas* attracted more and more listeners. The *Ventas* success gave encouragement to the printed press. The editor of the weekly tabloid the *Philippines Times* was arrested and jailed for subversion for linking the murders to the armed forces generals, but demonstrations, marches and Church and business opposition limited the extent of the government clamp down. One significant opposition factor was the use of business economic pressure. Businesses withdrew advertising from the three establishment papers, and one group of businessmen, in co-operation with and protected by the Catholic Church, started their own paper *Ventas*.[33]

The three national papers boycotted were the *The New Philippines Daily Express*, the *Times Journal* and *Bulletin Today*. The *New Philippines Daily Express* was held until 1986 by Roberto Benedicto who owned sugar-related businesses, hotels, a bank and broadcasting ventures. Benedicto was a golf companion of President Marcos and was Filipino Ambassador to Japan. The *Times Journal* was published by President Marcos' brother-in-law and then Ambassador to the USA. A third government-influenced national paper published by Marcos' former military adviser was the *Bulletin Today*. Other papers were also closely linked to the government including the *Evening Post* and the *Metro-Manila Times*.[34]

The key fact is that all large Filipino papers were attached to the government and big business. Until 1986 independent and opposition papers had much smaller circulations, for example *Ventas* sold

50,000 weekly. Regional papers tended to be more independent but publishers without the support that *Ventas* had from the Catholic Church and big business tended to be cautious in the face of draconian reprisals. Their continued existence depended upon American influence. American expenditures in the Philippines propped up Marcos' economy so when President Carter's administration applied pressures to increase press freedom, some opposition was allowed. However, self-censorship continued. Carter, unlike Marcos, had only a four-year term.[35]

When the Marcos' government financial scandal was unearthed in 1985 it was revealed in the permanently free American press, not in the temporarily half-free Filipino press. In California, the daily *San Jose Mercury-News* disclosed that the Marcos family had put together a real estate empire in Europe and America valued at a staggering $766 million.[36]

As with Japan's Tanaka affair in 1974, the revelation about the Philippines was made in the USA. As in Japan, the Philippines had had a press system modelled on the US system imposed on it. As in Japan, though for political not social reasons, the system had not worked. Press caution prevailed. In both countries press freedom's supposed watchdog function proved a sham. Massive financial abuses by those in power were covered up by a restrained press.

By late 1986, under the Cory Aquino government, over 20 new newspapers had been started whilst the pro-Marcos *Daily Express* floundered. Whilst many were sensational, the fragile political climate created similar incentives for editorial caution as existed under Marcos.

THE ARAB WORLD

Oil has transformed much of the Arab world. Made up of 18 countries and 150 million people with a common language, history and culture, this area has been the focus of much political and economic news in the last two decades with the rise and fall of OPEC. Its own news media, particularly the newspaper, is still undeveloped despite the rapid rise of incomes. The Middle East demonstrates that literacy, a common language and affluence alone are insufficient to induce the development of a mass newspaper industry.[37]

Only in Egypt is there a single daily newspaper with a circulation exceeding 250,000 and total circulation of the respected *El Ahram* was less than the circulation of many single Western dailies. Despite a common language, there is no international Arab newspaper.[38]

Low demand can be explained by a number of social, political and economic factors. Culturally and socially the perception of the role of the newspaper in the Arab world differs from that in the West. Arabs tend to be suspicious of the written word (except the Koran), and particularly of newspapers. They rely on oral communication and particularly 'shillas', small groups of trusted friends. Politically, since the nineteenth century, Arab newspapers have been associated with government. The need for national unity with the on-going Arab-Israeli conflict since 1948 has continued this trend. In addition, low advertising expenditures in the Arab press have encouraged a system of financial subsidies from political parties, government and other partisan interests wanting influence. There is government-controlled radio and television throughout the Arab world. The majority of consumers look to broadcasting for mass entertainment so that, since they distrust the written word for information and look elsewhere for entertainment, the scope for newspapers to inform and entertain is severely circumscribed.

LATIN AMERICA

In comparison to most of the African and Asian countries, the majority of Latin American countries are relatively affluent. The area consists of 23 countries with Brazil, Mexico, Argentina and Columbia dominating in terms of population, income and land area. Culturally, there is much in common with southern Europe, including the oral tradition.

Despite the fact that two languages, Spanish (220 million) and Portuguese (125 million) dominate the continent, unlike the diversity of languages in Asia and Africa, several factors still work against a large and vital newspaper industry. Unstable currencies and unstable governments have increased risks. Newsprint is imported so governments are able to control a vital input. The above factors are sufficient to deter entry to the industry by most profit-motivated entrepreneurs. The risk of repercussions and retroactive penalties is too high. But the most important factor working against the development of a newspaper industry with the relative scale of those of northern Europe, Japan and North America is radio and television. By 1985, Brazil had become a major exporter of television programmes. As in Africa and Asia, broadcasting has pre-empted the newspaper as a means of entertainment, diverted potential advertising dollars and hampered the development of a nationwide mass newspaper habit.

NOTES

1. Education Acts passed in Britain, France, Germany and the USA dramatically increased literacy.

2. In 1830 *The Times* cost five pence. The average weekly wage for a labourer was one hundred and twenty pence (ten shillings).

3. High tariffs added to world newsprint prices make newsprint prices comparable to those of the 1860s in the West when newsprint was rag-based.

4. One hundred years ago the art of advertising was in its infancy in the West. In the Third World there is no large consumer market in the 1980s for advertising to exploit and magazines like *Time* and *Reader's Digest* attract nearly half of what revenue is available.

5. *Gazette* (29) 1982, p. 58.

6. *Far Eastern Review*, 18 March 1985.

7. James Foss, *The Philosophy of Religion* (MacMillan, Toronto, 1979), p. 88.

8. Vernacular-language newspapers open and close with little fanfair so statistics have to be treated cautiously.

9. *Editor and Publisher Year Book*, 1985.

10. Less than two per cent of the population speak English.

11. *Far Eastern Review*, 18 March 1983.

12. G. Jones, *The Toiling World* (International Press Institute, Zurich, 1979), p. 63.

13. A 1984 documentary on PBS television, 'Nova', 25 November 1985, attempted to assess the impact on society of vintage American situation comedies shown to illiterate rural peasants.

14. *Nieman Reports*, Winter 1980, p. 32.

15. *The Economist*, 26 December 1981.

16. G. Jones, *The Toiling World*, p. 87.

17. Ibid., p. 91.

18. Stories of corruption in the Indian press are rife. Poor pay and poor profits make both journalists and editors vulnerable to those wishing to buy influence. Newspapers also bribe individuals with threats to expose stories about them in later issues. Potential victims then have the opportunity to buy silence. Both the state and business use advertising expenditures to buy a favourable press.

19. *New York Times*, 30 April 1984.

20. *Gazette* (33) 1984, pp. 193–201.

21. *Guardian*, 9 May 1984.

22. *The Economist*, 23 June 1984.

23. There are other similarities. Both produce newsprint, Canada has a horrendous problem with her Indians. However, Indians make up only two per cent of the population.

24. For example, in 1982, the Peoples' Action Party (PAP) lost its

monopoly in Parliament when the Workers' Party won a by-election. When one of the first questions the Workers' Party asked the ruling PAP in Parliament was why they hindered the free exchange of ideas, the Foreign Minister replied, 'We make our own rules . . . as to how the public issues should be discussed'.

25. *The Economist*, 23 April 1982.
26. Ibid., 24 June 1984.
27. *Editor and Publisher*, 10 October 1985.
28. *Far Eastern Review*, 28 February 1985.
29. *The Economist*, 23 November 1985.
30. *Time*, 28 November 1983.
31. *Far Eastern Review*, 29 November 1984.
32. Ibid., 23 May 1985.
33. Ibid., 6 April 1983.
34. *Macleans*, 22 March 1986.
35. *Far Eastern Review*, 25 January 1986.
36. *The Economist*, 25 January 1986.
37. Income and literacy vary dramatically throughout the Arab World from the illiterate Oman to the affluent United Arab Emirates.
38. W. Rugh, *The Arab Press* (Syracuse Press, New York, 1979), p. 43.

11

Conclusion

In this book I have attempted to analyse the major economic forces which affect the world newspaper industry in the 1980s. I have shown that the cheap-to-buy newspaper is by and large a product for the relatively affluent. Most newspapers are produced in the more affluent developed countries. Most of those newspapers which are produced in the Third World are produced for the affluent literate elite there, often in English. The reasons for this are straightforward. Since 1900 newspapers have been a medium by which advertisers reach consumers. They particularly wish to reach the affluent and so are prepared to spend the most in newspapers read by the affluent. It is newspapers like the *New York Times* and *The Times* of London which are most heavily subsidised by advertisers. Similar economic forces operate in the Communist world where the state wishes to control the flow of information to the population. They create a monopoly of the press and subsidise it, as necessary, to carry their messages to the audience they wish to reach. Quite simply newspapers are a medium to carry messages. Advertisers, the state, press owners and readers all pay to have their messages carried to those who are important to them. The adage, 'he who pays the piper calls the tune', applies to newspapers as much as to any other product.

Advertising is the major economic influence on Western newspapers, determining which will and will not survive. Advertisers discriminate against the poor and the left-wing reader because they are poor market potential for most products. However, so long as editorial content does not jeopardise sales of their products, advertisers for the most part are disinterested as regards newspaper content. It is reader demand which largely influences product quality in terms of editorial quality and format, modified to some degree by the wishes of owners, editors and the state. All advertisers want is the readers' attention.

Newspaper production in all countries is profoundly influenced by the state. Table 3.2 summarises many of the ways in which the state can either support or undermine the press. Without tax concessions, subsidies, state advertising and the like, the majority of the world's newspapers would have to cease production. Even with this support few competitive newspapers are viable. The cases examined from Chapters 4 to Chapter 10 illustrate many examples from around the world of both explicit and hidden state subsidies and supports for the press. They also illustrate how the state can inhibit the press. More generally, since Western newspapers depend on advertising and advertising depends on the level of economic activity, appropriate fiscal and monetary policies are essential for a healthy economy and the continued survival of the press. Economic mismanagement and balance of payments problems in many Third World countries in the past quarter century have justified state policies further jeopardising growth prospects for their already fragile newspaper industries.

Newspapers are only one medium within the media. The newspaper industry is an industry within the broader entertainment industry. It is a soft-edged industry critically affected by developments in the other media and developments in the past decade have been formidable. The advertisers, readers, owners and the state who use newspapers to carry their messages have been offered new substitutes in increasing numbers. In the 1980s many newspaper firms have successfully maintained demand with new newspaper products and product developments both to compete with and complement the other media. On the supply side the new technology has enabled newspapers to lower costs.

FUTURE PROSPECTS

I began this book with a quotation by Rupert Murdoch about the future of newspapers. Rupert Murdoch has shown considerable shrewdness in foretelling where the Western media industry will next develop. He continues to acquire newspapers. Cassandras have long forecast the end of the newspaper on the basis that the newer media will replace them. However, newspapers have unique qualities. They have the advantage of being disposable, tactile and requiring no hardware. The proliferation of new electronic communications and entertainments has created new opportunities for newspapers. Zipping and zapping television programmes has reduced television's appeal to advertisers. With remote control television, viewers are no longer captive to a channel but, without leaving their seat, can zip from an advertisement to another channel so abandoning the advertisers. VCRs enable the viewer to fast forward or zap straight through the advertisements. It is less easy to zip and zap newspaper advertisements. Likewise, fragmentation of television and radio, with dozens of new channels becoming available by satellite and cable in North America and Europe, has destroyed the simple broad reach that network broadcasting used to provide. The fact that television companies continue to buy up newspapers, that newspaper stocks continue to rise, and that total advertising expenditures in newspapers continue to increase all auger well for newspapers.

The future is not without risk. First, the newspaper market is mature. The prospects of any significant growth in paid-for circulation is small. In northern Europe, North America and Japan the market is virtually saturated and circulation has peaked. In Mediterranean Europe and Latin America economic growth has not been followed by widespread newspaper readership. Instead, broadcasting and weekly magazines have pre-empted newspapers. Similar trends can be discerned in the Third World where emerging middle classes do not acquire the newspaper habit. Second, new competition is a constant threat. Electronic means of delivering messages will become cheaper, more flexible and more user-friendly. This will create new demands but also erode the markets of the traditional media including newspapers. Newspapers will continue to take a smaller share of a growing entertainment and advertising pie. Third, in 1986 few competitive newspapers were profitable. The forces of the market encourage the take-over of the newspaper industry by large media corporations owning chains of monopoly newspapers. Virtually complete in Canada and Australia, the process continues in the United States and Europe.

All three forces were much in evidence in France in 1985 and 1986 where total newspaper circulation has been declining for over 20 years. France represents a market mid-way between the high circulation market (over 300 per 1,000) of northern Europe, North America and Japan, and the lower circulation markets (up to 100 per 1,000) of more newly developed countries like Spain, Italy and those in Latin America. Events in France in 1986 showed how unexpectedly quickly and dramatically the basic conditions of the market can change.

In France in 1986 videotext and electronic newspapers achieved an unprecedented success. Whilst in Britain and Germany in 1986 the respective state-run videotext systems languished, and in the United States Knight Ridder and Time-Mirror Co. abandoned videotext, in France videotext boomed. The French state, recognising that expensive videotext terminals had created an insurmountable obstacle elsewhere to the widespread use of videotext, kept its Minitel system simple and cheap. By 1985 the state had provided free terminals to over one million users. Intended primarily as electronic telephone directories, assorted entrepreneurs added 2,000 additional services. Amongst them, most of the major French newspapers added services enabling consumers to chat, send electronic mail and read the news electronically.

In France, television also underwent a transformation beginning in 1985 with ramifications for the already fragile press. The state television monopoly was ended. Franchises for two new private commercial stations were awarded and plans announced to privatise one of three existing state channels. In 1985 French newspapers enjoyed 49 per cent of France's $5.6 million advertising and television just 22 per cent. The advertising share, if not the absolute amount, going to newspapers must decline. In addition, plans were underway to expand both cable and direct broadcasting across Europe. Rupert Murdoch's Sky Channel in 1986 was the largest of Europe's 18 satellite channels reaching six million homes through cable systems. In 1985 he set up Media International to beam programmes directly to France and Germany from the French satellite TDF-1.

By 1986 French dailies like *Le Matin de Paris* and *Le Monde* were in financial difficulties. As newspapers' advertising share declined the forces to eliminate competition increased. Still, Robert Hersant continued to acquire newspapers in France and Belgium. In Paris, his *Le Figaro, France-Soir* and *L'Aurore* gave him 40 per cent of the national market. In Lyons, purchase of *Le Progrès* in 1985 and four other papers gave him a near monopoly in France's third-largest market. Hersant's *Le Dauphiné Libéré*, in typical Jackal fashion, had beaten *Le Progrès* into financial submission.

In France and much of Europe, severe government restrictions on television advertising diverted advertising to newspapers. This means of supporting newspapers declined in the mid-1980s as new broadcast franchises were awarded in Britain, France and Italy and satellite systems became increasingly able to leap national boundaries. Previously frustrated television advertisers who had not used newspapers, like Kelloggs, Coca-Cola and McDonald's began to advertise on satellite television in Europe in 1985, demonstrating that the new media finds new markets as well as supplanting the old. In the past newspapers survived and adapted to new competitors and give every indication of being able to do so again.

Newspaper chains continue to buy up smaller newspapers. Newspaper firms' shares continue to rise. In declining industries, like steel and tobacco, major companies seek to diversify out of the industry as share prices fall. The newspaper industry is a mature industry that does not fit such a scenario of decline. So long as total advertising expenditures rise, monopoly newspapers will maintain good prospects of profits. It is likely that to reach customers advertisers will undertake an increasing share of a newspaper's costs and many paid-for newspapers could become freesheets. But so long as advertisers in the West, and governments in the Communist world, wish to reach customers, newspapers will remain a medium of preference in the foreseeable future. In the Third World, so long as governments oppose newspapers, so long as incomes remain low, and so long as free broadcasting alternatives are available the prospects for growth are dim.

Select Bibliography

To list all the sources used to write a book on the world newspaper industry would be virtually impossible. Every day an avalanche of new primary sources appears in the daily newspapers and weekly news magazines. The most important of the books, reviews, reports, magazines, monographs, news weeklies and trade papers used are listed below.

BOOKS AND JOURNALS

Atwood, L. Erwin, 'Cankav Xiaoxi: News for China's Cadre', *Journalism Quarterly*, Summer 1982, pp. 240–8

Bagdikian, Ben H., 'Conglomeration, Concentration and the Media', *Journal of Communication*, Spring 1980, pp. 59–64

—— *The Media Monopoly* (Beacon Press, Boston, 1983)

Baistow, Tom, *Fourth Rate Estates: Anatomy of Fleet Street* (Comedia, London, 1985)

Berss, Marcia, 'Bingo!', *Forbes*, 10 September 1984, p. 40

Bishop, Robert L., 'The Decline of National Newspapers in the U.K.', *Gazette* 31 (1983), pp. 205–12

Black, Erroll, 'Freeing the Press in Canada', *Canadian Dimension*, January 1982, pp. 10–11

Blankenberg, William B., 'Newspaper Ownership and Control of Circulation to Increase Profits', *Journalism Quarterly*, Autumn 1982, pp. 390–9

—— 'A Newspaper Chain's Pricing Behaviour', *Journalism Quarterly*, Summer 1983, pp. 275–80

Bogart, Leo, *Press and Public* (L. Erebaum Associates, Hillsdale, N.J., 1981)

Boyd-Barrett, J. Oliver, *The International News Agencies* (Sage, Beverly Hills, Calif., 1980)

—— 'Western News Agencies and the Media Imperialism Debate', *Journal of International Affairs*, Winter 1982, pp. 247–60

Canada, *Royal Commission on Newspapers* (Supply and Services, Ottawa, 1980)

Canadian Business, 'The Irving Industrial Group', November 1983, pp. 41–58

Chu, James, 'The Gathering of News About China', *Gazette* (33) 1984, pp. 87–106

Colvin, Geoffrey, 'The Crowded New World of TV', *Fortune*, 17 September 1984, pp. 156–68

Compaine, Benjamin M., *Future Directions of the Newspaper Industry: The 1980s and Beyond* (Knowledge Industry Productions, White Plains, N.Y., 1977)

—— *Who Owns the Media* (Knolegate Industry Publications, White Plains, N.Y., 1982)

—— *The Newspaper Industry in the 1980s* (Knowledge, White Plains, N.Y., 1980)

Cudlipp, H., *The Prerogative of the Harlot* (The Bodley Head, London, 1980)

Curry, Jane L., 'Poland's Press: After the Crackdown', *Columbia Journalism Review*, October 1984, pp. 36–42

Curry, Jane and Dassin, Joan, *Press Control Around the World* (Praeger, N.Y., 1982)

Dizard, W.P., *The Coming Information Age: Technology, Economics and Politics* (Longman, New York, 1982)

Editor and Publisher, *International Year Book 1985* (Editor and Publisher, New York, 1985)

Edoga-Ugwuojo, Dympua, 'Ownership Patterns of Nigerian Newspapers', *Gazette* (33) 1984, pp. 193–201

Emery, E. and Emery, M., *The Heritage of the American Press* (Prentice Hall, New Jersey, 1984)

—— *The Press and America* (Prentice Hall, Englewood Cliffs, 1984)

Engwall, Lars, *Newspapers as Organisation* (Saxon House, Hants, 1978)

—— *Newspapers as Democracies* (Saxon House, Glamorgan, 1978)

—— 'The Structure of the Swedish Daily Press', *Swedish Journal of Economics*, (77) September 1975, pp. 318–28

Europa Year Book (Europa Publications, London, 1985)

Evans, Harold, *Good Times, Bad Times* (Atheneum, London, 1984)

Freiburg, J.W., *The French Press: Class, State and Ideology* (Praeger, New York, N.Y., 1981)

Fukutake, Tadashi, *Japanese Society Today* (University of Tokyo Press, Tokyo, 1981)

Giffard, C.A., 'Circulation Trends in South Africa', *Journalism Quarterly*, Spring 1980, pp. 86–91

Goldenburg, Susan, *The Thomson Empire* (Bantam Books, N.Y., 1984)

Great Britain, Monopolies and Mergers Commission. The Birmingham Post and Mail Holdings PLC (London, HMSO, 1985) Cmnd 9516

Great Britain, Monopolies and Merger Commission. Benham Newspapers and Reed International PLC (London, HMSO, 1982) HC402

Great Britain, Monopolies and Merger Commission. The Berrow's Organisation Ltd and Reed International PLC (London, HMSO, 1981) Cmnd 8337

Great Britain, Monopolies and Merger Commission. J. Andrew and United Newspapers (London, HMSO, 1980)

Great Britain, Monopolies and Merger Commission. United Newspapers and Fleet Holdings PLC (London, HMSO, 1985) Cmnd 9610

Great Britain, Monopolies and Merger Commission. West Somerset Free Press and Bristol United Press (London, HMSO, 1980) HC 546

Great Britain Royal Commission on the Press 1974–7, *Final Report* (HMSO, London, 1977) Cmnd 6810

Griffin, Tony, 'Technological Change and Craft Control in the Newspaper Industry: An International Comparison', *Cambridge Journal of Economics* (8) 1984, pp. 41–61

Hagner, Paul R., 'Newspaper Competition: Isolating Related Market Characteristics', *Journalism Quarterly*, Summer 1983, pp. 281–5

Henderson, Michael, 'The Indian Press — How Free?', *Nieman Reports*, Winter 1980, p. 32

Hird, Christopher, 'How Maxwell Got the *Mirror*', *New Statesman*, 17 May 1985, pp. 13–16

Hodgson, Godfrey, 'Private Power and the Public Interest', *Political Quarterly* (52), December 1981, p. 403

Holstein, Milton, 'Springer — Germany's Most Remorselessly Criticised Publishing Giant', *Journalism Quarterly*, pp. 35–40

Hynds, Ernest C., *American Newspapers in the 1980s* (Hastings House, N.Y., 1980)

Jones, G., *The Toiling World* (International Press Institute, Zurich, 1979)

Kariel, Herbert G. and Rosenvall, Lynn A., 'Factors Influencing International News Flow', *Journalism Quarterly*, Autumn 1984, 61 (3), pp. 509–15

Kellner, Peter, 'Really, No Really, Bad News', *New Statesman*, 3 September 1982, p. 5

Kerton, Robert, 'Daily Newspapers as Natural and Unnatural Monopolies', in *Canadian Perspectives in Economics* (Collier Macmillan, Toronto, 1972)

Koutsoyiannis, A., *Non-Price Decisions: The Firm in a Modern Context* (The Macmillan Press, London, 1982)

Laurenson, John and Barber, Lionel, *The Price of Truth, the Story of Reuters* (Mainstream, London, 1985)

Leaman, Michael, *Barefaced Cheek* (Hodder and Stoughton, London, 1983)

Lent, John A., *The Asian Newspapers' Reluctant Revolution* (Iowa State University Press, Ames, Iowa, 1971)

────── *Newspapers in Asia* (Heinemann Educational Books, Singapore, 1983)

MacBride, Sean, *Many Voices, One World: Report by the International Commission for a Study of Commuication Problems* (UNESCO, Paris, 1980)

Maxwell, Kenneth, *The Press and the Rebirth of Iberian Democracy* (Greenwood Press, Conn., 1983)

McDonald, Robert, *Pillar and Tinderbox* (Marion Boyars, Boston, 1983)

McQueen, Humphrey, *Australia's Media Monopolies* (Widescope, Victoria, 1977)

Merrill, John, *The Foreign Press. A Survey of the World's Journalism* (Louisiana University Press, 1980)

────── *Global Journalism* (Longman, New York, 1983)

────── *The Imperative of Freedom* (Hastings House, New York, 1974)

────── and Fisher, Hal, *The World's Great Dailies* (Hastings House, New York, 1980)

Merrillees, William J., 'Anatomy of a Price Leadership Challenge', *Journal of Industrial Economics*, March 1983, pp. 291–310

Meyers, William, *The Image Makers* (Times Books, N.Y., 1984)

Miller, W.L., Brand, J. and Jordan, M., 'On the Power of Vulnerability of the British Press: A Dynamic Analysis', *British Journal of Political Science*, 12, 1982, pp. 357–73

Needham, Douglas, *The Economics of Industrial Structure, Conduct and Performance* (Holt, Rinehart and Winston, London, 1978)

Pearce, Edward, 'Dial M for Murdoch', *Encounter* 2 (1982), p. 56

Penrose, E.T., *The Theory of the Growth of the Firm* (Oxford University Press, Oxford, 1959)

Picard, Robert G., 'State Intervention in U.S. Press Economics', *Gazette*

(30) 1982, pp. 3–11

Porter, W., *The Italian Journalist* (University of Michigan Press, Ann Arbor, 1983)

Robertson, Geoffrey, 'Toothless Watch-dog', *New Statesman*, 1 July 1983, pp. 9–10

Rothmyer, Karen, 'Letter from London', *Columbia Journalism Review*, October 1983, pp. 35–41

——— 'Mapping out Moon's media empire', *Journalism Review*, December 1984, pp. 23–31

Rugh, William A., *The Arab Press* (Syracuse University Press, Syracuse, 1979)

Sandford, John, *The Mass Media of the German Speaking Countries* (Oswald Wolff, London, 1976)

Schudsen, Michael, *Advertising: The Uneasy Persuasion* (Basic Books, N.Y., 1984)

Schultz-Brooks, Terri, 'Daily News: Can New Team Rout Rupert', *Columbia Journalism Review*, June 1985, pp. 55–62

Sheperd, W.G., *The Economics of Industrial Organisation* (Prentice Hall, Englewood Cliffs, N.J., 1979)

Sherrid, Pamela, 'Embarrassment of Riches', *Forbes*, April 9, 1984, pp. 45–9

Shue, Vivienne, 'China's Local News Media', *The China Quarterly*, June 1981, pp. 322–31

Siegel, Arthur, *Politics and the Media in Canada* (McGaw-Hill Ryerson, Toronto, 1983)

Siebert, Fred S., Peterson, Theodore and Schram, William, *Four Theories of the Press* (University of Illinois Press, Urbana, 1956)

Simpson, D.H., *Commercialisation of the Regional Press* (Gower, Hants, 1981)

Smith, Anthony, *The British Press Since the War* (David and Charles, Newton Abbot, 1974)

——— *Goodbye Gutenburg: the Newspaper Revolution of the 1980s* (Oxford University Press, 1980)

——— *Geopolitics of Information* (Faber, London, 1980)

Solman, Paul and Friedman, Thomas, *Life and Death on the Corporate Battlefield* (Signet, N.Y., 1982)

Stephens, Mitchell, 'Clout: Murdoch's Political Post', *Columbia Journalism Review*, July/August 1982, pp. 44–8

Stewart, Walter, *Canadian Newspapers: The Inside Story* (Hurtig Publishers, Edmonton, 1980)

Stigler, George, 'The Kinky Oligopoly Demand Curve and Rigid Prices', *Journal of Political Economy*, October 1947, pp. 432–49

Stoffman, Daniel, 'Citoyen Péladeau', *Canadian Business*, June 1985, p. 237

Supple, Barry, *The Experience of Economic Growth: Case Studies in Economic History* (Random House, New York, 1963)

Taylor, H.A., *The British Press* (Arthur Baker, London, 1961)

Tunstall, Jeremy, *The Media in Britain* (Constable, London, 1983)

Udell, Jon G., *The Economics of the American Newspaper* (Hastings House, New York, 1978)

Wheen, Francis, 'No Such Thing as a Free Lunch', *New Statesman*, 17 May 1985, p. 57

Young, Hugo, 'Rupert Murdoch and The Sunday Times', *Political Quarterly*, (55) December 1984, pp. 382–90

NEWSPAPERS AND MAGAZINES

Business Week, Christian Science Monitor, Columbia Journalism Review, Daily Telegraph, Editor and Publisher, Encounter, Fortune, Financial Post, Financial Times, Globe and Mail, Guardian, IPI Report, Journalism Quarterly, L'Express, Le Monde, Le Nouvel Observateur, London Illustrated News, Los Angeles Times, New Statesman, Newsweek, New York Times, Nieman Reports, Observer, Quill, Sunday Times, The Australian, The Economist, The Times, Time, US News And World Report, USA Today, Wall Street Journal, Washington Post.

Index

Page references in *italics* refer to figures or tables. Page references including 'n' refer to notes.